LABOR AND REINDUSTRIALIZATION:
Workers and Corporate Change

Edited by

Donald Kennedy

Department of Labor Studies
The Pennsylvania State University

Cover photo: U.S. Steel demolishes the blast furnace at its Ohio Works, Youngstown, Ohio, 1982 from the documentary *The Business of America* produced by California Newsreel.

CONTENTS

Preface

This is the second book published by The Pennsylvania State University's Department of Labor Studies in its monograph series on public policy issues of concern to workers as individuals and as members of trade unions. The goal of the series is to bring the best thinking of both academics and practitioners to bear on current problems, and to make their contributions accessible to as wide an audience as possible.

I believe this volume, *Labor and Reindustrialization*, is admirably suited to these ends. Its publication at this time will be a significant contribution to an important ongoing debate over the future of economic policy in this country. Workers and their organizations must be active participants in this debate. *Labor and Reindustrialization* will help to insure that they are.

Ronald Filippelli, Chairman
Department of Labor Studies
The Pennsylvania State University

Introduction

Donald Kennedy

Over 38 million American jobs disappeared in the decade of the 1970s.[1] These jobs were destroyed by the deindustrialization of the United States. Deindustrialization can be defined as "a widespread, systematic disinvestment in the nation's basic productive capacity." This disinvestment diverted capital from productive basic industries into speculative ventures, mergers and acquisitions, and facilities overseas.[2] This movement of capital is illustrated vividly by U.S. Steel's acquisition of Marathon Oil for $6 billion and by the exporting of capital by multinational conglomerates to locations outside the United States.

Deindustrialization closed many workplaces, phased down and "milked" others, relocated work, caused massive layoffs, forced early retirement for many workers, forced transfers of others, created a climate in which employees gave back to their employers wages and benefits and made other contract concessions, sabotaged the economic and social health of communities, and led to a deterioration of the physical and mental health of many Americans. This process also strained such programs as unemployment compensation, public assistance and other social services, and caused a loss of tax revenues and subsequent layoffs of public sector workers.

The economic and social devastation created by deindustrialization triggered a national debate over the best strategy to pursue in order to reindustrialize the United States. Reindustrialization can be defined as the recreation of the conditions necessary to reattract capital into productive investment and thereby create economic growth. The discussion of industrial policy is an important part of the deindustrialization/reindustrialization debate. Industrial policy can be seen as the process of designing a strategy or set of strategies which will recreate the conditions to attract capital investment, create jobs and restore economic health.

Donald Kennedy is on the faculty of the Department of Labor Studies at The Pennsylvania State University.

The debate over industrial policy has been sharp and there is strong disagreement over which policies the nation should follow. The collection of articles published here is a part of this debate. The debate itself has raised several important questions. Why did deindustrialization occur? Was it inevitable? How should government, labor, consumers, and communities respond to the American decline? What role will high technology play in reindustrialization? Should workers attempt to buy closed facilities and thereby save jobs? Should the concept of Enterprise Zones be pursued as a reindustrialization strategy? Will the adversarial approach to labor relations be replaced by new forms of cooperation at the workplace?

In the opening article of this collection Gerald Glyde examines the nature of corporate planning and why it is responsible for deindustrialization. He analyzes supply side economics which was offered by some as the answer to industrial decline. He concludes that the supply side approach is not the most efficient way for the nation to reindustrialize. Instead Glyde sees some sort of national democratic planning as the way for the United States to confront its most serious domestic challenge since the Great Depression.

To understand how America was deindustrialized, Charles Craypo analyzed plant closings and phase downs in South Bend, Indiana. Craypo's research demonstrates that cities lose their factories and workers because of the needs and decisions of large corporations. In most cases companies do not ask for concessions or contract changes and when such changes are granted they don't save jobs or workplaces. In fact, he finds that there is little if anything labor can do to prevent the deindustrialization of manufacturing industries in the United States. His article seems to suggest that workers will have to explore new strategies and forms of workplace control to create jobs and save their communities.

If deindustrialization is an inevitable fact of life, what weapons are available to workers to resist its harmful effects? Sharon Simon's analysis of the law of collective bargaining concludes that, at best, the law is a limited weapon in this struggle. Lawsuits may result in severance pay awards but only in the rare case would an employer be required to reopen a closed business. In the area of the relocation of bargaining unit work during a contract, she advises unions to negotiate strong contract language and to use the grievance procedure to protect the incomes and living standards of organized workers.

Arthur Hochner, is more optimistic about the strategy of worker ownership of industry as a partial response to deindustrialization. In his article Hochner lays out a blueprint for workers to follow when considering whether or not to open worker owned and operated businesses. Hochner concludes that employee takeover of industry is one strategy which can, in some instances, save jobs and become part of a larger plan of reindustrialization.

In the debate about reindustrialization some researchers and public officials have offered the concept of Enterprise Zones as the centerpiece for an industrial policy. Bruce Nissen examines their proposals carefully and concludes that this approach should not be pursued. He argues that such zones would be regional sweatshops in which workers would be forced to accept low-paying, unsafe, unskilled jobs from an employer which has shifted many of the production costs to the community and will, in fact, soon abandon the Enterprise Zone and move on. Nissen also surveys many of the proposals for reindustrialization which have been offered as alternatives to the Enterprise Zone approach.

Is high technology the answer to problems created by deindustrialization as many claim? Carol Haddad examines the promises made by many proponents of high-tech. She concludes that the high technology industries will not offer employment for all those Americans who have been displaced by the deindustrialization of basic industry in the U.S. Haddad also surveys strategies which workers, who find employment in the reindustrialized workplace, can pursue to protect their jobs, wages and quality of worklife in a high-tech environment.

Will labor and management create new forms of workplace cooperation as one step in the reindustrialization process? Will workplace cooperation be the foundation for a new era in labor relations in which cooperative workplace management will replace the traditional "adversarialism?" Robert Cole examines how unions can respond to experiments in workplace democracy. He argues that even though there is a faddish quality to much of the discussion surrounding employee involvement at the workplace, labor should take the phenomenon seriously. He argues that unions should explore the possibility of workplace cooperation and offers guidelines for labor to follow in its discussion with management about quality of worklife experiments.

In order to help unionists better understand the quality of worklife movement, William Parsons surveys the relevant literature, films, and support groups which are available for workers. Parsons also identifies some of the historical and historiographical developments in the field of workplace cooperation which will help workers become more informed and better able to evaluate management employee involvement proposals.

The authors in this collection suggest that a rational plan of reindustrialization is necessary if workers and communities are to avoid the harmful effects of corporate change. There is much that can be done in the area of public policy to minimize the social and economic disruptions and dislocations which are caused by corporate change.

The authors suggest that labor and other groups should play a prominent role in exploring strategies of reindustrialization which will protect communities and workers from economic disastor.

End Notes

1. Barry Bluestone and Bennett Harrison, *The Deindustrialization of America: Plant Closings, Community Abandonment, and the Dismantling of Basic Industry* (New York: Basic Books, 1982), pp. 6-7.
2. Ibid.

Managing Economic Change: Labor's Role

Gerald P. Glyde

Introduction

Labor's agenda does not unfold in a vacuum. External economic events, internal politics of unions, the behavior and financial condition of employers in their immediate industries, other unions' contract outcomes and negotiation experiences all shape this agenda. The economic environment dictates concerns for labor which include job security, unemployment, plant closures, concessions or givebacks, foreign competition, the "new" technology, union-busting, quality-of-worklife schemes, corporate restructuring, and the vivid memory of the recent inflation which reduced wages in real terms.

These diverse issues are all linked to the fact that our economy is presently in the midst of an industrial and economic shakeout. The term shakeout is not used lightly. It implies wrenching change, often resulting in a falling-out even among groups which previously may have had relatively stable relationships that permitted moderate changes to occur.[1] With the jolting change that takes place in a shakeout, some parties come out ahead while others lose; but few of the economy's participants proceed unaffected by the sweeping events.

In any major reordering, those players with economic and political muscle will "manage" the change, and will try to impose losses on the weaker players. A key question, then, is: who will manage our long-term economic change — including decisions to implement change, and decisions on adjustment to change once the implementation decisions are made? Much of this paper is devoted to this basic question and to labor's role in managing economic change.

The current economic shakeout has both short-term and long-term origins. The short-term dimension is associated with the devastating

Gerald P. Glyde is an Associate Professor in the Department of Labor Studies, The Pennsylvania State University.

recession that the country experienced in the early 1980s, when industrial capacity utilization fell to below seventy percent and, in industries like steel, capacity utilization fell to below forty percent. This "administered" recession, designed by government to combat inflation, created severe unemployment and produced jolting effects which will not recede quickly.

The "administered" recession appeared with the world in the midst of a technological and corporate reshuffling, and an economy becoming increasingly more international. Effective management of these major structural or long-term changes holds the key to any reindustrialization effort and sustained emergence from the shakeout.

At present, the long-term changes combine with short-term factors to produce negative effects that are multiplicative rather than additive. For example, the destructive effects of American firms moving parts of their business overseas in the long-term are compounded by short-term recession policy and vice versa. Together these changes produce more depressing effects — a shakeout — than the sum of their single effects.

Workers and their unions are often victims in any major shakeout since they do not control the basic levers of change. Rather, they are usually placed in the unenviable position of reacting to change. Moreover, in a period of basic structural change, unions are put in the situation where they are effectively "pushing on a string" as the scope of bargaining (the range of issues that unions can bargain over) is too narrow to provide adequate protection from jolting and unanticipated change.

What follows provides, first, evidence that there is a shakeout underway in the economy and some important implications of these changes for labor are noted. Second, the current inadequacies of overall economic management are explored. Finally, with this background, we consider some broad policy options for emergence from our economic dilemma and the implications of those options for labor. It should be noted that the focus throughout is on long-term problems and long-term policy options.

Evidence of Wrenching Change

In 1978, United States Steel had total revenues of about 11 billion dollars; 78 percent of this revenue derived from its steel-making or fabricating operations. In 1982, revenues rose to about 19 billion dollars, but only 28 percent came from steel-making. During this four year period U.S. Steel's oil and gas revenues went from zero to 51 percent of the company's revenue.[2] In 1979, preparatory to this major change in direction the company announced the permanent closure of 14 steel mills in eight states with a loss of 13,000 jobs.[3]

The actions of U.S. Steel are not unique. Armco diversified to the extent that it dropped the word "steel" from its title. Bethlehem Steel at the end of 1982 announced closure of its Lackawanna, New York plant with a loss of 7,300 jobs. National Steel has diversified into aluminum; and instead of being the nation's fourth largest steel maker, it is the fourth largest savings and loan company.

Outside of steel, the automobile industry recently closed over two dozen plants; the same number of tire plants were closed between 1975 and 1981. Closures such as these, and a seemingly endless list of others, are well documented by Barry Bluestone and Bennett Harrison in their book *The Deindustrialization of America*[4]. In this book empirical evidence is provided that indicates extensive corporate flight of basic industry from the United States into other countries. For example, General Electric in the 1970s grew world-wide by 5000 employees, but in a domestically disruptive way. It created 30,000 foreign jobs but destroyed 25,000 jobs in the United States.

Surprisingly, it is not just the stereotyped old brick factory that closes its doors. A recent study of "Fortune 500" company plant closures, found that one-third of the closures were of plants not over six years old. The median age of plants closed was 15 years.[5] These rapid moves are evidence of destabilizing change; many of the attendant costs are borne by those who have no role in the management of change.

The recent spate of corporate mergers is further evidence of major and profound underlying change in our economy that has a significant impact on labor. Examples of such mergers include: ITT's acquisition of Avis and Sheraton Hotels, NBC's purchase of Hertz, ARCO's acquisition of the London Observer, Standard Oil's acquisition of Kennecott Copper, LTV's acquisition of Jones and Laughlin Steel and subsequent merger with Lykes, and Mobile's acquisition of Montgomery Ward.[6] In 1979, U.S. corporations spent more money on acquisitions and mergers (40 billion dollars) than they did on research and development.[7]

In 1982 there were signs that corporate acquisitions across industries were being replaced by divestitures, although this might have been a temporary trend related to the recession. Thirteen percent of 875 major divestitures were larger than 100 million dollars in that year. One example is Beatrice Foods, a 10 billion dollar a year conglomerate which plans to sell 50 of its companies.[8] What is clear about both mergers and divestitures, is that they are disruptive and are confounding to labor since collective bargaining structure tends to follow industrial structure. Mergers of firms across industries and multinational growth causes disarray in bargaining structures. On the other hand, a reversal of the merger trend would also provide a shock to unions who are responding to conglomeration by merging themselves.[9]

Additional evidence of an economic shakeout is the rapid internationalization of the U.S. economy. In 1970 direct investment (investments in land, buildings and equipment) in the U.S. by foreigners was 13 billion dollars. By 1981 it had risen to 90 billion dollars. U.S. direct

investment in other countries was 76 billion dollars in 1970 and reached
227 billion dollars by 1981. Exports from the U.S. to other countries
rose from 71 billion dollars in 1973 to 236 billion in 1981; imports to the
U.S. from other countries went from 71 billion dollars to 264 billion
dollars in 1981.[10]

Specific examples of foreign direct investment in the U.S. involving
many well-known companies include the following: Savin, in the
office equipment field, is 57 percent Canadian, Great West Life is 96
percent Canadian, ABDick is 100 percent British, Howard Johnson is
100 percent British, Moore Business Forms is 100 percent Canadian,
Lever Brothers is 100 percent Dutch, Miles Laboratories is 100 percent
German, Euclid is 100 percent German, Timex is 100 percent Norwegian, Nestle's is 100 percent Swiss, American Motors is 46 percent
French, and Mack Truck is 20 percent French.[11]

In the other direction, the 100 largest U.S. multinationals are dependent on their foreign direct investment. J.P. Morgan has assets of 59
billion dollars; 56 percent of those assets are outside of the U.S. Xerox
has assets of 7.7 billion dollars, 46 percent are outside of the U.S.
Johnson & Johnson has 41 percent of its assets held outside of the U.S.
Thirty-eight percent of H.J. Heinz assets are outside of the U.S. Other
companies with over 30 percent of their assets held outside of the U.S.
include: Colgate-Palmolive, Scott Paper, Gillette, Firestone, Texas
Instruments, Quaker Oats, Kellogg, NCR, Goodyear, Union Carbide,
Minnesota Mining and Mfg., Sperry, and Burroughs.[12]

This internationalization has destabilized domestic markets that had
become accustomed to a more closed and predictable sales environment. Industries developed pricing practices that made market shares
and sales more predictable. In addition, collective bargaining gained
some stability from this domestic market tranquility and balance. The
upsetting of this equilibrium via rapid internationalization of markets
in the 1970s thus rendered collective bargaining more unstable as well.

Inflation

The uncertainty of price changes and periods of rapid inflation in the
1970s and early 1980s also contributed greatly to the economic shakeout. The consumer price index rose from 100 in 1967 to 289 in 1982, a
189 percent increase in average consumer prices.[13] For low income
persons the index is much higher since they spend proportionately
more of their budget on items that had the highest rates of increase —
medical care, food, energy and housing. The energy price index went
from 100 in 1967 to 416 in 1982, a whopping 316 percent rise and clearly
destabilized large segments of the economy.[14]

In this inflationary environment many unions negotiated seemingly
adequate money wage gains only to have members disappointed by
wages in real terms (adjusted for inflation) that were actually declining, especially when tax and social security deductions were taken
into account. In 1974 compensation per hour for all workers in the

nonfarm sector rose by 9.4 percent while in inflation adjusted terms compensation actually fell by 1.4 percent. In 1979 compensation rose by 9.3 percent; in inflation adjusted terms it fell by 1.7 percent. In 1980 inflation adjusted compensation per hour fell by 2.9 percent, and in 1981 it fell by .7 percent.[15] At a 10 percent rate of inflation, pay in real terms is cut in half in about seven years.

Inflation, fueled by energy cost increases, encouraged firms to push forward their plant closure plans. That is, if a firm contemplated closing a string of plants over a 15 year period, unexpected increases in costs, especially energy costs for energy intensive firms, may push those closures far ahead. The effects on workers and communities are disasterous, especially when the closures are regionally concentrated as well as concentrated in time due to the combined effects of inflation and "administered" recession. Massive closures are effective disciplinary measures to use against workers — all part of the symptoms of a shakeout period.

Unemployment

Even though inflation is destabilizing to workers and their unions, unemployment is more devastating. In the decade between 1973 and 1983 two major "administered" recessions drove unemployment to 9.2 percent in May, 1975 and to 10.8 percent in December of 1982.[16] In a recession jobs are lost, incomes decline, on-the-job training is disrupted and the underutilized capacity ensures that productivity growth will not be high. The 1982-83 recession was particularly devastating since it was laid on top of other long-term factors that have been discussed above — the formula for bringing on a shakeout.

Employers appear to be reluctant to bring back laid off workers when business picks up. Instead, more of them raise production by improving labor-saving technology. Although there are positive aspects to capital innovation, it clearly adds to the "shakeout" phenomenon of a recession by leaving a residual of workers and communities "high and dry" in any subsequent expansion. This form of unemployment is known as structural unemployment and it appears to be a growing problem. From 1965 to 1969, the unemployment rate averaged 3.8 percent; from 1970 to 1974, 5.4 percent; from 1975 to 1979, 7.0 percent. The first four years of the 1980s produced an unemployment rate average over 8.0 percent.

In a recent meeting of the U.S. Business Council — an association of executives of major U.S. corporations — the prevailing view was that few of those workers laid off during the 1982-83 recession would be rehired. For example, Union Pacific Corporation, a giant transportation company, had 6,000 of 44,000 employees on layoff. The company's president indicated that, compared to 20 years ago, 40 percent more freight could be handled with one-half as many employees. In any subsequent upswing, few of the 6,000 workers would be returning to their jobs in his estimation. The president of DuPont noted that of the company's 174,000 world-wide workforce, seven percent were on layoff. Even in a robust economy, he felt few of the unemployed would be rehired due to automation.[17]

New Technology

Another major contributor to the economic shakeout is the rapid movement toward use of the microprocessor at the workplace. The silicon chip, which is a miniature system of integrated circuits, has provided for technical change based on advanced and enlarged computing power. A silicon chip is one square centimeter in size and can perform millions of multiplications per second and store vast quantities of information. So-called "super chips" will expand this computing and industrial machine control (and worker control) capacity greatly in the next decade. Calculations which cost 80 cents to perform in 1950, now cost less than a cent; and auto manufacturers can operate robots at about six dollars per hour which is less than one-half the rate for human labor.[18]

The impact of microprocessors is felt in both manufacturing and in services and has revolutionized the storage and processing of information. Its introduction has the potential for good and bad as has past technology — but this new technology promises to be more sweeping than some other invention-innovation. When agriculture mechanized, workers went to manufacturing; when manufacturing automated, workers went to services. With a new technological shock to manufacturing and services simultaneously, and an increase in foreign competition, coupled with a recession, the effects on employment and unemployment may be large. Some knowledgeable people, such as Wassily Leontief, a Nobel laureate economist, consider current technologies based on the chip and integrated circuits to be close behind the wheel and equal to the steam engine in achievement. For labor he makes a pointed observation: "What will happen will be quite analogous to what happened to horses after we got the tractor. I hope the solution will be different."[19]

Technology represents a major change that creates structural unemployment and uncertainty. When this effect is combined with a job destroying recession, the shakeout effects can indeed be wrenching. And if labor has little input or control of this process, it plays a minor role in the management of change. Whether technology works for or against labor in the long-term will depend on labor's ability to participate fully in its management.

Labor and Economic Change

There are clearly a number of important related events that are creating change — an eratic inflation, energy price increases, two major unemployment-causing recessions, extensive plant closures, a wave of corporate mergers and acquisitions, an opening up of world trade and competition, world-wide corporate direct investment activities, and a new technological breakthrough in computing and machine control. These events create major readjustments in old and established relationships. In this shakeout environment, each economic actor attempts to protect its own position, often at the expense of others. The "others" may often be workers.

To what extent will labor participate in these decisions which render important change? That is, will labor, through collective bargaining, and political action be able to promote an orderly adjustment process in response to necessary change so that its interests are taken into account? To what extent will labor be left behind as these decisions are made solely by business and by government-business consensus? These are basic policy questions that labor needs to address. This is especially true given the inadequacies of our current and past performance in managing change.

Inadequate Management of Economic Change

We have always had change in our economy, and implicit if not explicit ways to deal with it. But the established methods of management are inadequate to handle the sweeping change associated with the current economic shakeout. In fact, the methods of managing economic change have always been inadequate for those who need protection from wrenching change — the difference now is that the changes are more widespread and are felt by more people and communities than in the recent past.

Our failure to manage change has six dimensions. First, we have failed to come up with an alternative short-term strategy to the contradictory policy of moderating inflation by causing recession and unemployment. Reaganomics, as practiced in 1981 and 1982, provides an excellent example of this contradiction. Second, we have failed to engage in effective long-range planning. By planning we do not mean rigid top-down planning; rather, planning that is participative and encourages harmonious change. Planning implies looking openly at available options and the impact of decisions on all groups affected by that decision and their response. Third, related to inadequate planning, we have failed to take proper account of the social costs of industrialization in the period of rapid growth following World War Two. This neglect has resulted in inadequate preparation for our economic shakeout.

Fourth, firms (management) have not performed well in adjusting to and managing long-term change; they appear to have focused heavily on the short-term. Fifth, a rather narrow scope of bargaining for labor has left it with insufficient power to participate in the management of change. Decisions which were at one time seemingly remote management prerogatives — investment, plant closing, technical change, etc. — are now seen as having direct and immediate impacts at the workplace for labor. Sixth, given little protection or economy-wide planning, groups who perceive their position to be eroding, or expect major change to take place, have taken on a zero sum mentality.

Short-Term Planning by Government
The short-term solution for inflation in our economy has been for the government to bring on a recession. To put it bluntly, we create unemployment on purpose to take pressure off price increases. The reasoning is based on the view that most inflation is caused by too much spending power (in the hands of government, business, and consumers) relative to the productive capacity of our economy. Excess of spending power over ability to produce will force prices up. Therefore, the reasoning goes, to reduce inflationary pressure (average price increases), the government should reduce spending power. It does this by raising interest rates and cutting back on its own expenditures. The result is predictable; unemployment goes up.

The major "administered" recession of 1974-75 attacked inflation and produced an unemployment rate of 9.2 percent. Ronald Reagan managed the most recent inflation by producing our worst post-World War Two recession, with a peak unemployment rate of 10.8 percent.

This method of managing an economy in the short-term produces a roller coaster effect that curbs our ability to grow in the long-term. More importantly, the policy is obviously unfair in its distributional effects and it does not really get at the major sources of inflation. The unemployed obviously suffer the most, and unemployment is not equally distributed. And, as structural factors such as energy and corporate structure play a larger role in price and productivity changes, recessionary policy becomes less effective unless unemployment rises even further. The unemployment and inflation record since the early 1970s is testimony that our current short-term economic planning program for inflation and employment is bankrupt. Difficulty in finding an alternative policy may be related to our willingness to consider long-term planning.

Long-Term Planning by Government
Gunnar Myrdal, the Swedish economist, wrote of this country's intense interest in the short-term and its lack of long-term vision nearly four decades ago in *The American Dilemma* and again two decades later in *Challenge to Affluence*.[20] In the more recent book he suggests that we can't be progressive unless we take a better look at the "bigger picture" and the long-term implications of our policies. Although twenty years old, the following quote by Myrdal is an apt statement of a current need in our society:

> "Only by writing on the wall in definite and concrete figures the opportunities that could be realized by a change in policies can America be made to wake up to its old ambitions and new necessities."[21]

The argument over whether to engage in governmental economic planning has ebbed and flowed over time in the United States and Western Europe. When economic depressions hit there was always more interest in planning. Also, in time of emergency such as war, we have engaged in more planning without getting into ideological conflict over the concept.[22] It is not surprising that in the state of economic malaise in the early 1980s, the concept of economic planning is once again more open to discussion.

It is really a moot question as to whether to plan or not. Whenever a major economic decision is made by government which affects the future course of our country, "implicit" and partial planning is already occurring. But the alternative choices are not being aired along with their implications, and the decision is not a participative one. A dollar spent one way, by definition, means that it cannot be spent elsewhere. "Explicit" planning would consider openly the lost or foregone opportunities of that dollar and the impact (costs and benefits) of where the dollar is spent — and encourage participation by the affected groups.

Our society does engage in some "explicit" planning but it is corporate in nature rather than democratic planning. Corporate planning is guided by the needs of firms; it is elitist, secretive, closed, and partial, and the planners are not directly accountable to the public.[23] Corporate planning has important impacts on other groups, but they are not part of that planning process. For example, unions and their members have an obvious stake in the corporation plan — especially when a plan involves plant closures, capital mobility out of the country, or major technological change. However, worker participation in these decisions is rare.

A rejection of governmental planning, or a more participative corporate planning, does not mean that we are free from planning. As John Kenneth Galbraith emphasized in *The New Industrial State*, we are very much subject to the planning whims of large corporations.[24] They spend too much money to allow things to evolve due to chance. According to his view, carefully orchestrated advertising and planning have often ensured a market for a new product. Although these campaigns may sometimes fail, and are now confronted in some cases with more foreign competition, huge corporate product plans clearly direct a large part of our lives. The choice of having competitive markets does not exist and has not existed for some time in many sectors.

The main purpose of these remarks is to point out that we have done little in the way of public economic planning, or participative corporate planning. Given our more complex economy, and current problems, we may have to consider moving at least in the direction of more "explicit" planning than in the past. Planning is no panacea, but at present we do less of it than any of our competitors who out perform us. At a minimum we should engage in explorative social and economic surgery on the merits and demerits of more "explicit" planning without letting the ideologies decide the issue. Planning is consistent with any political philosophy.

Social Costs of Growth and Change

As a consequence of our unwillingness to engage in more "explicit" planning, and because of the narrow scope of collective bargaining, we have failed to adequately take account of the social costs of production or the social costs of industrial change. Specific examples of social costs are production costs such as pollution and health hazards created at the workplace. These costs are largely borne by workers and society; the firm does not pay for the social costs unless there is some form of regulation. In general, social costs are costs imposed on others by firms as a consequence of their industrial behavior.

Private costs, such as wage and fringe benefits, are costs that firms pay for as a direct consequence of their production. Since the firm obviously pays for these costs, it is in its interest to keep them low, or at least to compare labor costs with alternative technological possibilities. In this sense there is a natural tendency for firms to implement technical changes at the workplace to lower private costs because it is the firm which directly benefits from a new technology. But the same incentive to reduce social costs does not exist.

If workers breathe toxic air at the workplace, but the harmful effects are delayed and show up later in retirement or after the worker has moved to another job; it will be the worker, his family, and society who pay for these less obvious costs of production. Since the firm does not pay for these hidden or social costs, the price of the product involved does not adequately reflect the true costs of production. In effect the worker, his family, and society are thus subsidizing the production of the product and, therefore, also subsidizing the firm and the consumers of that product.

As our economy has matured, there are considerable social costs associated with the industrialization process — pollution; health hazards such as chemicals, heat, and noise; plant closures, where communities and workers are left to pick up a substantial part of the cost of closing; job stress; mental health; and alcoholism. To the extent that these problems are related to the production process, or to changes in the production process, there will not be the same incentive for firms to reduce them as is the case for private costs of production. The bias towards reducing private costs and ignoring social costs is a natural flaw in the market mechanism and it can cause important technological twists to occur such that the most efficient technology is not employed. This is not to say that firms never consider safety but the incentive for firms to reduce social costs is not strong relative to their desire to reduce private costs.

The concept of social costs is a very important one. These costs occur in a wide range of economic activities and particularly when economic change occurs. Inadequate management of these social costs is part of the overall inadequacy of the management of economic change. Our historical failure to devise ways to identify and properly handle social costs of industrialization has left us particularly vulnerable to the

damage caused by an economic shakeout. Any plan for reindustrialization should recognize the social cost problem. It was perhaps possible to cover-over this problem in a period of generally strong economic
growth, but the shakeout has imposed large social costs on many more
groups than previously. More general unemployment and community
disruption associated with this shakeout clearly demands better management and recognition of these social costs.

Corporate Management of Change

After World War II, U.S. firms dominated world markets as potential
competitors had been ravaged by war. The U.S. had a growing domestic market and we provided almost 20 percent of world exports in 1951;
imports made up only three percent of our GNP. There was, then, an
era of relative comfort for U.S. industry. Companies set up administered pricing arrangements where one dominant firm would be the
price leader, and others would follow; occasionally another firm might
try to become the price leader, but that was the extent of the price
competition. What competition there was came through advertising
and product differentiation. More often the product differences were
imaginary rather than real. One important aspect of this corporate
behavior was that firms were not used to change and their behavior
was not conducive to innovation — the incentive was not there. While
other countries' steel and auto industries were making a "comeback"
and technological strides in the 1960s, our industries were "laying
back" and did not want to be confronted with change; they seemed
content to split the growing domestic market.

But as global competition increased, U.S. producers were faced with
inevitable foreign competition — in steel, autos, rubber, and electronics. The management response to inevitable change was inadequate.
Via strong lobbying, firms tried to keep all sorts of imports out of the
country. If American firms took the grace period and revitalized their
domestic plants, industry specific protection might be worthwhile. But
the response to protection, tax incentives, loan guarantees, and other
federal largesse, was for firms to practice "paper entrepreneurship" or
"portfolio management" or "merger mania." That is, their response to
new competition was to worry about short-term gains and thus put
their assets where the greatest short-term return was. They acted more
like banks, buying and selling securities for short-run dividends.

These myopic corporate decisions have contributed to America's
long-term productivity growth problem. For example, manufacturing
productivity rose at a rate of 2.5 percent per year in the U.S. from 1960
to 1979. During the same period, the annual rate of productivity
growth averaged 8.3 percent in Japan, 5.5 percent in Sweden, 5.4
percent in West Germany, 5.6 percent in France, and 6.1 percent in
Italy.[25] During this same period, hourly compensation in the U.S. rose
more slowly than in any of these countries. Foreign countries achieved
this productivity edge despite the fact that they are more dependent on

oil imports than the U.S. and they are generally more heavily regulated.

The focus on short-run profit by American managers reflects a structural problem of business. During the "bigger is better" era corporations became multiplant, multifirm and multinational. The way to check profitability in multiple business corporations that were decentralized was to check profits or rates of return by plant or firm in the short-run.[26] Low return subsidiaries were dropped and a search made for higher yield properties regardless of industry lines or expertise of management in different areas.

In this process large firms with multiple plants in multiple domestic and foreign locations, and conglomerates, with multiples of these firms played the "portfolio" game of selling, buying, and closing plants. These actions were taken instead of modernizing facilities and planning to confront international competition in a changing marketplace.

Scope of Collective Bargaining

The scope of bargaining refers to the range of issues that unions can expect to negotiate. At present, firms do not have to bargain over the decision to close a workplace, although they are required to negotiate over the consequences of a closure. Firms do not have to bargain over investment decisions (plant locations are part of investment); they do not have to bargain over mergers and acquisitions; they can build plants and replace old equipment without decision-making input from workers.

It was perhaps not so important that labor participate directly in the management of change during the two decades after World War Two. The domestic economy grew rapidly. Foreign competition was less threatening. There were more technological limits to tapping lower labor costs around the world by U.S. multinationals — and there were less multinationals as well. In this environment a more limited scope of bargaining was understandable.

However, improved technology in transportation and communications, along with the appropriate multinational and conglomerate structure has lowered the relative costs of moving facilities, managers, and information — this is part of the microprocessor revolution. Combine this lower cost of mobility to move with a world-wide workforce that currently expands by about 30 million workers per year and the prediction of "change" is a safe one. Technology has had this effect before within our country; it has shifted to a world stage now.

If we look ahead and agree that technology will continue to lower mobility of capital costs, then an important result follows. Firms will be able to (and if world markets are highly competitive, they may be forced to) move their facilities or production in response to smaller and smaller cost differentials both among and within countries. When this technological possibility is combined with a short-term "portfolio" management mentality, the outcome has serious consequences. Some of these effects are already evident in the form of the shakeout described earlier — for example, plants closing after only six years of existence.

This tendency for increased competition tends to put worker against worker within a country as well as among countries. Destructive aspects of wage competition have always been a problem for labor; the internationalization of this process raises the stakes. The ability of firms to make decisions in an international context rather than a national context increases the power of the corporation over its home country, its regions, as well as over labor.

Both government and labor are more likely to be held hostage to the demands for concessions when firms are more "footloose." State and local governments already compete vigorously for favorable locational decisions by firms — tax breaks, industrial parks, finding a "union-free" environment, etc. With the locational competition stakes rising, due to expanded competition, and the costs of capital mobility falling, the pressure on labor costs increases and the possibility of plant closures rises.

Another negative aspect of mobility of firms is the tendency for over capitalization — that is, for regions or countries to be subject to the boom and bust cycle of global competiton. If the costs of moving are reduced, for technological reasons, then leader firms will move toward these lesser cost (and low regulatory) countries. These areas will be subject to boom conditions and wages will rise, and so will profits for the initial firms, but if other firms follow, they will tend to drive wages higher and profits lower. Soon there will be too many firms and those engaged in the race will pull up stakes and look for the next low cost, low regulation arena. The loser region will now be in the bust phase of the boom-bust cycle.

Given that there is little public control of domestic or international economic change, and given that firms have not done a good job in adjusting to major economic change, and are able to impose substantial social costs on workers, there is an argument for expanding the scope of collective bargaining. The results of this expansion would be to raise the cost of economic change for firms such that they would consider the effects of their decisions on workers more carefully. For example, firms might still close, but the costs for community and worker disruption would be borne more fully by the firm making the move. Expansion of the scope of bargaining would tend to push these costs back into the cost calculations (private costs of the firm). The firm can still act on its own but will more fully pay for its actions.

Zero Sum Mentality (In Positive Sum World)
Under the conditions described above, it is no wonder that labor and other groups see themselves in a zero sum game. A zero sum game refers to a situation where one party feels that the sacrifice that it makes

is simply offset by gains to the other side. Making accommodations is not perceived to increase the total economic pie; concessions mean "you lose X amount and someone else gains X amount." You are worse off, and you and your opponent together are no better off, even though your opponent benefits from your loss. A perception of a zero sum game would lead toward actions that prevent change. This is rational if you can't see any benefit, now or in the future, for a current sacrifice.[27]

In the context of our earlier discussion, which indicated a haphazard approach to managing change, this zero sum mentality is relevant, especially in the collective bargaining arena. If unions view management as unwilling to expand topics for bargaining and as unwilling to provide information to negotiators in times of rapid and major change; if labor views management as aggressive; if government does not appear willing to help ease change, but instead appears to be making labor's job more difficult; and if labor history graphically suggests an adversarial and combative atmosphere, it is no wonder that labor tends to perceive the world in a zero sum light.

We need to develop ways to recognize change with positive sum possibilities, and develop ways to manage change so that everyone involved can benefit. To do this will require that we address: the planning question; the notion of social costs of growth and change; the adequacy of corporate decision-making and how decision-making varies according to the competitiveness of industry; and the scope of collective bargaining. Working toward solutions to these issues will permit intelligent progress and reduce the zero sum mentality.

Policy Directions for Managing Change

We have focused mainly on the problems because a better understanding of them enables readers to judge for themselves the merits and demerits of particular solutions that are offered. Moreover, addressing problems suggests at the same time areas that policy must deal with. It is not the purpose of this section to evaluate numerous specific and varied proposals held up as answers to our dilemma. Rather the purpose is to identify alternative long-term policy directions or broad choices that are available to us to solve our problems, and to consider their implications.

There are basically two broad policy options to choose from. First, we can follow a more "free and unencumbered market" philosophy, which is a major part of the supply side-free market school. This approach implies a reduced role for government, the "freeing-up" of private enterprise and markets, which translates into a policy of more open competition and all that entails for workers and unions.

Second, we can follow a structuralist policy which moves us toward a more conscious and admitted recognition of interdependencies and market imperfections in our economy and the world economy. This view calls for a more active role for government, more selective regulation of markets in the public interest, and increased cooperation among and meaningful participation by economic players. For labor this means more participation in government decisions and in a range of decisions previously treated as management prerogatives — a broadening of the scope of bargaining.

From the tone of the discussion throughout this paper, it is clear that a structuralist interpretation of the problem is preferred. But the supply side-free market view has converted many. For this reason we provide an overview of the supply side-free market interpretation of our economic problem and its policy prescription.

Supply Side-Free Market Policy

The supply side-free market interpretation of our economic problem is that government has become too large — this charge seems to be leveled most strongly at the federal government in Washington (those distant bureaucrats). The allegation that government is too large is consistent with and part of the view that the growth of the private sector has been stifled by the government sector.

Professional economists such as Milton Friedman, author of *Free to Choose*, and more popular writers such as George Gilder, author of *Wealth and Poverty*, represent the same sort of position.[28] As they see things, over the last few decades, markets and people have become over-regulated, over-taxed, and government deficits have "crowded-out" private free market investment. The government has bid away resources from the private sector which, together with its spending policies, has diminished people's desire (need) to work, pushed interest rates up and dampened investment. In short, according to this view, the government does not have the potential to be very efficient.

According to this school, then, our problems stem from a government which over-regulates, and spends too much so that resources taken from the private sector raise interest rates. Firms, faced with affirmative action, health and safety regulations, and pollution rules, have had their costs increased. Moreover, increased tax payments have reduced their profits. From this scenerio it follows that if costs go up and revenues go down, firms' profits will fall. And this leads to a reduction in investment as firms see less of a payoff for taking risk.

The motivational problem exists in the workforce too, according to this way of thinking. Rational individuals do not find it worthwhile to seek work or stay at work if unemployment insurance, added to welfare, foodstamps, and other government transfers, and increased taxes make it easier not to work. This type of behavior by the labor force, added to the lethargy of firms brought on by government activity, has reduced our productivity rate according to the supply side-free market school of thought.

This explanation of our problem has a predictable view of unions and their effect on the economy and productivity. In short, unions are viewed as monopolies and antimarket institutions. The monopoly view of unions holds that unions raise wages above competitive levels and therefore there are less jobs in union workplaces than otherwise, because firms put more labor saving technology in those job sites in response to the higher wages. Unions, according to this view, institute work rules and thus reduce productivity. Their actions produce costly strikes, which reduce output. They increase wage differentials by raising wages of their more skilled workers. They discriminate in the rationing of scarce job slots. Their monopoly position encourages corrupt and undemocratic practices.[29] From this list of allegations it is not difficult to foresee what supply side-free market advocates would have in store for unions if their long-term policy preferences were to be followed.

The absence of strong market competition, caused by increased government usage of private resources and regulation, explains in large measure why our economy has performed so poorly — according to the supply side-free market view. This is why plants have closed, joblessness has risen and why our country falls behind the foreign competition. Of course there are variations on this theme and different emphases. But what is important is that the underlying explanations are all close to the above scenario in terms of general direction.

As we consider supply side-free market policies, keep in mind that as the word supply implies, its proponents are attempting to increase supply — supply of output by firms, supply of work effort by employees, supply of savings, supply of investment. They hope to do this by reducing taxes and the government "take" of private resources. This reorientation is the cornerstone of their policy direction.

Since government is a major culprit according to the supply side-free market view, the long-term solution is for it to shrink — use proportionately less of our total resources. Tax cuts and government spending cuts are thus in order. But, whereas demand side tax cuts like the Kennedy-Johnson tax cuts of 1964 were meant to stimulate consumption (demand), the supply side tax cuts were aimed at increasing savings and investment. Therefore, the cuts give more to higher income than lower income people, because in theory low income people would spend their cuts, whereas high income people would save much of their cut and it could go into investment.

Cutting taxes for high income earners was the objective of Reaganomics but politically it was hard to sell this "trickle down" approach — give the money to those who already have plenty and they will save (invest) it. More funds will be available for expansion (investment) and the less well off will be hired in the jobs resulting from the expansion.

Consequently, the supply side tax cuts of the early 1980s were packaged somewhat differently — everyone would get a cut in taxes. But the real objective was to substantially lower the rates for those in the top bracket. As David Stockman, Director of the Office of Management and Budget, told the *Atlantic Monthly*:

"The hard part of the supply-side tax cut is dropping the top rate from 70 to 50 percent the rest of it is a secondary matter. The original argument was that the top bracket was too high, and that's having the most devastating effect on the economy. Then, the general argument was that, in order, to make this palatable as a political matter, you had to bring down all the brackets. But, I mean, Kemp-Roth was always a Trojan horse to bring down the top rate."[30]

A major tax cut reduces government resources and, therefore, the long-run policy of the supply side-free market approach is to cut government programs. The Congressional Budget Office estimates that cuts decided on in 1981-82 will lower government spending by 240 billion dollars during 1983-86. These cuts are in nondefense areas such as: medicaid, medicare, food stamps, education, and job training.

The implications of the supply side-free market approach are clear. The economic players — consumers, firms (some firms), workers, and unions are going to have to fend more for themselves. There is likely to be little planning of the "explicit" kind to which we referred earlier, since this would represent interference with private decisions. Whatever planning takes place will be "implicit" or closed planning.

Social costs will receive less attention, since the market mechanism is not well suited to handling them. This suggests that with respect to issues such as plant closures, it will be the market which decides when, where, and how a firm closes. The argument is that firms must not be prevented from moving their capital when they see fit. To interfere with this process would be antimarket. Placing public policy in the way of these closures ". . . seeks to destroy one of the few remaining vestiges of the free market . . .," that right being the "right to close shop."[31] Similarly, worker health and safety, affirmative action, and pollution control involve social costs and, therefore, would be expected to receive much less emphasis.

In the supply side-free market model, the responsibility for the management of change would clearly go more toward firms. Its adherents think this is well and good, since in their view, consumers through their spending decisions reward firms that do well (are efficient) and punish those who do poorly (are inefficient).

The supply side-free market advocates see the zero sum mentality, mentioned earlier, as a problem. Their solution is to get us out of that mold by force. The force will be markets. If people and institutions are subject to markets and have no political or regulated protection, they may have a zero sum mentality but they will have no power to prevent change. Markets thrive on change and an enforceable zero sum position is antimarket. A way out of the zero sum problem, therefore, is to make changes in regulations, the law, or collective bargaining, so that groups cannot resist change.

A major move in the direction of the supply side-free market philosophy will mean, in effect, a narrowing of the scope of collective bargaining. As changes occur, labor will have less say or participation in those changes, or in the adjustment to those changes. This view follows from the fact that if the government encourages firms to act more freely from government restraints, then firms will be encouraged to break away from restraints put on them by nongovernmental institutions such as unions. Firms facing unions who are protecting members' interests by slowing change will be given implicit if not explicit sanction by government to break through those restraints.

In short, according to this view, firms and others will be "free to choose" — the title of Friedman's book mentioned earlier. Free to move, free to locate overseas, free to hire who they want, free to pay the wage that they want, constrained only by the dictates of the market. Workers, likewise, are free to accept or reject a wage, free to accept or reject a risky job. There are, of course, restrictions that supply side-free market advocates would allow, but in terms of broad policy direction their position and the implications stemming from that position are clear. The management of change is to be left to the market.

Another implication of this model is that there exists a "natural" rate of unemployment. If we do the things advocated above, the natural rate will fall towards full employment automatically. The government should not take an activist role in this regard — just make the market work better by reducing government's role.

The supply side-free market approach would depend much more on market competition to manage change, and greatly reduce the role of government. Its policy for reindustrialization is one of "hands-off" or laissez-faire. The economic system is seen as being "competitive enough," given the reduction of government activity, taxes and regulation, to provide for our individual and collective future welfare. This philosophy is not new, but a move in this direction would represent a significant departure from the post-World War Two trend.

Structuralist Response and Alternative Policy

A common view, which links up sometimes divergent positions under the structuralist heading, is that in many fundamental ways markets do not manage change adequately. To put too much faith in mythical free markets in essential parts of the economy is to ignore the realities of a complex and interdependent economy. The structuralist position is not necessarily antimarket — it is simply open to explore ways to make our system perform more in the public interest through an activist public policy or institutional guidance.

The structuralist position would move us in the opposite direction from the supply side-free market approach. We would move toward a more selective "hands-on" policy, and a more cooperative approach through increased and broadly based participation in the management of change. Structuralist policy is explored further below, first, by providing some direct responses to the supply side-free market position as outlined above and, second, by discussing additional policy alternatives and their implications.

Structuralist Response

In response to the supply side-free market view of government and markets, the following points should be noted. First, the federal government has not grown as much as some people think. Second, compared to other countries, including our foreign competitors, we are already a very "unregulated" and low tax country. Third, government activity has not "crowded-out" private investment to any meaningful degree. Fourth, regulation and government activity are not inherently bad or inefficient.

In 1960, paid civilian employment in the federal sector was 2.4 million; 20 years later in 1980, it was 2.9 million.[32] This represents a 16 percent increase over the 20 years in which the labor force grew by a whopping 48 percent from 72 million to 107 million.[33] The proportion of federal employees located in Washington has remained at about 12 percent over this period.

Another indicator of long-term growth in the federal sector and in regulation is the proportion of gross national product (GNP) that is spent by the federal government. During the period 1960-1964 the federal budget was 19 percent of GNP, 19.7 percent during 1966 to 1969, 20.1 percent from 1970 to 1974 and 21.9 percent from 1976 to 1981.[34] The relatively high recent growth in the federal budget as a share of GNP is largely due to the back to back recessions, that resulted in falling revenue and a need for recession — related government expenditures.

Another measure often used to illustrate that our long-term economic problem is over-regulated and "big" government is the growing federal deficit. This argument has been part of the supply side-free market argument for some time. It is pointed out that our federal deficit has grown three times from 1950 to 1981. This seems to be significant until it is mentioned that during this period corporate debt rose about 13 times, consumer installment debt increased 16 times, mortgage debt rose 13 times and local government debt rose 14 times.[35]

Since the end of World War Two, our federal deficit as a percent of GNP has declined from 96.9 percent in 1950 to 58.3 percent in 1960 to 39.5 percent in 1970 to 35.6 percent in 1980.[36] It should also be pointed out that government debt is different from consumer debt. If a family borrows, it pays the debt to someone else — it is not paying the right hand with the left. The federal debt (unless foreigners hold it and they do not hold much) is owed to our collective domestic family. It also matters what the federal debt is used for. If it creates jobs, roads, bridges and future growth, when there is slack in the economy, then we will all be better off and so will future generations who have to pay it (receive it).

Compared to other developed countries, the U.S. does not tax at a high rate; and this is an indication of regulation. In West Germany, transfer payments amount to over 25 percent of GNP, whereas in the U.S. they are about 10 percent. In the U.S., government revenue raised in taxes, as a percent of GNP, is 28 percent. In other countries the comparable figures are: U.K. (33%), West Germany (37%), Sweden (44%), France (37%), Canada (34%), Japan (23%), and Norway (46%). All of these countries have exceeded ours in manufacturing productivity growth for about two decades.[37] And virtually all of them have more regulation of business activity, especially in labor matters.

Big government, according to the supply side-free market view is supposed to "crowd-out" the private sector's ability to invest. But real corporate investment (as a percent of GNP) was 9.1 to 9.4 percent in the early 1960s; in the late 1960s it averaged between 10-11 percent, as it did between 1970 and 1979. In 1980, 1981, and 1982, corporate investment exceeded 11 percent.[38] The investment is there, however, much of its energy is going into mergers and acquisitions.

The comments above suggest an exaggerated claim that government soaks up resources and stymies private economic activity. Government activity certainly might be inefficient in many areas, but its growth has not been responsible for our long-run economic problems — except, of course, in as much as government recessionary short-term policy creates unused capacity and, therefore, discourages investment.

The supply side-free market approach argues, the less government, the better, and, therefore, the more latitude that firms have, the better. The structuralist approach does not have so much faith in the workings of so-called free markets. The following quote coming, surprisingly, from Felix Rohatyn, an influential banker-businessman captures part of the problem:

> ". . . the price of our energy is not freely set, nor is the price of our food, or the price at which we borrow money. Free markets are clearly desirable but we do not live in a free market economy and never will."[39]

This quote suggests a very important point. The choice before us, according to supply side-free marketers is that we can have either "free markets" or "something else." Setting up the choice this way begs the question, for what we do have, and have had for the relevant past, is the "something else." The "free market" choice is really a myth; the real debate should be over understanding the "something else" and selecting the correct mix of institutional guidance versus markets within the inevitable "something else" — to make it work for us, not against us.

Given this reality, the structural approach welcomes an innovative, efficient, expanded, and cooperative role for government in the management of change. Institutional guidance is not viewed as being negative per se. In fact, it is needed so that the marketplace serves better the public interest. But regulations are not "the" answer — although effective ones are welcome. They will have to be complemented with the creation of a more cooperative environment between business and labor, an environment that government can help foster.

Public Policy Alternatives

Earlier in this paper we described in some detail how we currently mismanage economic change. Structural policy directions to reduce this mismanagement would include steps to: (1) generate full employment in the short-term and find alternatives to "administering" recessions to beat down inflation (2) explore the benefits of "explicit" and participative planning in key areas of our economy (3) take account of the social costs (benefits) of private economic behavior so that the notion of what is "efficient" or "productive" change is more comprehensive and equitable (4) reduce the discretion that firms have to implement destructive change, and set conditions to encourage long-term decision making instead of the short-term "portfolio" approach (5) expand the scope of bargaining so that labor can more fully participate in the management of change and (6) reduce the zero sum mentality by providing an environment for positive sum sharing agreements.

The distinctions between the supply side-free market view and a more structural approach are now quite apparent. With respect to the first five policy statements above, the supply side-free market view would move in the reverse direction. On the sixth policy statement, the supply side-free market approach would try to reduce the zero sum problem too, but the method would involve the "stick" as opposed to the "carrot" approach.

The first policy step above suggests a goal of full employment and an alternative to the administered recession solution to inflation. The Employment Act of 1946 and the Full Employment and Balanced Growth Act of 1978 have been passed already. If we followed the spirit and letter of those Acts we would have unemployment of four percent. Full employment is a basic requirement for sustained growth. We just do not put enough resources and intellectual energy into the commitment to keep people on the job. Instead we lay them off in the fight against inflation. This is an archaic policy that requires us to raise unemployment ever higher and higher, in order to reduce inflation.

If moderately rising unemployment were effective in stopping price rises, we would have had a moderate inflation record in the 1970s — we clearly did not, even with extensive unemployment. This is because most of the inflation was not related to excessive spending or wages. Rather, inflationary origins were in energy costs, corporate pricing practices, and overall productivity problems. We need a commitment to full employment and a fair incomes (price-wage control) policy that labor participates in fully. This could be the beginning of a more rational use of our economy with selective institutional guidance as part of the long-term strategy which recognizes the complexity and interdependence of our economy and the world economy.

An increase in democratic planning is the second policy step suggested above. This policy would be an experimental one at first, with business and labor directly involved. It would be flexible, change-oriented, informational, educational, explorative and open. At first, there could be a good deal of explorative economic and social surgery, to determine where many of our problems are. It is in this forum that issues like foreign trade would be addressed and coordinated with discussion of issues such as trade related plant closures, unemployment, technical change and foreign investment. The details of such a step are not so important as is the decision to move in this more logical direction. It is a political problem not an economic one that stands in the way of experimentation along these lines.

The creation of a reindustrialization board, with considerable power and financial resources would be a crucial aspect of any planning effort. This board — with genuine participation guaranteed for labor and business — would have considerably more flexibility and tools in its investment behavior than the private sector would. It could make loans, it could invest directly, it could give tax concessions, it could make selective regulatory concessions or it could create new regulatory conditions in order to elicit certain behavior from borrowers. It could also lend to private or public concerns, insist on more input from labor and communities as a condition for loans, give trade relief as a condition for certain behavior, and encourage the use of pension funds for investment. Most of all it could provide investment with a long-term, public interest focus.

One area that planning would hopefully address is the notion of social costs, our third policy step. These are costs or consequences of production for which firms do not pay. Since markets do not perform well in handling them, and they occur across a wide range of areas — plant closures, internal pollution, external pollution, occupational accidents and disease, etc., we need to set up a public balance sheet to account for social costs. This accounting is very important during the best of economic times. It is even more important during times of change and in periods of economic shakeout.

To not consider fully the social costs of new technology, or of a change in investment, or plant location, or foreign investment, or trade concession, is to encourage truly inefficient and nonproductive uses of our resources. Bringing social costs more into economic calculations can be expected to create resistance since some people will lose (those who could previously ignore the social costs) and others will gain (communities and workers who previously had no choice but to pay the social costs).

The plant closure legislation debate centers around the willingness to consider or weigh social costs. The supply side-free market view would oppose such legislation as being antimarket. This view would encourage "free choice" for the firm, with no strings attached. Structuralists, like popular economist Lester Thurow would provide financial and training cushions for individuals and communities in recognition of social costs, but leave the firms free to move. In recognition of social costs, and noncompetitive destructive industrial mobility, some economists such as Bluestone and Harrison would move to control capital investment (including plant closures) much more in the public interest. They view deindustrialization in the U.S. as the destructive effects of capital competition around the world and they would control that mobility in the public interest.

Both Thurow's and Bluestone and Harrison's solutions to the plant closure problem address the social cost problem. And both are concerned with the management of change, although with emphases in different places. Recall that we suggested that the management of change came in two parts — the decision to change (to close the plant), and the decision on timing of and adjustment to change (early warning of plant closing and compensation and retraining). Bluestone and Harrison would control the actual closure decision in the name of social costs. Thurow would control the adjustment aspect of a closure. Both policies would affect the management of change, one directly, the other indirectly. In contrast, the supply side-free market approach would do little to address this problem, preferring to let markets manage the change.

The fourth policy step is consistent with steps two and three. That is, if we look more openly at long-term economic options via some form of planning, and considered more explicitly the social cost problem, then firms will have less discretion to implement socially destructive change. In addition, considering long-term factors and social costs would tend to move firms away from the short-term "portfolio" management approach. Again, the details of how we reduce the discretion that firms have to implement destructive change is not as important as deciding that a policy move in the direction of step three is required.

The fifth policy step suggested above is expansion of the scope of collective bargaining. This policy is suggested so that labor can more fully participate in the management of change. An expanded scope of bargaining fits in with policy steps two, three, and four, since workers are one group that suffers directly from inadequate planning, from suppression of social costs, and from destructive change resulting from unencumbered behavior of firms.

Contrary to the supply side-free market approach, the structural view does not consider unions as a major source of our economic problems. Instead unions are viewed as being beneficial organizations, making up for the deficiencies of the market and as an offset to corporate power. Whereas the supply side-free market approach would tend to narrow the influence of unions, the structural approach would enhance the role of unions.

There are essentially three avenues open for labor to expand its influence on the management of change. One is by being an autonomous and major partner in a new planning effort along with government and business. Assuming that we made some serious efforts in this direction, labor's position would be enhanced. Second, if the items which are bargained at the negotiating table are expanded to capture factors such as new technology, plant closures, new investment plans, etc., that clearly affect "conditions of employment" then labor would have more influence. Third, if labor participated on corporate boards there would be another channel for input into the management of change.

As issues surrounding change become more complex, and are caught up in international, national, conglomerate, and multinational decision-making, it is clear that labor must have more input into these processes if it is to remain a viable force. These three methods to provide more labor input could result in more enlightened change. Social costs of change can be well represented by labor if it is an expanded role. If allowed this input, labor will not have to play the obstructionist role as much and this will lessen its zero sum mentality.

The sixth policy step is concerned with reducing the zero sum mentality and creating an atmosphere whereby positive sum opportunities can be enhanced. Steps two through five would lead toward that end. If these were implemented, there would be less concern that labor's sacrifice in economic change would simple be treated as a corporate gain.

The essential point is that potential losers in economic change have to be adequately compensated by potential winners. Only then will potential losers be more willing to submit to change. With this principle in force, the potential winnings have to be substantial enough to compensate and still make the change worthwhile. That is, there has to be a positive sum potential for change to occur.

At present, we do not have enough information or mechanisms for communication and compensation to put this principle into practice. Therefore, the understandable resistance to change. The supply side-free market approach will reduce the zero sum problem by force — the market in practice will dictate change without compensation.

A structural approach would create channels of compensation and would provide a framework where the full "public" or social costs of change could be more fully recognized. Some experience with this approach could be expected to make workers more secure — as are West German workers, who more fully participate in change and, therefore, have reduced their view that change is of a zero sum nature. In the U.S., workers and other groups have plenty of incentive to be obstructionist given the way we currently manage change.

Conclusions and Implications for Labor

This discussion began with suggestions that labor's agenda is shaped by the environment in which it operates, an environment currently marred by concerns about unemployment, plant closures, union security, etc. These concerns have been determined by the current economic shakeout we are in, combined with the fact that labor does not participate in the management of change.

The current methods of managing change have been found to be deficient and have placed labor in a defensive position especially during a period of economic shakeout. Labor's current role in the management of change does not form a solid basis for an independent and autonomous role in any reindustrialization effort. Following the supply side-free market alternative for reindustrialization would weaken labor's role even more. The structural approach appears to address some basic long-term policy questions that labor and others must consider as a basis or framework for improving the management of change.

Long-term policy directions include the need for more planning, more accounting for social costs, more responsible decision-making by managers, more participation by labor through a broader scope of bargaining and an autonomous role in any planning scheme, and more compensatory change or control of change to reduce the zero sum problem. Serious developments along these lines would provide for a more civilized long-range basis for reindustrialization than would the supply side-free market alternative. The decision as to which route to follow is a political one more than an economic one. It seems clear that a structionalist approach offers labor the most sane environment in which to participate in reindustrialization.

End Notes

1. Piori calls this stability a form of "regulation," a ". . . . system of institutions that keeps an economy in balance and ensures its further growth and development." See: Michael J. Piore, "American Labor and the Industrial Crisis," *Challenge* (March/April 1982), p. 6.
2. *The New York Times*, February 21, 1983.
3. Barry Bluestone and Bennett Harrison, *The Deindustrialization of America* (New York: Basic Books, 1982), p. 4.
4. *Ibid;* see also Richard J. Barnett and Ronald E. Miller, *Global Reach: The Power of the Multinational Corporation* (Simon and Schuster: New York, 1974).
5. Roger W. Schmenner, "Every Factory Has a Life Cycle," *Harvard Business Review* (March/April, 1983), p. 121.
6. Walter Adams, "Mega-Mergers Spell Danger" *Challenge* (March/April, 1983), p. 12.
7. *Ibid.* p. 13.
8. *The New York Times*, July 3, 1983.
9. Charles J. Janus, "Union Mergers in the 1970's. . . . ," *Monthly Labor Review* (October, 1978), pp. 13-23.
10. Council of Economic Advisers, *Economic Report of the President* (Washington, DC: U.S. G.P.O., 1983), p. 279.
11. *Forbes*, July 4, 1983, p. 101.
12. *Ibid.* p. 118.
13. *Economic Report of the President*, p. 221.
14. *Ibid.*
15. U.S. Department of Labor, *International Comparisons of Manufacturing Productivity. . . . ,* 80-322, May 22, 1980, p. 2.

16. U.S. Department of Labor, *Monthly Labor Review* (February, 1983), p. 60, and (February, 1976), p. 68.

17. *The New York Times*, May 16, 1983.

18. Sar A. Levitan, "The Future of Work: Does it Belong to Us or to the Robots," *Monthly Labor Review* (September, 1983), p. 10-14.

19. *The New York Times*, May 8, 1983.

20. Gunnar Myrdal, *Challenge to Affluence* (New York: Patheon Books, 1962); see also his *An American Dilemma* (New York, Harper, 1944).

21. Myrdal, *Challenge to Affluence*, p. 91.

22. Neil W. Chamberlain, *Private and Public Planning* (New York: McGraw-Hill, 1965), pp. 1-4.

23. Robert B. Reich, "A Path For America," *Dissent* (Winter, 1983), p. 25.

24. John Kenneth Galbraith, *The New Industrial State* (Boston: Houghton Mifflin, 1967), ch. XVIII.

25. *International Comparisons of Manufacturing Productivity*, p. 7.

26. Robert H. Hayes and William J. Abernathy, "Managing Our Way to Economic Decline," *Harvard Business Review* (July-August, 1980), pp. 67-77.

27. Lester Thurow, *The Zero Sum Society* (New York: Penguin Books, 1981).

28. Milton and Rose Friedman, *Free to Choose* (New York: Harcourt Brace Janonovich, 1980); and George Guilder, *Wealth and Poverty* (New York: Basic Books, 1981).

29. Richard B. Freeman and James L. Medoff, "The Two Faces of Unionism," *The Public Interest* (Fall, 1979), pp. 69-93.

30. William Greider, "The Education of David Stockman," *The Atlantic Monthly* (December, 1981), p. 46.

31. *The New York Times*, August 26, 1983. See also Richard McKensie, "The Case for Plant Closures," *Policy Review* 15 (Winter, 1981), pp. 119-133.

32. U.S. Department of Commerce, *Statistical Abstract of the United States: 1982-83* (Washington, DC, G.P.O., 1982), p. 265.

33. *Ibid.* p. 374.

34. U.S. Department of Commerce, *Statistical Abstract of the United States: 1981*, p. 245.

35. Ray Marshall, "Understanding the 'Supply Side' Fallacy" *Federationist* (June, 1981), p. 5.

36. U.S. Department of Commerce, *Statistical Abstract of the United States: 1982-83* (Washington, DC, B.P.O., 1983), p. 246.

37. Robert Heilbronner and Lester Thurow, *Five Economic Challenges*, (Englewood Cliffs: Prentice Hall, 1981), p. 57.

38. *Economic Report of the President*, p. 263.

39. Robert LeKachman, *Greed is not Enough: Reaganomics* (New York: Pantheon, 1983), p. 197.

The Deindustrialization of a Factory Town: Plant Closings and Phasedowns in South Bend, Indiana, 1954-1983

Charles Craypo

Introduction

Factory towns in the Northeast and Great Lakes states are being deindustrialized. The writers most closely identified with the term deindustrialization define it as "a widespread, systematic disinvestment in the nation's basic productive capacity."[1] Closings and phasedowns of business establishments are the principal consequences of such disinvestment. For a single community, this can mean the loss of plants, mills, and offices at a rate too rapid to be offset by the start of new establishments and the expansion of existing ones.

A case study of one community enables us to identify and explain in detail the reasons for industrial dislocation, the role of union-management relations, and the impact on workers. The task of the informed case study, in other words, is to describe and interpret actual events and, on that basis, to construct a political economy analysis of what happened, why it happened, and how its happening affects individuals and organizations. Separate cases are then considered together for empirical evidence of general patterns and new directions in the structure and behavior of American industry.

This is a study of plant closings and phasedowns in the South Bend, Indiana area during 1954-1983. It describes and analyzes 27 docu-

Charles Craypo is Professor of Industrial and Labor Relations, Extension Division, New York State School of Industrial and Labor Relations, Cornell University. The author is indebted to Keith Knauss, Jerry Paar, and Lawrence Mishel for help in identifying plant closings in South Bend-Mishawaka and for their comments and suggestions on this paper. He also wishes to acknowledge the kind cooperation and valuable assistance of the staffs of the South Bend Public Library, and the South Bend Tribune Library. Initial research in the study was supported by a grant to the Indiana History Project from the Indiana Committee for the Humanities and was conducted with the assistance of students in the Division of Labor Studies, Indiana University at South Bend.

mented shutdowns. Individual case descriptions are developed from background information of the industries and firms involved, local newspaper accounts of shutdowns and labor relations, primary documents obtained from interested parties, and interviews with some of the participants. The analysis uses two contributions of structural economics: industrial organization theory and the theory of relative bargaining power between labor and management.

The Economic Environment

Indiana is an industrialized Great Lakes state. Manufacturing in Indiana accounts for about 40 percent of personal income and 30 percent of the jobs. The state's manufacturing wages are comparable with those of others in the Great Lakes region, but its average nonmanufacturing income is below the average. Therefore, per capita income in Indiana is lower than that in every other Great Lakes state.

Indiana's economy is cyclical because its manufacturing sector is centered in slow-growth, recession-prone industries — primary metals, transportation equipment, and electrical products. Moreover, it has not kept pace with either regional or national growth trends in population, jobs, and income. The rate of change differs within the state, however. Indiana's rural and semi-rural communities have fared best, while most of its urban areas barely hold their own and others, like South Bend, fall farther behind the national patterns.[2]

Indiana is politically sympathetic to business. Recent surveys by a leading industrial location consultant rank Indiana's pro-business climate second in the nation when those factors over which state and local government have control are measured. It easily outranks each of its neighboring Great Lakes states. Indiana's chief attractions are its low levels of wages, workers' compensation benefits, welfare expenditures, and business and personal income taxes.

These findings are consistent with Indiana's current industrialization strategy. State and local economic development agencies promote Indiana as being the most pro-industry state within a highly unionized and regulated region. The South Bend-Mishawaka Area Chamber of Commerce and its economic development agency, Project Future, have been trying to lure businesses from other Great Lakes states, especially from Michigan, which finished forty-fifth in the same industrial climate survey.[3] The Chamber points out that a majority of the local employers with one-hundred or fewer workers operate nonunion, and that larger firms produce in "a very mature union climate" in which union leaders and members understand that they must work with employers to preserve industrial jobs.[4]

South Bend Labor and Deindustrialization

Located 90 miles east of Chicago, and straddling the St. Joseph River as it flows north into Lake Michigan, South Bend is an early Indiana industrial center. Basic commodities like plows, clothing, and wagons were made in the city before the Civil War. Studebaker carriage works began producing automobiles shortly after the turn of the century and South Bend then took on the image of a "metal working" auto town.

The Labor Force.
South Bend workers are included in a standard metropolitan statistical area (SMSA) which encompasses St. Joseph and Marshall counties. The area's two major population centers are South Bend and Mishawaka, which borders South Bend to the east. The rest of the SMSA is sparsely populated and largely rural. At the beginning of 1983 it had a labor force of 138,300 persons, 122,200 of whom were employed, for an area unemployment level of 11.5 percent.

During 1961-1963 the South Bend area workforce experienced a dramatic change in the ratio of manufacturing to total employment. This shift is shown in Table 1. Total employment rose 29 percent, but the number of manufacturing jobs fell by 22 percent while nonmanufacturing jobs increased by nearly two-thirds. At the end of the period manufacturing employment accounted for only 26 percent of total employment compared to 42 percent at the beginning, a drop of sixteen percentage points.

Table 1
Employment in the South Bend Standard
Metropolitan Statistical Area, 1961-1983

Employment	1961	1970	1980	June, 1983*
Total wage and salary	82,400	94,200	110,800	106,500
Manufacturing	34,800	32,500	30,700	27,200
Percentage of total in Manufacturing	42%	34%	28%	26%
Nonmanufacturing	47,600	61,700	81,100	79,300
Percentage of total in Nonmanufacturing	58%	66%	73%	74%

*Preliminary figures.

Sources: Indiana Employment Security Division, South Bend, Indiana, "Indiana Labor Market Letter" (various issues); preliminary June 1983 figures estimated by Kathy Zeiger, Labor Market Analyst, IESD, South Bend office.

Thousands of these manufacturing jobs were lost in three stages of economic dislocation. First, the 19 plant closings which occurred during 1954-1979 directly displaced more than 14,000 hourly and salaried employees in manufacturing. Second, in South Bend the most recent economic recession began in 1979; it had a severe impact on auto-related manufacturing, and was still rampant in mid-1983. Third, seven additional plant closings and several permanent plant phase-downs occurred in the area during 1980-1983, the latter because a number of national firms relocated local production to their southern plants. The second and third stages of dislocation together accounted for a net loss of 3,500 manufacturing jobs in less than four years. This loss rivals the loss of 4,100 manufacturing jobs during the preceding two decades.

For the economy as a whole, the number of manufacturing jobs increased during 1961-1980, although the ratio of manufacturing to total employment declined. Manufacturing jobs rose by 24 percent nationally, compared to the 12 percent drop in South Bend. The share of manufacturing jobs to total employment decreased from 30 to 22 percent nationwide, but in South Bend the decline was greater, from 42 to 28 percent. South Bend thus did not share in the economy's generation of new manufacturing jobs. As an indicator of deindustrialization, the failure to share in this gain is as important as a net loss of manufacturing jobs.

Industrial Shutdown and Worker Income.

The change in job ratios undoubtedly affected family and community incomes. Northern manufacturing jobs normally are in the "primary" labor market for blue-collar workers, which means they are unionized, pay high wage and benefit levels, have low employee turnover rates, and provide economic security. Nonmanufacturing jobs, by contrast, are frequently in the "secondary" labor market, which is the reverse of primary employment — nonunion, low wage and benefit levels, high turnover rates, and economic insecurity. This is especially the case with service sector jobs, which in 1980 accounted for nearly three-quarters of nonmanufacturing employment in the South Bend SMSA.[5]

The shift from primary to secondary employment decreases total community income. Figures comparing occupational earnings within the South Bend-Mishawaka SMSA during the first quarter of 1980 show estimated gross average weekly earnings of $365 for manufacturing and $225 for nonmanufacturing employees. Average yearly earnings on that basis would be $18,980, and $11,700 respectively, a difference of $7,280 more for each manufacturing worker. If the 1961 ratio between manufacturing and nonmanufacturing employment had remained constant through 1980, it would have meant a net addition of 15,000 manufacturing jobs. The effect of maintaining this job ratio would have been a gain of $109 million in direct income (15,000 jobs x $7,280 average earnings differential = $109,200,000). Additional indirect income would have been generated by the consumption multiplier effect of a higher proportion of manufacturing jobs.[6]

Deindustrialization.

The South Bend area was effectively "deindustrialized" during 1953-1983. Since South Bend is a factory town, deindustrialization meant mostly the shutdown and phasedown of manufacturing facilities and the displacement of hourly production workers. Table 2 shows the employment changes that occurred during this time among the eight largest area manufacturers. These firms provided 43,000 jobs in 1953; thirty years later three of them had been closed and the other five together employed eight thousand. More than thirty thousand jobs were lost at just three facilities, which underscores the importance of large corporate employers in the deindustrialization process.

Table 2
Employment Changes Between 1953 and 1983 in the Eight Largest South Bend-Mishawaka Manufacturers

Company	Average Employment, 1953	Average Employment, April 1983	Net Employment Change
Studebaker	20,524	Closed	-20,524
Bendix	11,762	5,700	- 6,062
Uniroyal	5,300	1,130	- 4,170
White Farm	1,500	<100*	- 1,400
Singer	1,500	Closed	- 1,500
Wheelabrator-Frye	900	493	- 407
Dodge-Reliance-Exxon	900	534	- 366
Wilson Bros.	750	Closed	- 750
Total	43,136	7,957	-35,179

*Estimated number of employees by the UAW local union.

Sources: Figures for 1953 are from Robert Gold, *Manufacturing Structure and Pattern of the South Bend-Mishawaka Area* (Chicago: University of Chicago, Department of Geography, 1954), p. 75; those for April, 1983 were compiled by "Project Future," South Bend-Mishawaka Chamber of Commerce, April 20, 1983 (mimeo).

Of the 13,000 jobs that were phased out during 1953-1983, few will ever be restored. White Farm went through bankruptcy and is now a subsidiary of the privately owned TIC Corporation; it is not likely that TIC will refurbish the aging South Bend plant and install new product lines. Bendix, Wheelabrator, and Dodge are each transferring local production to their southern plants. Uniroyal reportedly has stabilized employment and added non-tire rubber products at its Mishawaka facility.

Table 4 shows the distribution of jobs among major employers in the South Bend area in 1982. Chamber of Commerce figures indicate that the largest ten manufacturers provided slightly more than 13,000 jobs, while the ten largest nonmanufacturing employers reported nearly 14,000. Comparable figures for nonmanufacturing employment in 1953 are not available, but they certainly would not have exceeded or even approached the level of manufacturing jobs at that time.

Plant Closings
Indiana experienced frequent plant closings during the 1970s. A partial listing of shutdowns statewide for 1975-1980, compiled by the "Save Our Jobs" campaign of the Indiana Citizens Action Coalition,

Table 3
Plant Closings in the South Bend-Mishawaka Area, 1954-1983

Company	Product	Year of Closing[1]	Number of Employees at Closing[1]	Historical Peak Number of Employees[1]	Stated Reason for Closing[2]
Singer	Sewing machine cabinets	1954	1,200	2,600	Moved operations closer to wood sources.
Kingan	Meat processing	1954	150	N.A.[3]	Insufficient level of operations.
Bike-Web	Elastic garments	1959	200	350	Moved operations to improve efficiency.
Curtiss-Wright	Heavy construction equipment	1961	200	3,000	Insufficient share of the product market.
Studebaker	Auto	1963	8,500	22,000	Forced out of product market.
H. D. Lee	Clothing	1964	230	650	Deteriorating plant and equipment.
South Bend Tackle	Fishing gear	1965	90	N.A.	Labor-intensive plant and equipment.
Essex Wire	Automotive wire products	1968	N.A.	550+	No stated reason.
Rockwell	Auto bumpers	1967	700	700	Inefficient operations.
Roth Plating	Electroplating	1967	75	100+	Noncompetitive operations.
Empire Box	Paper cartons	1967	125	200	Marketing and operating difficulties.
Cummins	Diesel engine castings	1969	1,000	1,000	Necessary plant modernization too costly.
Drewrys	Beer	1972	250	500	Not competitive in product market.
Wilson Bros.	Clothing	1973	100	2,000	Necessary plant modernization too costly.

Company	Product/Service	Year	Employees[1]		Reason
Genner Packing	Meat processing	1973	80	100+	Forced out of product market by low operating level.
Ward Baking	Baked goods	1974	85	N.A.	High labor costs and outdated equipment.
Associates	Loans and insurance	1975	550[4]	550	Advantages of Southern location.
AM General	City buses	1978	780	780	Not competitive in product market.
H.B. Skinner	Industrial pipe clamps	1978	40	80+	Products outdated.
Weyerhaeuser	Paper products warehousing and distribution.	1979	60	100+	Marketing reorganization.
Schumacher & Sons	Building construction	1980	N.A.	N.A.	High labor costs and interest rates; business slump.
Whitehouse	Health care apparel	1982	32	80+	Market conditions.
South Bend Range	Commercial ovens	1983	30	200+	High labor costs and inefficient plant.
South Bend Tool & Die	Machine tools	1983	35	450	High cost of labor and new equipment.
South Bend Screw	Precision machine parts	1983	N.A.	60	No stated reason.
Garvey Pattern	Precision machine tools and fixtures	1983	40	100	Downturn in market and union problems.
Torrington[5]	Industrial bearings	1983	164	1,000+	Excess production capacity.

[1]Reported numbers of employees include both hourly and salaried workers.
[2]As reported in the local press.
[3]Information not available.
[4]Associates' computer operations remained in South Bend, consisting of 700 additional jobs — mainly technical employees.
[5]The closing was announced in October, 1983, to be effective in 1984.

Sources: South Bend City Library historical files, and *South Bend Tribune* library files.

identified 144 separate closings. More than half of them occurred in the northern tier of Indiana counties, which includes the industrial communities of Gary, Michigan City, Elkhart, Fort Wayne, and South Bend.

Table 4
Employment in the Largest Ten Manufacturing and Largest Ten Nonmanufacturing Firms in South Bend-Mishawaka, 1982

Manufacturing:	Approximate Number of Employees, September, 1982
1. Bendix	5,800
2. AM General	2,000
3. Uniroyal	1,380
4. Wheelabrator-Frye	860
5. Dodge-Reliance-Exxon	700
6. Allied Products	550
7. Torrington	501
8. RACO	498
9. Wheel Horse	450
10. Miles Laboratories	300
Total	13,039

Nonmanufacturing:	Approximate Number of Employees, July, 1982
1. University of Notre Dame	3,500
2. South Bend Schools	2,336
3. Memorial Hospital	1,697
4. St. Joseph Medical Center	1,400
5. South Bend City	1,391
6. St. Joseph County	1,118
7. Indiana Bell Telephone	745
8. U.S. Post Office (South Bend)	562
9. Mishawaka Schools	550
10. Penn-Harris-Madison Schools	542
Total	13,841

Sources: "Project Future," South Bend-Mishawaka Chamber of Commerce, September 16, 1982 (mimeo); Research Department, South Bend-Mishawaka Chamber of Commerce, July 16, 1982 (mimeo).

South Bend-Mishawaka has been suffering from plant closings since the mid-1950s. During 1954-1983, at least 27 facilities were permanently closed. Many others also are said to have closed, such as local bakeries and dairies and small retailers, but relatively few jobs were involved and their demise went unnoticed in the local press.

The 27 shutdowns are listed in Table 3. All but two of them are manufacturing plants. The number of workers they displaced cannot be determined precisely because figures are not always available or reliable. An estimated 15,000 hourly and salaried jobs disappeared at the time of closing, and close to 40,000 jobs were lost if reported peak employment estimates are considered. Either way, more than half the lost jobs were the result of a single plant closing, the Studebaker shutdown in 1963. Studebaker dominates all the aggregate job figures in this study, which suggests how hazardous it is for factory towns to be dependent on one employer.

Table 5
South Bend-Mishawaka Plant Closings
According to Change in Operations and
Ownership Structure, 1954-1984

A. Relocation of established operations by a multi-plant, absentee owner.

1. Singer	4. Ward Baking
2. Bike-Web	5. Weyerhaeuser
3. Essex Wire	6. H. D. Lee

B. Termination of established operations by an absentee owner.

1. Curtiss-Wright	4. Cummins
2. Studebaker	5. AM General
3. Rockwell	

C. Relocation of acquired operations by a multi-plant, absentee owner.
   1. Kingan (Hygrade) [H]*
   2. Empire Box (Packaging Corporation of America) [H], (Tenneco) [C]**
   3. Wilson (Enro Shirt) [H], (DWG Corporation) [C]
   4. South Bend Tackle (Gladding) [H]
   5. Roth Plating (Buckeye) [H]
   6. Drewrys (Associated) [H], (Heileman) [H]
   7. Associates (Gulf + Western) [C]
   8. Skinner (Textron) [C]
   9. Whitehouse (Opelika Mfg.) [H]
   10. South Bend Tool + Die (Rehnberg & Jackson) [H] or [C]
   11. South Bend Screw (Kawneer) [C], (AMAX) [C]
   12. Bantam (Torrington) [H], (Ingersoll-Rand) [C]

D. Relocation of established operations by a multi-plant, local owner.
   1. South Bend Range (Escan)

E. Termination of established operations by a single-plant, local owner.

1. Gentner	3. Garvey Pattern
2. Schumacher	

---

*Horizontal acquisition.
**Conglomerate acquisition.

Table 5 groups the 27 plant closings into five categories based on the type of operational change, the nature of plant operations, and the structure of ownership.

Firms' stated reasons for closing are also included in Table 3. These reasons can be vague and even misleading, however. More important to an understanding of the closings are the individual firm's structural and operational characteristics and its labor relations. Specific issues become relevant to the analysis. Is the plant locally or absentee owned? Is the owner a single or multi-plant producer, and is it a single or diversified product company? Are plant production workers unionized, and, if so, are there labor cost differentials between the local plant and other facilities that are owned by the same firm or to which the firm has access? Is plant production being terminated or relocated? Was the plant established or acquired by the owner?

The answers to those questions determine which of several categories of plant closing is the appropriate classification for a particular shutdown; they also indicate the role of unions and collective bargaining in the plant shutdown process. Three broad categories have been defined here for that purpose. They distinguished the plant closing cases according to the employer's corporate structure and production operation:

1. Plant closing by absentee owners,
   a. terminate production,
   b. relocate production,
2. Plant closings by absentee owners following acquisition,
   a. terminate production,
   b. relocate production,
3. Plant closings by local owners,
   a. terminate production,
   b. relocate production.

A production termination, for example, implies that the employer has failed to overcome operating disadvantages, such as an inadequate share of industry sales, and is not able or chooses not to manufacture the product elsewhere. A production relocation, by contrast, suggests that the employer has the ability to produce profitably or even to increase profits by moving its operations, perhaps to pay lower labor costs.

Shutdown of Established Plants by Absentee Owners

Eleven of the 27 closings listed in Table 5 were by absentee owners of established rather than acquired operations. Six of them involved production relocations to other plants owned by the firm. The remainder were production terminations by large metal manufacturing corporations. The first group displaced fewer than two thousand employees; the latter dislocated nearly twelve thousand.

Production Relocation

Singer.

The South Bend closings began in 1954 when the Singer Company stopped making wooden cabinets for its home sewing machines at a 53-year old plant. Singer said it was consolidating all its cabinetmaking operations and moving them closer to natural wood sources in the South.

Production operations at Singer were labor intensive. Relocation to places where labor was cheap offered a way of reducing operating costs. In addition, Singer had experienced recent but separate strikes in South Bend and its sewing machine manufacturing plants in Connecticut and New Jersey. The electrical products workers union (IUE) was pressuring Singer to negotiate a master agreement covering the three plants. Had the company agreed to this consolidated bargaining structure, union power would have been enhanced.

As it turned out, the South Bend plant was the first of the three facilities to be closed. By the late 1950s, Singer's share of world sewing machine sales had dropped sharply and the company responded by phasing down that business and diversifying into new industries. After quitting South Bend, Singer acquired firms in the business machines and consumer appliance industries. Most of these were later divested in the wake of a 1975 change in Singer's management strategy. The decision was made to revive global production of consumer sewing machines and transfer industrial sewing machine production from Europe to Elizabeth, NJ. Singer also diversified into high-tech products.

The Connecticut sewing machine plant was closed after having been reduced to minimum operations. In 1981 the IUE local in Elizabeth agreed to contract givebacks in return for company promises to modernize the aging plant and keep it operating. Then, in 1982, Singer shut it down anyway. The plant had once employed 10,000 workers, but in 1973 was down to 3,500, and at the time of closing to only 400 workers. The union charged breach of contract, and Singer was found liable for damages and ordered to reimburse displaced workers for the concessions, an estimated $2 million. The union wanted the court to make Singer reopen the plant, but the judge ruled that was not practicable. Shutdown of the New Jersey plant left Singer with a single domestic sewing machine site, a nonunion assembly operation in South Carolina.[7]

Bike-Web.

Bike-Web came to South Bend in 1929 when its parent company, Kendall, built a plant to manufacture elastic goods; it was one of nine elastic web loom factories operated by Kendall. In 1937 the Textile Workers Organizing Committee was certified to represent the plant's 175 hourly workers. Production employment, which was mainly female, fluctuated between 250 and 350, but had fallen to 200 when the plant was closed in 1958. Kendall closed that and two other elastic products plants in the North and moved operations entirely to an acquired facility in Seneca, SC. (In 1972 Kendall was acquired by Colgate-Palmolive and is now one of its most profitable domestic operations.)

A one-week wildcat walkout had occurred in 1944 and a two-month strike over new contract terms in 1951, but labor relations at the South Bend plant were described as being harmonious. Although separate contracts were negotiated for the three northern facilities, wages and benefits among them were comparable.[8]

Essex Wire.

Essex Wire was a Midwest auto parts supplier which began diversifying heavily in the mid-1960s. In 1974, after it had become Essex

International, it was acquired by United Aircraft, itself a highly diversified company which later became United Technologies. During its diversification and acquisition period, Essex closed several northern manufacturing plants, sometimes during or after bitter confrontations with local unions, and relocated their operations in the South and Southwest.

A 102-day, violent strike occurred at its Hillsdale, MI plant in 1964. It began as a contract dispute over wages and benefits, in which the IUE local tried to match the wage at Essex's Fort Wayne, IN plant. Essex conceded that wages were low in Hillsdale, but said that was why they had come to the rural Michigan community in the first place.

A riotous atmosphere developed. The union organized mass picketing outside the plant; the company continued production using supervisors, imported strikebreakers and armed guards. Beatings and assaults occurred almost daily at the plant gates, until Michigan's Governor ordered the facility closed and sent in the National Guard. A four-year contract eventually was signed, but the plant later closed.

Also in 1964, Essex purchased an empty Studebaker plant and began warehouse operations in South Bend. Soon it started manufacturing wire harnesses for auto fittings and by early 1966 was employing more than 500 mostly women workers. Essex closed its main fittings plant in Detroit, which it had acquired three years earlier, and transferred part of the work to South Bend.

Labor relations in South Bend were stormy. In 1966 a wildcat strike erupted over production standards, which the workers alleged were "physically impossible" to meet. It resulted in the firing of 45 strikers. (Almost simultaneously a similar wildcat strike broke out among women workers at another of Essex's Indiana plants; that one too ended with the firing of strike leaders.) There was also considerable unrest in South Bend over recurring occupational health problems in the plant. Finally, in late 1967, less than three years after it had begun operations in South Bend, Essex sold the facility and soon afterward stopped production altogether.

While Essex was having labor difficulty in South Bend, it committed an unfair labor practice at another wire plant. It threatened to shut down the Kansas facility if workers failed to ratify a contract settlement. A company attorney told them that Essex had taken long strikes elsewhere over wages. He recalled one instance in which the company was forced to meet union wage demands after a 60-day walkout, but later closed the operation. "Fellows," he said, "this is what the company offered and I don't think they will go any higher if you go on strike. I suppose, as they don't have much invested here, they will close the doors and move out of the country."[9]

Ward Baking and Weyerhaeuser.
One of the nation's leading bakery chains, Ward started baking in South Bend in 1920 after years of having shipped baked goods into the

area from Chicago. It had acquired the plant of a failing local bakery. The South Bend facility was expanded and renovated and by 1955 it claimed to be using the latest technology and producing at maximum capability.

Ward Baking meanwhile diversified into other food processing and distribution lines and eventually was reorganized to become Ward Foods, Inc. Investment in the South Bend bakery lagged while resources went into Ward's seafood, dairy, meat, candy, and frozen food ventures. In March, 1974 the parent company announced the plant would be closed in less than a week. High labor costs and outdated equipment were reasons given for the shutdown. South Bend area retail outlets again would be supplied from Ward's Chicago bakery.[10]

A large, diversified natural resources company, Weyerhaeuser located its Midwest paperboard processing and distribution center in South Bend's new Airport Industrial Park in 1961. Huge rolls of paperboard were received there from western and southern mills, and were then cut to specified dimensions and shipped to Midwest customers.

In 1965 the operation was expanded for the second time and by 1969 some 46 persons were employed. Employment peaked at about 100 during the 1970s. But in 1979 Weyerhaeuser announced it was reorganizing its paperboard distribution system and no longer needed the South Bend facility. The workers were organized, but neither the union nor labor costs were mentioned as a factor in the decision.[11]

H. D. Lee.

Lee was one of the nation's largest manufacturers of work clothes in 1917, when it purchased and modernized a local plant being vacated by Singer. South Bend production grew rapidly and within a few years more than 500 hourly workers were employed, most of them young women working as sewing machine operators. The plant turned out garments for distribution in eleven midwest and southern states and by 1936 it was the largest of Lee's six regional production facilities.

Lee had never experienced a labor disturbance in South Bend. This may have been due to its benevolent labor policies. Like other progressive employers before and after World War I, it practiced what the labor historians call "welfare capitalism." A 1919 newspaper article on Lee described the local work environment.

> Every attention had been given to the comfort of the employees in the adaptation of the buildings, and the welfare work of the company includes, besides provision for wholesome recreation during the free hours and at noon, educational advantages. . . . The women employees all dress in the comfortable garment which the company manufactures, the Lee Unionall.

Later the plant would be organized by the United Garment Workers, a conservative craft-bound union which concentrated on organizing the work clothing industry and in establishing harmonious labor-management relationships. There were no disruptions under UGW representation. So, when the company announced in 1964 that it was closing the plant and relocating the production, workers were given a three-month notice "because of the excellent relationship we've had with our employees in the past," according to Lee's corporate director of labor relations.

Lee blamed the closing on its aging South Bend plant. Even if it were to build a new facility in the city, however, the company said a shortage of skilled sewing machine operators in the area discouraged future operations there. A few years after the shutdown Lee was acquired by VF Corporation, the parent owner of Vanity Fair clothing. As a VF subsidiary, Lee presently gets its garment production mostly from southern and southwestern plants.[12]

Termination of Production by Absentee Owners

Five large companies closed motor vehicle and construction equipment operations in South Bend during 1961-1978. Production was terminated because of insufficient product sales in four instances and because the parent firm decided to obtain component parts from outside sources rather than produce them. Labor cost differentials and labor relations disputes do not appear to have been crucial or even relevant considerations in the decision to terminate operations except possibly in one instance.

Curtiss-Wright.

The first of these closings involved the South Bend plant of Curtiss-Wright, an aircraft manufacturer that tried unsuccessfully to enter the highway construction equipment industry against the established firms. In 1958 the company leased a large plant from Studebaker and began making huge road scrapers and earth movers in South Bend. Plant equipment and machinery were shipped into the city by rail from a California plant which Curtiss-Wright had acquired. The South Bend site was preferred, the company said, for its central location to steel supplies and equipment buyers. Although employment quickly reached 3,000, Curtiss-Wright never achieved its target share of the market. Anticipated sales were also curtailed when an expected upsurge in federal highway construction failed to materialize in the late 1950s.

In early 1961 the company gave workers and the community about two weeks notice that the plant would be closed. Labor was not mentioned as a contributing factor even though the UAW local had struck for five weeks the preceding year over seniority issues. When the city asked Curtiss-Wright to locate a new electronics assembly operation in South Bend — instead of in Arizona as planned — the company declined, saying that would not be practical.[13]

Studebaker.

In late 1963 Studebaker Corporation announced it was permanently ending domestic production of autos. Its only manufacturing plant was located in South Bend and employed about 8,500, down considerably from a peak of 22,000 in the early 1950s. Within two weeks of the announcement the last Studebaker rolled off the assembly line. Both workers and the community were stunned.

Studebaker began operations in South Bend in 1852 as a wagon maker and blacksmith. Soon its wagons became all-purpose vehicles of Midwest farms and were used to carry settlers across the Western prairies. In 1902, the company started producing automobiles which were known for their advanced styling and quality engineerng. When the plant closed, it was by far the city's largest manufacturing employer. Its complex of red brick buildings occupied a wedge of land adjacent to the business district and surrounded by modest, but well-kept working class neighborhoods, the kind which housed most of the city's ethnic labor force.

Studebaker Labor Relations.

Studebaker's first labor contract was negotiated without a strike in 1937 by the CIO auto workers union (UAW). The company was coming out of receivership and could not afford a production stoppage.[14] Soon after Studebaker negotiated an incentive system that was unique in the industry, but which raised Studebaker's direct payroll costs much above the industry average. Company strategy was to pay premium earnings in return for productivity performance above industry averages. It paid high wages and good fringe benefits, but it never got the superior productivity.

Over the years Studebaker agreed to costly interpretations of production standards in order to avoid confrontations with the militant local union. Moreover, company officials relished the firm's reputation of having trouble-free labor relations. At the time the South Bend plant closed, hourly labor costs were conservatively estimated to be one-fourth greater, and per unit labor costs one-third higher, than those of other auto makers.

Beginning in 1947, the company sought union concessions. That year Studebaker was profitable because pent-up, postwar consumer demand had produced a seller's market in new automobiles. In view of this prosperity, the union refused to concede. All through the 1950s, however, Studebaker repeated its demands. Finally, in 1954, the local union leadership recommended making modified givebacks, but the members voted them down. Management promptly announced that the plant would be closed in two months if the workers continued to resist. Another vote was taken and this time the changes were ratified by a nine-to-one margin.

The following year Studebaker merged with Packard Motor. Packard executives took charge of the combined company and, among other things, pledged themselves to eliminate Studebaker's labor cost differential. First they imposed unilateral work rule changes which threatened to displace every sixth production job; the workers responded with wildcat slowdowns and stoppages. Then they demanded new contract concessions; this time the workers elected militant local officers and formally struck the plant. A month later, the international union ordered the strikers back to work and entered into the negotiations. A new settlement contained substantial union concessions in work rules and some fringes. Despite their having voted down earlier givebacks, the members narrowly ratified the contract.

A short work stoppage also erupted during 1958 negotiations when management tried to get a settlement that was below the current Big Three economic pattern. Studebaker tried to exempt its negotiations with the union from the productivity and cost-of-living standards that were normally used in auto wage determination and instead wanted to peg future pay increases to company profits. Although the union was able to deflect this important shift in economic bargaining practice, the union did agree to make temporary concessions in supplemental unemployment benefit levels, annual improvement factor (productivity) payments, and employer pension fund contributions. This was the third time the union had made contract concessions in four years.

Over time, the UAW local had negotiated the best pay provisions in the industry, but Studebaker's marginal status as a producer prevented them from becoming industry standards. Considerable pressure was coming from both the company and the international union (and eventually also from the community) to bring Studebaker's terms and conditions closer to those of the industry.

In the 1961-1962 contract talks, Studebaker negotiators were determined to eliminate the remaining labor cost differences between South Bend and Detroit. When the union presented its economic demands in December 1961, the company rejected them on grounds they would increase costs prohibitively and jeopardize continued domestic production. Management countered with an economic package aimed at bringing South Bend pay in line with Big Three rates and eliminating certain time-paid-not-worked benefits.

Claiming that Studebaker's offer left union negotiators "no room for movement," the local struck at the beginning of 1962. Management broke off the talks and estimated publicly that Studebaker dealers had a 70-day supply of unsold cars. Six weeks later the parties resumed serious negotiations and soon reached a three-year agreement. It narrowed further, but did not eliminate entirely, the company's labor cost disadvantage.[15] The plant shutdown occurred late the following year.

Displaced Studebaker workers did not fare well in the months following the closure. The shutdown revealed that the pension fund was 80 percent underfunded. As a result, workers under age 40 got nothing, regardless of how many years of service they had with Studebaker, and those aged 40-60 received lump sum severance pay which averaged less than $600. The Studebaker supplemental unemployment benefit fund also was exhausted.

Immediately after the closing, South Bend's unemployment rate shot up to a postwar high of 9.1 percent. Studebaker workers had been the highest paid in the community and two-thirds of them owned homes there. Eight months later about one-third of the 8,500 who had been displaced were still without jobs, a little more than half had found employment, and the rest were either retired or performing phase-down tasks at Studebaker. An estimated 500 of them left the South Bend area within two years of the closing.[16]

Labor costs were certainly a factor in the closing, but they were not the major cause. Company executives often criticized the union public-ly, but they never claimed it was responsible for the shutdown. Studebaker could not be a profitable producer because it did not sell enough cars to operate the plant efficiently. Making fewer than 80,000 units a year, as it did in 1963, Studebaker could not get the economies of large-scale production necessary to offset overhead costs.

Studebaker and the Big Three.

Studebaker did not sell enough cars to operate at profitable levels. It had failed to hold its market share in the postwar years, after lucrative war contracts and the rising market for new cars had revived the company from a period of bankruptcy during the depression. In 1948 and 1949 Studebaker reported the highest profit margins among major auto makers. The following year it reached a postwar peak in auto production with 268,000 units. But the next few years were devas-tating. Its sales ratio fell from 5 to 1 percent of industry revenue during 1950-1962. In 1953 Studebaker showed the industry's lowest profit level and made only 170,000 vehicles; then, although 1955 was a banner year for the Big Three, Studebaker experienced a negative 22 percent profit rate and turned out fewer than 100,000 cars. When it closed in 1963, it was building 68,000 cars a year.

Management responded to this deterioration in auto by diversifying into unrelated product lines. Conglomeration was a means of reducing the firm's dependence on auto revenues and, possibly, undertaken in preparation to leaving the industry altogether. During 1959-1963, Studebaker acquired at least eleven companies and entered into merg-er talks with several others. The acquired firms were medium-sized concerns doing business in fields ranging from electrical products to air transportation. After the South Bend shutdown Studebaker continued to make autos in Canada until 1966. Eventually the company was reorganized as the conglomerate Studebaker-Worthington. It had succeeded in getting out of South Bend and an industry in which it had not been an effective competitor, and in entering into unrelated but more promising lines of business.

Second-tier companies in industries dominated by the few largest firms, such as the Big Three in auto, fail for a variety of reasons.[17] Some of these are of their own making, but others are not. In the case of

Studebaker, management mistakes and above-average labor costs were largely the company's fault, but it is questionable whether the firm could have survived with competent administration and comparable labor costs. Secondary auto companies generally had to conform to industry practices established by the Big Three. These favored high-volume producers at the expense of smaller firms, and added considerably to the per unit cost of vehicle production.

The key to auto industry profitability and stability in the postwar years was its pricing policy. General Motors, which regularly captured 40-50 percent of domestic auto sales in those years, set its prices on the basis of cost-plus-profit. Per unit costs of production, which include material, labor, and overhead, were estimated on the basis of an anticipated "standard volume" of production and a "target rate of return" on net worth. According to the Congressional testimony of GM executives, the standard volume at that time was 80 percent of plant capacity and the target rate of after-tax profit was 20 percent of net worth. The target profit margin was added to the production cost of each car in order to arrive at the final product price. In this way profits were included as part of the cost of making and selling cars.

Ford and Chrysler were price followers. They normally priced comparable models within 1-3 percent of GM cars and settled for 10-15 percent average net rates of return on equity. Actual net profits for GM during 1947-1967 averaged 21 percent, compared to 13 percent for each of the other two. Studebaker, by contrast, averaged 24 percent net profits on equity during 1947-1952, and 31 percent net loss during 1953-1959.

In place of competitive pricing, Big Three companies substituted design changes and promotional advertising. During the late 1950s the combined cost of these practices amounted to roughly one-fourth the cost of producing a middle-sized car. The large auto makers could average this huge expense over the hundreds of thousands or even millions of units produced annually, while secondary firms like Studebaker had to do so for only a fraction of that volume. The latter had neither the financial resources nor the production size to compete effectively with the Big Three on the basis of product image.

The UAW was able to negotiate high wages and benefits under the nonprice competitive system. Administered pricing treated labor costs as one element in the "cost-plus-profit" price formula; negotiated labor cost increases were simply included in vehicle prices. But this practice also made the auto union a convenient scapegoat for higher auto prices and contributed to cyclical layoffs of auto workers.[18] When consumer demand for new cars slumped, the companies responded with production cutbacks and layoffs as a means of restricting supply and maintaining price instead of with price reductions as a way of selling auto inventories. Congressional economists estimated in the mid-1950s that GM could produce at less than one-half of its factory capability and still not lose money.

Ironically, the administered price system eventually made the Big Three uncompetitive with emerging overseas producers. Unaccustomed to price and quality competition, GM, Ford, and Chrysler were easy targets for Japanese and German auto makers. While General Motors busied itself with styled fenders, its foreign rivals developed front wheel drive, disc brakes, and fuel efficient engines. The weakest of the surviving domestic companies, Chrysler, soon found itself in a market position like that of Studebaker's in the 1950s. This time, however, union concessions and government-backed loans provided the necessary time and money for Chrysler to weather the storm until it can merge with or otherwise be integrated organizationally with a stronger company. But the industry characteristics that contributed heavily to Studebaker's shutdown in 1963 surely were a factor in the estimated 300 domestic auto assembly and parts plants that closed after 1970.

Rockwell, Cummins Engine, and AM General.
    Three additional transportation vehicle producers shut down South Bend-Mishawaka plants during 1967-1978. Rockwell Standard's sudden closing of an eleven-year old, highly mechanized auto bumper manufacturing plant in 1967 was attributed to inefficient, unprofitable operations and a loss of customers for products manufactured there. Both sides agreed publicly that labor was not the problem and that instead the closing was part of a reorganization and consolidation of Rockwell's 28 automotive parts plants. Rockwell had not competed successfully with other auto bumper suppliers.
    In addition Rockwell was then negotiating merger terms with American Aviation. These talks would result in the formation of Rockwell International, a conglomerate firm that was more committed to aircraft and aerospace production than to the auto supply business. In retrospect, it appears that Rockwell was one of the first auto suppliers to diversify away from that uncertain industry and into more stable product lines.[19]
    The world's largest independent manufacturer of diesel engines, Cummins began making castings in the old Studebaker foundry in 1964 as an alternative to purchasing them from outside suppliers. Five years later it abandoned the facility, explaining that physical improvements in the foundry, which had been constructed in 1923 and refurbished in 1952, were financially prohibitive. A one-month notice was given the approximately 1,000 employees.
    Upon occupying the South Bend foundry, Cummins officials had said, "we look forward to working out a contract with the union." Subsequent negotiations were strike-free and when the plant was closed a company statement emphasized that "our relations with the union have been excellent and the caliber of the work force has been high." The problem was inability to make castings in South Bend at costs that were competitive with those of supplier firms. "Cummins

cannot justify the large captial investment that would be required . . . to reverse what has proved to be an unsatisfactory performance," an official said. The company would get castings from independent producers.

The South Bend plant closing was one of several production reorganizations made by Cummins after the mid-1960s. New southern plants were opened to perform work transferred from other locations and diverse joint ventures and licensing arrangements resulted in overseas production of Cummins engines and components. By the 1980s the company had major plants in eight states and was getting production in at least seven other countries.[20]

AM General was formed in 1970 when the automaker American Motors acquired Jeep Corporation. With its Jeep production located in Ohio, in 1973 the company began manufacturing city buses in Mishawaka. At its zenith AM General had about one-third of the domestic market, but by 1977 had lost much of this to the more established firms, General Motors and Flxible.

Nevertheless, AM General claimed to have had the lead in development of the "transbus." This was a transit vehicle for elderly and handicapped riders which the federal government reportedly planned to require cities to purchase when using government funds to buy equipment. But because the decision to make the "transbus" mandatory was being delayed, in June 1978 AM General announced it was leaving the industry.

The bus plant has remained largely unused. But in 1983 AM General won a potential billion-dollar defense contract to build an all-terrain military vehicle called Hummer. Full-scale production eventually would provide an estimated 1100 jobs, but the work was to be done under the terms of a substantial concession agreement which AM General had negotiated with the UAW local several weeks earlier. The new contract was a factor in the Pentagon's decision to award the contract because it would narrow labor cost differentials between AM General's Mishawaka plant and those of its major competitors in the South, General Dynamics and Teledyne.

Less than 24 hours after the Defense Department announcement, American Motors disclosed it was selling the subsidiary in order to raise cash for its auto and jeep operations. A group of local investors attempted to purchase AM General, but LTV, the Texas-based conglomerate, was the successful bidder.[21]

Shut Down of Acquired Establishments

The largest category of plant closings in the South Bend-Mishawaka area involves the shut down of acquired establishments by parent companies. Twelve such cases occurred during 1954-1983. Nine of them were local employers who had been bought out in horizontal acquisitions, that is, by larger companies doing business in the same product markets. Most of these takeovers were part of consolidation trends occurring in certain industries as a result of changing production technology, marketing methods, or corporate structures. When such changes occur, large firms begin acquiring smaller ones in order to integrate them into their production systems. Or, they shut down plants which are old, or which have outdated technology or high labor costs, in order to eliminate excess production capacity.

Horizontal Consolidation

Kingan, Empire Box, South Bend Tackle and Roth Plating.

An early example of this type of closing was Kingan & Co. During World War II Hygrade Food Products acquired Major Bros. Packing of Mishawaka, a family owned meat processor in the city since 1897. Hygrade, which operated processing plants east of Chicago, later acquired another large packer, Kingan, whose production was in southern and western states. The acquisition made Hygrade a national producer and the fifth largest firm in the industry.

A year after the merger, Kingan was given operating control over Major. It began processing a full-line of meat products under the Kingan label for distribution in Northern Indiana and Michigan. But new processing methods and marketing practices were shifting the operating advantage in meat packing from medium-sized to large plants. The result was that independent producers went out of business while the leaders consolidated operations. At the end of the war the industry consisted of more than four thousand slaughtering and processing plants; by 1977 there were an estimated 1300.

Less than a year after Kingan assumed management of Major, the latter was closed, displacing 150 employees with no advance notice. The reason given for shutting down the plant was its failure to increase slaughter operations beyond that which had been diverted to Mishawaka from Kingan's larger plant in Indianapolis. Hygrade later reopened a part of the plant for use as an animal feed and fertilizer processor; it employed 14 workers. Hygrade experienced declining profit margins and in 1976 was acquired by Hanson Industries, a privately held conglomerate.[22]

Empire Box moved one of its two plants from Chicago to South Bend in 1927. The company made paper board boxes for food packaging cartons. By 1936 the local plant employed more than 130 workers — most of them skilled males — whose wages compared favorably to those of printers.

In 1954 Empire was acquired by Ohio Boxboard, one of the nation's leading flat paper board manufacturers. Ohio Boxboard merged five years later with two other leading flat paper makers and fabricators, American Box Board and Central Fibre Products, to form Packaging Corporation of America. This consolidation resulted in the shutdown of certain plants, including Empire Box in South Bend, which was phased out over several months. The local manager said "economic marketing and operational problems" were responsible, without elaborating on it. Packaging Corporation of America itself had been acquired by the conglomerate Tenneco in 1965 and made part of Tenneco's packaging products division. In 1983 Tenneco operated six paper carton plants, considerably fewer than the number operated by the three firms when they merged to create Packaging Corporation.[23]

South Bend Bait began operations in the city during the 1890s and in time became a leading full-line producer of fishing rods and tackle. Its "Oreno" line of lures was highly regarded by fishing enthusiasts. In 1958 South Bend Tackle, as it was called then, was acquired by outside interests, which immediately reorganized it as a holding company for two other rod and tackle producers, and also gradually transferred production from South Bend to Iowa.

Nevertheless, four years later new owners brought the firm back to South Bend and added new product lines. They returned to the city, in their words, for its "better labor market," an apparent reference to the need for experienced workers in the industry at that time. In 1964, however, the company again changed hands. This time its name was also changed, to Gladding Corporation, and four previously independent rod and tackle companies were consolidated along with South Bend Tackle. Reorganization of Gladding's production operations followed shortly afterward, including the shutdown of the South Bend plant over a two-month period. Gladding continued to manufacture fishing tackle for awhile, but by 1983 it had become a diversified producer of marine gear and athletic wear.

Gladdings' chairman emphasized at the time that the South Bend shutdown decision was not due to problems with the Furniture Workers Union, which represented the workers, or to labor costs. There had been no history of work stoppages or disturbances. Instead, he explained, the South Bend plant was "uneconomical" because new production methods in the industry required capital-intensive, automated plant and equipment.[24]

A provider of metallic electroplating services to local metal manufacturing companies, Roth Plating opened in South Bend in 1946. It located there because of the city's central location to auto and appliance manufacturers, and occupied the factory formerly used by the South Bend Watch Company, which had stopped manufacturing in the 1920s. Roth was one of thirty small firms that located in the area that year, according to the Chamber of Commerce. Six years later it expanded operations into the old South Bend Brewery works, and increased its employment to 70 persons.

In 1965 Roth was sold to local businessmen, who in turn sold the company two years later to Buckeye Products, an electroplating firm located in Michigan. Upon acquisition of Roth, Buckeye transferred production operations to Michigan, displacing 75 South Bend employees without notice. Roth owners said they had accepted Buckeye's financial offer because of the "great competition" in electroplating caused by the introduction of electroplated plastics. They also claimed that federal government regulations on auto safety restricted the use of interior "bright trim."[25]

Drewrys Beer.
At the end of World War II South Bend boasted three breweries, but the last of them, Drewrys Beer, closed in 1972.[26] Some 250 employees lost jobs. A regional brewer, Drewrys had been acquired by Detroit-based Associated Brewing in 1965 and then by Heileman Brewing when that company bought Associated in 1972.

Such acquisitions and shutdowns were part of a postwar consolidation of the beer industry. National brands had captured sales from regional and local brewers with aggressive price-cutting, saturation advertising, and exclusive marketing arrangements with wholesale distributors and taverns. This new competition completely transformed the industry. National firms became larger and small producers were driven out. In 1950, 407 companies brewed 82 million barrels of beer and the largest five of them accounted for one-fourth of industry sales; by 1979 only 41 firms were left, but they brewed 175 million barrels and the top five now controlled nearly three-quarters of the market.

The largest beer companies seldom close plants. Instead, they expand existing facilities and build new ones. Except for Heileman, their policy is to grow through internal sales expansion, not through acquisition of rival brands. During 1958-1975, Anheuser, Pabst, Schlitz, and Miller together made ten beer acquisitions compared to 38 made by the 13 regional companies and 50 by the rest of the industry. When breweries are closed, therefore, it is usually due to business failure or operational consolidation following regional and local mergers.

The South Bend Drewrys plant is an example of consolidation and shutdown. Heileman's acquisition of Associated (Drewrys) was challenged by the Antitrust Division of the Justice Department on grounds it would lessen competition in the Great Lakes area. A federal court approved the merger, however, and also ruled that Heileman could close one of Associated's breweries for economy purposes. Heileman promptly announced that the South Bend plant would be closed. Reasons given to the press were that it was noncompetitive with rival breweries and that advertising by major competitors had eroded Drewrys sales markets. But former Drewrys employees, both from the bargaining unit and from technical and supervisory ranks, claimed in interviews that Drewrys sales began to fall after Associated acquired it and then underpriced its own major brand, *Pfeiffer*, in areas where Drewrys had always been a large seller. In other words, they claim Associated acquired Drewrys and began to eliminate it as a competitor in certain market areas.

Labor relations at South Bend Drewrys had been stable and harmonious. Except for a brief walkout in 1968 over the length of the contract, no strikes occurred and the grievance process was said to function smoothly. Local union demands normally followed the pattern settlements made in Chicago breweries prior to Associated's acquisition of Drewrys. Following that, the South Bend settlement was patterned after those in Associated's Evansville, Indiana Brewery, with South Bend lagging somewhat. The terms of this regional pattern did not match the standards negotiated by the Brewery Workers at Associated's St. Paul, Minnesota, and Chicago facilities, and did not approach those bargained by other unions in the Budweiser and Miller master agreements.

In 1966, the Brewery Workers international tried unsuccessfully to achieve coordinated bargaining among its Associated locals as a way of standardizing and improving contracts within the company. Union strategy was to establish common or compressed contract expiration dates among the bargaining units and then to coordinate their negotiations on certain items of mutual interest, such as pension improvements. The St. Paul and Chicago locals demurred, however, because they preferred to pattern themselves after the superior settlements in their areas. And the South Bend and Evansville locals were immobilized by an international union disclosure that Associated was planning to close one of the two Indiana facilities.

It was assumed inside the union that Associated would choose the Evansville plant for shutdown. Twice in recent years the South Bend local had made contract concessions to save jobs. Extensive mechanization of product handling in the plant after the mid-1950s had reduced the peak number of production workers from 550 to 350. Additional displacement would affect mainly the regular employees because most of the temporary handler jobs had disappeared. In response, the local union took a one-year freeze on wage raises and fringe benefit improvements in 1965 and agreed to modest deferred wage increases over the next two years. Still, the number of jobs continued to decline, due mainly to falling sales rather than mechanization.

Then in 1972, amid rumors of a possible plant shutdown, the local again agreed to freeze wages and benefits during the first of a two-year contract. Five months later Heileman acquired Associated and announced the South Bend closing. Local management and union issued a joint statement in which collective bargaining was exonerated from responsiblity for the shutdown: "The Company stated that the closing was not attributable to labor problems or union activity and expressed appreciation for union efforts to keep the plant open."

Worker attention shifted to the severance pay they would receive under the contract. As early as 1955, the South Bend local had negotiated a pension-severance plan to assist displaced workers by providing them with a lump-sum of money in lieu of regular monthly pension benefits upon retirement. The plan allowed individual members of the bargaining unit, who were vested in the retirement plan, to receive a predetermined payment based on years of service in the event of permanent job loss. Later, in 1968, when there was talk of a possible shutdown, the provision was changed to liquidate the entire pension fund if the plant closed. Only severance payments would be made in that event. Each displaced worker was to be given one week's pay for every two years of service at the South Bend plant. The clause also required the employer to give 12 weeks notice of a planned shutdown and to offer available jobs at its other breweries to workers who are willing to relocate.

Wilson Bros.

A family owned men's clothing manufacturer, Wilson Bros. moved its production operations to South Bend from Chicago in 1887. By 1926 it employed 1,600 persons in what was now its main plant, and that year brought in another product line. Wilson Bros. officers explained the new addition:

> The management of the company debated where to locate but found that labor conditions in South Bend are so ideal, our relations with labor so pleasant, that South Bend was preferable to any other city. There is plenty of labor here and it is of high quality.

Like H. D. Lee, Wilson Bros. was a progressive employer for its time. In 1919 some 1,200 women were employed in the South Bend plant, where, according to a contemporary newspaper account, "they are given every pleasure that is in the power of the company to give them," including cafeteria meals, medical and dental care, comfortable work areas, and a company-sponsored employee club.

Plant employment peaked at 2,200 in 1929. Even during the depression of the 1930s, however, shipping and sales jobs were transferred to South Bend from Chicago. New product lines also were added so that total employment there remained close to the pre-depression high.

After the war Wilson Bros. made two acquisitions, including Enro Shirt Co. of Louisville, Ky. In 1952 a new president was named who, for the first time, was not a member of the Wilson family. He resided in South Bend rather than Chicago, where the Wilson family had always lived, because he considered South Bend "the focal point" of the company. Five years later, however, Wilson Bros., was acquired by an outside investment group whose stated goal was "to initiate development and diversification of the company." Within months most of the South Bend operations had been transferred to Louisville and the Wilson produce brands integrated into a new company called Enro Shirt Incorporated. Only Wilson's pajamas and bathrobe lines remained in South Bend. Company headquarters soon followed the production and located in Louisville. In 1973 the phased-down South Bend plant was closed altogether, displacing 81 employees. Today Wilson Bros. operates as a division of DWG Corporation, making diversified clothing items in Louisville, North Carolina, and rural Pennsylvania.[27]

Whitehouse, and South Bend Tool & Die.

The Whitehouse division of Opelika Manufacturing, a multiplant producer of textile linen products for the health care industry, was closed over a three week period in December 1982, after having cut back employment by more than half during the previous three months. The displaced workers were mostly women sewing machine operators.

Opelika is a relatively small company that grew in the industry through horizontal acquisitions. Whitehouse was its first acquired property, in 1951. It owns and leases manufacturing plants in four southern states and Barbados in addition to California and Illinois, where it is headquartered.[28]

The closing of South Bend Tool & Die, one of the city's oldest remaining manufacturing concerns, represented the passing of an important part of local industrial history. News of the closing "swept through the machine tool industry here the way Studebaker Corp.'s closing 20 years earlier stunned the community," observed *Tribune* busness writer Ray Leliaert, Jr. Despite the heavy loss of manufacturing operations, South Bend is still thought to be the nation's largest machine tool center after Detroit, boasting more than one hundred companies operating in some aspect of the industry.

South Bend Tool was the landmark company. Organized in 1929, it serviced the machine tool needs of Bendix, Studebaker and other large, expanding companies in the area. The nature of that industry is such, however, that middle-level managers and supervisors, themselves skilled toolmakers, could easily leave the company and go into the business for themselves. They diverted contracts from South Bend Tool by taking advantage of personal contacts they had developed with buyer representatives. At least twenty current tool and die shops and designers in the area were established by former South Bend Tool employees.

In 1977 the company was merged with a closely-held firm in Illinois. Headquarters remained there, even though the other company was operated as a division of South Bend Tool. Four years later the fabricating component of the South Bend plant was closed and the facility offered for sale. Then, in 1983, the main operation was closed with a one-month notice. It was necessary, said the owners, because of high labor cost and the expense of having to invest in new equipment if the plant stayed open. "We've had two years of losses, and financially competition is too keen and we just can't make it," the parent company president claimed. "One of the hardest things I've done is close down a company that's been in business 54 years — you've got good people working there," he added. Thirty-five persons reportedly lost jobs. Because the acquiring firm is privately held, it is uncertain whether this acquisition and shutdown represents a horizontal consolidation and a relocation of production.[29]

South Bend Screw

A manufacturer of precision machine parts for the auto and aerospace industries, South Bend Screw was founded in the city in 1928. In 1959 it employed 60 persons. That year the company was acquired by Kawneer of Niles, Michigan, which is located a few miles north of South Bend. Kawneer, a manufacturer of architectural aluminum products, was moved to Niles from Kansas in 1907 as a result of an industrial development campaign which included plant construction for incoming firms.

In 1962 the company was acquired by AMAX. Years later AMAX consolidated its aluminum-related subsidiaries to form ALUMAX, a half interest in which was later sold to Mitsui of Japan. In 1975 Kawneer stopped manufacturing in Niles, leaving only the subsidiary headquarters. That too is now being moved to Georgia. Officials indicated at the time that the acquisition was part of a "long range program of integration and growth."

Two years after Kawneer acquired South Bend Screw, it relocated operations in a South Bend industrial site along the river. The land was leased to the company for $1,000 a year for 10 years. Then, in 1983, after Kawneer indicated its subsidiary might leave the area, the city offered to lend the parent company $500,000 to relocate South Bend Screw in the Airport Industrial Park and expand its operations. Besides, the city wanted the riverside property in connection with a redevelopment project. Before the transaction could be finalized, however, Kawneer sold the plant's machinery and equipment to unidentified investors who planned to relocate them. The workers were given a one-month notice.

Torrington.

In October, 1983, Torrington announced it was closing its South Bend bearings plant. The announcement culminated a two-year period in which the company at first denied it was contemplating the transfer of production to its southern plants, but then indicated that ultimately the decision rested on the willingness and ability of South Bend workers to make the local operation efficient. Management meanwhile unilaterally initiated Quality Circles in the plant and introduced a "cell manufacturing" process which combined job classifications and mixed department boundaries contrary to existing contract language. When the UAW local negotiating committee resisted these actions by filing grievances and NLRB unfair labor practices charges, it lost membership support and was eventually voted out of office. Five months later the shutdown announcement was made.

The bearing plant came to South Bend in 1928, when Bantam Ball Bearing Co. dismantled its 30-year old manufacturing facility in Connecticut and moved 15 rail cars of machinery to a new facility in South Bend's recently completed Belleville Industrial Development area. Bantam made the move in order to be nearer its customers in the auto and machine tool industries. It was one of several companies, including M.B. Skinner and Empire Box, that were attracted to South Bend during that time by an active Chamber of Commerce campaign to bring industry into the area through the offer of donated land and various financial incentives, along with the promise of "free and efficient labor conditions."

A year later, Bantam was acquired by engineers and executives formerly with Studebaker. They consolidated the company's entire operations in South Bend and increased its capitalization in order to finance new machinery and more efficient production methods. So successful were they, that Bantam remained profitable and twice expanded its operations during the depression. This prosperity attracted outside interests and in 1935 the Torrington Company, a Connecticut bearings manufacturer, acquired Bantam. South Bend eventually became the headquarters for Torrington's heavy bearings division. Torrington was later acquired by the conglomerate Ingersoll-Rand.

By 1982 Torrington had built two new bearing plants in the South. Meanwhile, several hundred employees at South Bend had been laid-off due to the recession and the movement of work to the new facilities. To allay worker fears that local operations were being phased out, Torrington's president went to South Bend in July and, in a speech from the plant loading dock, assured the work force there was no present intent to close the place. But, he told them, future output there would depend on productivity. "The cost of manufacturing quality into a product should be in the neighborhood of three to four cents," he said. "South Bend's cost is three times that and this has a direct effect on the amount of work which comes into this plant."

The local union refused to make concessions on a controversial wage incentive system in the plant, but otherwise cooperated with the company's productivity efforts except for the unilateral changes mentioned above. In any event, management claimed that productivity was on the rise. The layoffs continued, however, and in August, 1983, Torrington announced it was moving division headquarters from South Bend to Connecticut. Then, two months later, the plant shutdown was announced. By that time, only 164 employees remained of the more than 700 in 1980. Production was moved to plants in Union, S.C., and Shiloh, N.C.

In making the announcement, Torrington officials praised the efforts of its South Bend workers. "We gave them a productivity challenge and they did a fantastic job," said the division manager. "If we had returned to a normal economy" after the recession, "this decision may not have had to be made."[30]

Conglomerate Acquisitions.

Large conglomerate corporations acquired two South Bend firms and later closed them shortly after the acquisitions. By far the largest shutdown involved Associates Commercial Corporation, a finance and insurance company, which was founded in South Bend in 1918 and grew to become one of the largest firms in the industry. In 1968 it was acquired by Gulf + Western. Friction arose between Associates' top management and parent company officials over the subsidiary's location and relationship with local financial institutions. According to Congressional reports, Gulf + Western policy was to sever existing financial ties of acquired firms and instead link them to Chase Manhattan, the New York bank which financed its acquisitions.[31] South Bend Associates apparently resisted this and other restrictions on its operations.

In an unusually critical editorial which opposed the move from South Bend to Dallas, Texas, the *South Bend Tribune* observed that "Associates hasn't been 'our' local company in fact, despite an attempt to maintain an outward appearance that it is, since it was sold to Gulf + Western. . . . Decision making for the company shifted increasingly to Gulf Western headquarters in New York." Indeed, two years earlier Associates management had promised to construct a new commercial building in South Bend, one which would be the centerpiece of a downtown renewal effort. The project was suddenly cancelled by Gulf + Western as part of its corporate ban on new construction.

When it left South Bend, Associates employed 1,250 nonunion employees. Some 700 of them remained in the city to operate the company's nationwide computer services network. (Forty-one jobs were eliminated in 1983 when the company consolidated certain computer operations in Dallas.) The reasons given publicly for the move involved business advantages in the South: pro-business environment, favorable labor markets, low energy costs, financial resources, superior air transportation facilities, no corporate income taxes, and a better quality of life for employees.[32]

Skinner.

Another conglomerate shutdown involved one of South Bend's smaller but more celebrated manufacturers. In 1927 M.B. Skinner brought his hardware opperation to South Bend from Chicago. Skinner was an innovative producer and an imaginative employer. He devised and manufactured metal repair clamps for industrial pipes which allowed repairs to be made without having to shut down plants or destroy good pipe.

Skinner's factory was designed so that every workbench faced a window, and every window looked onto green lawns and trees. Flower beds, ornamental pools, stone benches, and well-kept hedges and shrubbery graced the plant's spacious grounds and elegant gardens. These were available to all employees during their lunch and rest breaks. In this and other respects Skinner epitomized welfare capitalism in labor relations. Although the plant was enlarged more than once in later years, the number of employees probably never exceeded 80.

Textron acquired Skinner and in 1961, five months after acquiring Sprague Meter, which also manufactured and sold pipeline repair devices, Skinner was made a division of Sprague. Sometime after the acquisition, Skinner hourly workers chose to be represented by the Steelworkers Union. No labor disputes were reported locally until a brief strike in 1977 over wages. The following year, Textron closed Skinner with about two months notice, on grounds the cast iron clamps Skinner produced had been made obsolete by widespread use of inexpensive plastic pipes. Some 40 persons were displaced; Textron offered them jobs at Sprague's Kentucky plant.[33]

Shutdown of Locally Owned Plants

Four of the 27 plant closings identified in the survey were locally owned at the time of shutdown. In one instance the company built a new plant in the South and eventually relocated production there from South Bend while keeping its main offices in the city. The other three are instances of local firms going out of business.

South Bend Range.

South Bend Range was established in 1898 as a manufacturer of coal and wood ranges for the home. It remained locally owned and over time became a major producer of commercial and institutional cooking equipment. During the early 1970s management reported record sales and employment in excess of two hundred persons. The company introduced several new product lines and also modernized and expanded its plant and equipment. It said it could not meet the growing demand for restaurant equipment caused by increasing numbers of Americans eating out, and even built a small production plant in Arizona to produce for that part of the country.

The second facility did not seem to detract initially from employment in South Bend, where the number of jobs rose to three hundred by 1973. Later, however, employment began to decline, eventually to about one hundred in 1977. Convinced their work had been diverted away from South Bend, the unionized workers there demanded a contract clause prohibiting the contracting out of production work and in 1978 their local struck the plant for seven weeks to get such a guarantee.

Following that confrontation, South Bend Range began building a much larger plant in North Carolina. As it was being built, company officials tried to alleviate local concerns about the future of the South Bend plant by announcing that the new facility would involve only new production. When it was completed, however, manufacture of convection ovens was moved from South Bend to North Carolina. Still, management insisted the firm would not leave the city. "We are moving ahead at this time because of the success of our new facility in North Carolina, the availability of assistance from local government agencies [there], and to provide needed space now in the face of escalating construction costs," said a company spokesman. But then another product line was transferred to North Carolina in early 1980, leaving a single major line in South Bend. The new move cut the remaining number of local jobs to about fifty. This time the company did acknowledge that labor cost differentials were an important consideration in the relocation, plus the fact that the South Bend plant was old and had "a tremendous amount of inefficiencies." Nevertheless, "We don't have any plans at all to completely leave South Bend," promised a company officer. Cooking broilers would remain the primary product line in the local plant, he said.

Late the following year broiler production was also transferred south. According to management, the latest decision was made following a comparison of productivity performance in the two plants. "The future really rests on our ability to get our productivity up in South Bend," the company president remarked.

In 1982 South Bend Range was reorganized after it acquired a Canadian cooking equipment manufacturer. The new firm was named Southbend Escan. Two months later Escan announced it was terminating production in South Bend. By now only 30 production and supervisory employees were working. A company statement explained the decision as "the need to improve efficiency, eliminate duplicate facilities and management, and to consolidate purchasing, production and shipments in a location better serving growing domestic and international markets."

Three months later Escan disclosed plans to locate its corporate headquarters in South Bend's Airport Industrial Park. The company would assume the $465,000 industrial revenue bond of a bankrupt electronics firm; the original bond had been reduced from $550,000 by the electronics company during the past three years. Some 65 to 70 headquarters jobs remain in South Bend.[34]

Gentner Packing, Schumacher, and Garvey Pattern.

Family owned Gentner Packing closed its doors in 1971, more than a half century after its opening in 1915. It processed beef for wholesale distribution throughout northern Indiana. The company gradually increased employment from a dozen workers prior to WWII to approximately one hundred in the 1960s.

In 1971 Gentner received loans and loan guarantees from the federal Economic Development Administration and local financial institutions. The purpose was to expand its daily slaughtering operations from 350 to 500 cattle and to hire an additional 50 workers. Less than two years later, however, the company announced it was closing for the duration. Its South Bend plant was, it said, the largest meatpacker east of the Mississippi. The reason given was the firm's inability to purchase cattle at low enough prices to make processing worthwhile. The plant never reopened.[35]

Peter Schumacher-Sons started in the South Bend-Mishawaka construction business in 1910. It grew steadily to become one of the area's leading general contractors, over the years building schools, hospitals, factories, office buildings, and apartment dwellings. Then, like many other large contractors it diversified into related activities during the 1960s, including heavy machinery and equipment hauling, industrial engineering, and real estate development.

Historically a family owned company, Schumacher was taken over in 1978 by the principal owner of a local engineering firm. The new owners divested Schumacher of its subsidiary enterprises and instead confined its activities to general contracting. In early 1980 the company was put in receivership by a local bank for having defaulted on loans made in 1976-1977. This was shortly after the firm had laid off its employees and offered to sell its office building. Schumacher's chairman attributed the failure to high operating costs associated with unions, high interest rates, and generally poor industry conditions. The divested businesses were unaffected by the shutdown. Schumacher Realty, in fact, reportedly was the selling agent for the construction firm's office building.[36]

Garvey Pattern was closed in September, 1983. At 69 years of age, principal owner George Garvey decided to close the facility, he said, because of declining business conditions and differences he was experiencing with the Pattern Makers union. He organized the firm in 1956 after having left another South Bend pattern producer that he cofounded in 1937.[37]

The Deindustrialization Process

Absentee owners closed 23 of the 27 plants in this study. They did so in response to problems in their product and labor markets. Sometimes they relocated established operations from South Bend to low-wage, nonunion places, or, less often, to geographically more convenient sites. These were mostly firms in garment or other labor-intensive industries which were in the process of relocating production to the South. At other times, absentee owners terminated established operations because they were not selling enough of the product. This happened mainly in concentrated industries, where second-tier companies were not competing effectively against the dominant firms. But most frequently, absentee companies acquired local establishments and shut the plants in the process of consolidating production operations.

There is more than one kind of plant closing in response to adverse product market conditions. For the absentee owner, one solution is to stop making the product and instead to transfer capital resources into other product lines. This approach makes the individual plants and divisions of multi-plant, diversified companies vulnerable to shut down. Their operating performance is measured not only against that of rival companies in the same industry, but also against alternative capital investments by the parent company. When short-term profit expectations are greater for petroleum products or financial services than in basic steel, for example, U.S. Steel and Republic Steel disinvest in steel and invest, respectively, in an oil company and a savings and loan institution.

When multi-industry companies shift capital this way, from one product area to another, often involving unrelated businesses, the intensity and velocity of capital mobility is greater than when single-product firms make the changes. When the latter move capital out of declining industries and into more profitable ones, the process occurs over an extended period of time, during which the less profitable enterprise contracts and the increasingly profitable one expands. (It is also possible that new firms may enter the more profitable industry.) In this instance, workers and communities have time to adjust. But when capital transfer occurs within a single firm, the process is usually abrupt and secretive, and affected parties are unable to adjust quickly and adequately. Termination of product lines and corporate diversification into other products and industries characterize the plant closings by Studebaker, Curtiss-Wright, Rockwell, and Cummins, and probably also the shutdown at AM General. It is easier for large, diversified corporations to disinvest out of threatened product lines and buy into new ones, than it is for them to stay and meet the competition; it is easier for them to close a plant than to keep it open and cooperate with the community to make the plant more competitive.

A second option available to an absentee owner having product market problems is to consolidate existing plant capacity. Previously independent firms are acquired during consolidation drives in the industry, and their plants subsequently closed in order to reduce or redistribute production capacity. Plants disappear, in other words, so that available market shares can be concentrated among fewer producers. This is the reverse of closing a plant for competitive reasons — the plant is shut down as part of a drive toward cooperative or collusive pricing and production practices among the dominant firms. Plants are closed in order to restrict the supply of the product or to widen profit margins by shifting production to low-cost operations.

Tactical plant closings have been an industry response to excess supply in the domestic steel industry, for example. From the formation of U.S. Steel in 1901, with its subsequent shut down of several newly acquired plants, to the 1983 combination of Jones & Laughlin (LTV Corp.) and Republic Steel, with its anticipated closing of duplicate and overlapping facilities, steel managers have curtailed output by consolidating and closing facilities.[38] In this study, Empire Box illustrates the point. It was part of a larger consolidation trend in the paper board industry, in which dozens of independent producers were consolidated into a handful of dominant suppliers. The purpose was to eliminate firms and make it easier to control price and output. In 1979 they and several smaller firms declined to contest antitrust charges against them for fixing prices of folding-carton products; together they agreed to reimburse purchasers for more than $200 million in overcharges. The federal court indictment, which included Packaging Corporation of America, claimed the price-fixing had occurred over the previous 14 years.[39]

Relocation of production following horizontal consolidation or conglomerate takeover of local plants occurred in at least nine other instances: Kingan, Wilson Bros., Roth Plating, Drewrys, Associates, Skinner, Torrington, Whitehouse, and South Bend Screw. It cannot be determined how production was reorganized in two other instances: South Bend Tackle and South Bend Tool & Die, but in each case plant equipment was relocated elsewhere. In any event, relocation of acquired operations by absentee owners easily was the most frequent type of closing found in the study.

Plant closings are also operational responses to problems in the labor market. From the perspective of the individual employer, differences in labor costs among multi-plant facilities or between it and its product market rivals, represent a "labor problem." The employer does not want to terminate production but to shift it elsewhere. Multi-plant, absentee owners are much more capable of closing plants to rid themselves of burdensome wages and benefit levels and restrictive union work rules than are single-plant, local firms.

At least ten of the South Bend closings and three of the current plant phasedowns involve relocation of production operations to the South.[40] The implication of this is that states which try to attract or hold manufacturing employers by reducing the social wage will not succeed in the long-run. There is always another location, here or abroad, where wages are lower and regulations on business more relaxed. The Bluestone-Harrison data in fact show that the chances of a given plant being closed during the 1970s were greater in the South than in any other part of the country. But because firms were also opening southern plants, and relocating operations there from the North, the actual extent of dislocation in the South was obscured.

Until recently, high wages and union contracts were infrequently mentioned by employers as causes for the South Bend-Mishawaka plant closings. In practice, however, they probably were a contributing factor in the Singer, Bike-Web, Essex, and H. A. Lee shutdowns, all of which used labor-intensive production methods. The Escan shutdown also resembles this type of closing except it is locally owned. It and the Essex case may also have been motivated by an anti-union animus.

During 1980-1983, however, excessive labor costs almost invariably were cited as major reasons for shutting plants and phasing down and relocating metal manufacturing operations. This shift in emphasis by local and absentee owners may reflect a change in public opinion regarding the effects of unions and collective bargaining. The perception that unionism is acceptable or even desirable, because it helps create and sustain high standards of living, appears to have given way to the reverse view, that it is undesirable because it makes American industry uncompetitive and is mainly responsible for our global economic decline.

The study shows, however, that South Bend-Mishawaka unions were generally willing to assist ailing firms at the bargaining table in order to avoid plant closures. Local unions at Singer, Studebaker, and South Bend Range could be accused of bargaining intransigency, but even in these cases that interpretation is questionable. The UAW at Studebaker resisted contract concessions in certain instances, but in others it agreed to major givebacks. The IUE local at Singer was participating in the international union's attempt to establish coordinated bargaining at several of the company's plants. The Steelworker local at South Bend Range appears to have acted defensively when it struck to win a no-subcontracting clause in response to the erosion of its bargaining unit at a time when the company claimed increasing production nationwide.

Plant closings are part of a current employer labor market strategy to solve what it sees as the "labor problem." Historically, American employers have perceived obstinate Yankee mechanics and artisans, undisciplined immigrant laborers, militant skilled craftsmen, and, most recently, powerful industrial unions, as being labor problems. To the employer, organized as well as unorganized labor resists regimentation, standardization, and exploitation, and constantly undermines and challenges management's use of labor as a productive factor.

Managers have tried to solve the labor problem with job deskilling machines, formal systems of supervision and discipline, psychological testing, welfare capitalism, police action, and wage incentives. At times, the solution included plant closings and production relocations, as in the garment, shoe and textile industries, and in the metal manufacturing foundries which escaped unions in New England by moving inland and south. But until now, employers were unable to solve the labor problem created by the CIO's organizing and bargaining successes during the 1930s and the accompanying resurgence of traditional craft unions. Plant closings and phasedowns, as well as the threat of them, represent a solution to the latest labor problem.

It is historically ironic that southern communities are now doing to South Bend what that city did to Chicago and others during the early decades of this century. South Bend manufacturers were able to control their largely immigrant work forces during the early periods of industrial labor unrest. In 1885, Polish workers rioted outside the gates of Studebaker and Oliver Chilled Plow in support of some loosely defined form of industrial unionism. The workers distrubance was put down with armed force and South Bend's factories remained open shops. Railway brotherhoods and AFL craft unions survived, however, and between 1900 and 1920 they conducted serious strikes, including one by Studebaker harness stitchers at the turn of the century. Manufacturing employers meanwhile established and maintained a city wide job referral system, which made it unnecessary for laborers to travel from one factory hiring office to another, but also enabled industry to screen-out the "troublemakers."

The specter of revolutionary industrial unionism worried South Bend's respectable citizens. In Chicago, only 90 miles away, the Industrial Workers of the World was rampant. But, in South Bend, railway, street car, and construction strikes were broken, sometimes with strikebreakers, and the city acquired a reputation for low-wage, non-union employers at a time when other cities were becoming union bastions.

Labor conflict elsewhere was seen as an opportunity for South Bend. Local businessmen began promoting the city as ideally situated, hospitable to industry, and having skilled, reliable workers. "We have no labor troubles in South Bend," boasted the Chamber of Commerce in 1922, "for this city is peopled largely by home owning folks." In 1927 the Chamber announced an ambitious industrial development program to rival those of other cities inside and outside Indiana that were in competition for manufacturing operations. The development package consisted mainly of building sites donated by a local realtor and guaranteed loans for new plant and equipment. A number of firms did locate in South Bend as a result of these efforts, some of the same operations that were later acquired and relocated in southern industrial development parks.[41]

Conclusion

The principal finding of this study is that large, diversified corporations are responsible for a majority of plant closings. Eighteen of the 27 closings are clearly of this kind. Furthermore, these shutdown decisions are made for reasons that are internal to the needs of the companies, but which result in substantial social costs to the affected parties. Yet, workers, unions and communities have little say in the matter and virtually no influence over either the process or the outcome. Most of the closings had tactical significance relevant to product market shares or labor market costs, or both. Without exception, the reasons were only vaguely communicated to local area residents and organizations.

Productive capital was taken from the community in these closings, but the workers stayed behind. They and their factory towns had to make the adjustments, not the people and the organizations that made the decisions. Looked at this way, a plant closing is a matter of relative control over the economic environment, not a situation in which workers and owners alike are the hapless objects of inexorable market forces. Workers, unions, and communities have little means of control over the plant closing environment because they are of no further use to the owners in the production process. Absentee owners have a great deal more control. They alone make the investment choices. Because they are diversified concerns that do business in a variety of industries, or have the capacity to do so if they choose, their mobility allows them to take advantage of the fact that some industries are declining while others are expanding, and that some geographic regions are at a stage of industrial development in which labor earnings and social wage costs are high while others are in the low-cost stage. The result is that corporations can pick and choose strategically among industries and locations, while workers and communities cannot.

Studies of plant closings at the national, state, and metropolitan levels show patterns similar to those in this case. Large, diversified corporations account for a disproportionate share of the closings. They close plants in all industries and in every part of the country, usually on short notice, and at little cost to themselves in compensation to affected parties. Their mobility gives them both opportunity and motivation to close facilities which smaller, specialized employers might try to keep open.[42]

The key determinant in the incidence of closings and phasedowns is whether absentee owners continue to invest in local plants. A survey made of 171 plant closings by the nation's largest five hundred corporations during the 1970s shows that inefficient or outdated facilities and equipment was the reason given most frequently. (High labor costs and militant unions were mentioned less than half as often.) The author concluded that "the clear culprit in closings of both new and old facilities is inefficient production technology. In nearly half of all closings the factory slipped — or perhaps we should say was allowed to slip — into poor technological and management practices."[43]

If the problem of plant closings is largely one of absentee control and capital disinvestment, then solutions for workers and communities must include, in addition to a national economic policy of full employment, some forms of local ownership and guarantees of plant reinvestment. Staughton Lynd calls this "reindustrialization from below," to distinguish it from the kind proposed by financier Felix Rohatyn and analysts Lester Thurow and Robert Reich.[44] In this view, influence or control over the ownership and investment function is critical to power and self-determination in the market economy. Therefore, if communities are to shape their own industrial fortunes, they must influence or control investment. Whether they will achieve this on a scale approaching that needed to offset the dislocation which has already occurred in places like South Bend remains to be seen.

There are signs of movement in that direction, however. These include the passage of community and regional laws which penalize employers who close plants arbitrarily; the use of eminent domain by local governments to acquire and operate production facilities which are in danger of being permanently closed or arbitrarily relocated by absentee owners; the adoption of area economic development programs that make industrial location subsidies and tax abatements conditional upon genuine and lasting job-creation rather than on temporary production-relocation; trade union initiatives in employee pension investment decisions; experiments with alternative production efforts aimed at preserving rather than dismantling established metal-working skills and facilities; leveraged buyouts of closed or declining plants by local businessmen and managers with the assistance of local financial institutions; and direct worker ownership under Employee Stock Ownership Plans.

Finally, it must be emphasized that a prerequisite of local investment and managerial control is for community and worker organizations to understand that they are in common predicament, that neither is the enemy of the other, and that they need to build political coalitions and work together in their common interest.

End Notes

1. Barry Bluestone and Bennett Harrison, *The Deindustrialization of America: Plant Closings, Community Abandonment, and the Dismantling of Basic Industry* (New York: Basic Books, 1982), p. 60.

2. "Hope in the Heartland," *Indiana Business Review* (October 1981).

3. Ray M. Leliaert, Jr., "Indiana's Industry Climate Best in Great Lakes Area," *South Bend Tribune*, January 31, 1982.

4. Robert F. Dixon, "South Bend Spruces Up For Business," *Indiana Business* (December 1981), p. 13.

5. For a general discussion of the dual labor market theory, which defines and analyzes primary and secondary labor markets, see, David M. Gordon, *Theories of Poverty and Underemployment: Orthodox, Radical, and Dual Labor Market Perspectives* (Lexington, Mass.: D.C. Heath, 1972). A specific treatment is in, Michael J. Piore, "The Dual Labor Market: Theory and Implications," in D. M. Gordon, editor, *Problems in Political Economy: An Urban Perspective* (Lexington, Mass,.: D. C. Heath, 1971).

6. Figures on the estimated income loss to the area were prepared by Michael Lawrence and Carol Ives, "Changes in Labor Force and Income in the South Bend-Mishawaka SMSA," (unpublished paper), December 17, 1981.

7. Paula Borenstein and Sarah D. Wolfe, "The Last American Sewing Machine," *In These Times*, (February 11-17, 1981), pp. 16-17; Neil Hood and Stephen Young, *Multinationals in Retreat: The Scottish Experience*, "Singer in Clydebank" (Edinburgh: Edinburgh University Press, 1982), pp. 42-60; "Arms Output Cut Forecast, Singer Union Official Predicts Lack of Demand," *South Bend Tribune*, April 27, 1952; "Singer Ordered to Pay Workers in New Jersey For Breach of Contract," *Wall Street Journal*, May 17, 1982.

8. The major source of information on plant operations and shutdowns in South Bend-Mishawaka is the *South Bend Tribune* (SBT). Most articles cited were written by two *Tribune* business writers, Ray Gregg, and, after 1968, Ray Leliaert, Jr. In order to avoid unduly lengthy citations, their bylines and story titles are not always included in the documentary end notes. Another South Bend newspaper, was the *South Bend News-Times* (SBN-T), which disappeared after World War II.

Material on Bike-Web is taken from these issues of the two papers: *SBN-T*, March 26, 1929; *SBT*, August 27, 1937, July 17, 1951, August 31, 1958.

9. *SBT:* June 15, 1964, March 18, 1966, July 8, 1966, August 30, 1966, June 25 and December 27, 1967, July 12, 1977. The Hillsdale strike is described in, "Michigan Gov. Orders State Troops to Hillsdale to End Strike Violence at Essex Wire Corp.," *Wall Street Journal,* May 29, 1964, and "Essex Wire Workers Accept New Contract Ending 102-Day Strike," *Wall Street Journal,* June 10, 1964. The unfair labor practice in Kansas is the issue in *Essex Wire Corp.,* 164 NLRB No. 48 (1967). Other labor law violations by Essex subsidiaries, including an illegal plant closing threat, are in *Controls Division of Essex International,* 221 NLRB No. 126 (1975); *NLRB v. Essex Wire Corp.,* (US CA,6) 80 LRRM 3166 (1972); *Essex International,* 192 NLRB No. 75 (1971).

10. *SBT:* October 16, 1955, and March 6, 1974.

11. *SBT:* August 28, 1961, and February 13, 1962.

12. *SBN-T:* February 23, 1919; *SBT:* February 24, 1964; *Moody's Industrials, 1983.*

13. *SBT:* October 19, 1958, and March 16, 1961.

14. Labor relations at Studebaker from the 1930s until shortly before shutdown are discussed in, Robert Macdonald, *Collective Bargaining in the Automobile Industry* (New Haven: Yale University Press, 1963).

15. Information on the 1962 strike and settlement is from the *Wall Street Journal:* January 2, 3, 17, and 29, and February 12, 1962.

16. John Palen and Frank J. Fahey, "Unemployment and Reemployment Success: An Analysis of the Studebaker Shutdown," *Industrial and Labor Relations Review* (January 1968).

17. For a discussion of product pricing in concentrated industries see, John M. Blair, *Economic Concentration: Structure, Behavior and Public Policy* (New York: Harcourt Brace Jovanich, 1972), pp. 403-522. Structure conduct and performance in the auto industry during the Studebaker years is described in Robert F. Lanzillotti, "The Automobile Industry," in Walter Adams, editor, *The Structure of American Industry,* Fourth Edition (New York: Macmillan, 1971). Other sources used here include two reports of the Subcommittee on Antitrust and Monopoly of the Committee on the Judiciary, U.S. Senate: *Administered Prices: Automobiles,* 85th Cong., 2d Sess., November 1, 1958 (Washington, D.C.: GPO); *A Reorganization of the U.S. Automobile Industry,* 93rd Cong., 2d Sess., February 28, 1974 (Washington, D.C.: GPO).

18. William Serrin, *The Company and the Union: The "Civilized Relations" of the General Motors Corporation and the United Automobile Workers* (New York: Alfred Knopf, 1973).

19. *SBT,* June 27, 1967. "Rockwell International," in Michael Katz, and Robert Levering, editors, *Everybody's Business: An Almanac* (San Francisco: Harper & Row, 1980), pp. 697-699. *Moody's Industrials, 1983.*

20. *SBT:* April 13, 1964, and February 14, 1969. *Moody's Industrials, 1983.* "Cummins Engine," in Moskowitz,Katz, and Levering, *Everybody's Business,* pp. 282-284.

21. *SBT:* June 1, 4, and 28, 1978; January 29, 31, February 25, and March 22, 23, and 24, 1983.

22. *SBT:* April 26, 1942; October 11, 1952; October 7, 1953; February 19, 1954; March 24, 1955. On industrial consolidation in meatpacking, see, U.S. Congress, Hearings Before the Subcommittee on SBA and SBIC Authority and General Small Business, House of Representatives, "Small Business Problems in the Marketing of Meat and Other Commodities: Part 3 — Concentration Trends in the Meat Industry," 96th Cong., 1st Sess., May 1, 2, 14, and June 4, 1979 (Washington, D.C.: GPO, 1979).

23. *SBN-T:* March 21, 1929. *SBT:* April 23, 1928, October 11, 1929; September 10, 1945; July 17, 1954. A clipping of the *Tribune* article on the shutdown is in the Packaging Corporation of America folder in the South Bend City Library, but it is undated. "Three Paperboard Firms' Plan to Consolidate Approved by Holders," *Wall Street Journal,* July 13, 1959.

24. *SBT:* December 8, 1958, August 7, 1962, July 2, 1965; "Gladding Corporation," *Dun's Million Dollar Directory,* Vol. I, 1983.

66   Charles Craypo

25. *SBT:* September 22, 1946, November 31, 1951, August 1, 1967.
26. This description is based on a previous study: Charles Craypo and William I. Davisson, "Plant Shutdown, Collective Bargaining, and Job and Employment Experiences of Displaced Brewery Workers," *Labor Studies Journal* (Winter 1983).
27. *SBN-T:* February 23, 1919; *SBT:* August 8, 1926; December 31, 1931; January 15, 1934; February 16, 1934; January 15, 1957; May 9, 1957; March 23, 1975.
28. *SBT:* December 9, 1982. *Moody's Industrials, 1983.*
29. *SBT:* August 16 and 28, 1983.
30. The South Bend Screw acquisition and shutdown is described in, *SBT:* October 8, 1959; February 25, June 10, and July 28, 1983. Torrington's history and closing are reported in *SBN-T:* February 14, 1928; May 4, 1931, May 30, 1935; Letter from Department, South Bend Public Library, South Bend, Indiana, May 21, 1940; *SBT:* February 14, 1928; February 6, 1929; July 21 and September 30, 1982; August 9, 1983, and October 13 and 14, 1983; Letter from UAW Local 590 Negotiating Committee to Local Members, South Bend, Indiana, May 6, 1983.
31. U.S. Congress, Antitrust Subcommittee of the Judiciary Committee, House of Representatives, Staff Report, *Investigation of Conglomerate Corporations,* 92nd Cong., 1st Sess., (Washington, D.C.: GPO, 1971), pp. 169-183.
32. *SBT,* November 13 and 14, 1975, and October 6, 1983.
33. *SBN-T:* September 28, 1927. *SBT:* June 31, 1947; June 30, 1950; February 3, 1978. "Textron's Corporation," *Moody's Industrial Manual,* 1968.
34. *SBT:* January 1, and November 30, 1972; May 21, 1973; November 29, 1979; April 24, 1980; December 5, 1981; October 30, and December 2, 1982; February 17, 1983. Interview with Robert D. Oswald, Chairman and Chief Executive Officer, Southbend Escan, *Outlook,* Madison Center, Inc., Summer 1983.
35. *SBN-T:* February 28, 1937. *SBT:* August 3, 1971, and April 6, 1973.
36. *SBT:* May 29, and October 16, 1961; April 27, 1980.
37. "Garvey Pattern to Close Sept. 30," *SBT,* September 16, 1983.
38. Thomas F. O'Boyle, "LTV to Pay $770 Million for Republic; Industry Shakeout, U.S. Steel Duel Seen," *Wall Street Journal,* September 29, 1983.
39. "Carton Producers Settle Trust Case for $200 Million," *Wall Street Journal,* September 14, 1979.
40. Establishments in which production was relocated to the South are: Singer, Bike-Web, Essex, H.D. Lee, Wilson, Associates, Skinner, Whitehouse, Torrington, and South Bend Range. That of Empire Box and South Bend Tackle may also have been transferred there. Plants being phased down and operations moved to southern plants, include Bendix, Dodge, and Wheelabrator-Frye.
41. Patrick J. Furlong, "Riot at Oliver's," *The Old Courthouse News,* Northern Indiana Historical Society (Winter 1976-1977). Jack Detzler, *South Bend, 1910-1920: A Decade Dedicated to Reform* (South Bend, Indiana: Northern Indiana Historical Society, 1960), pp. 86-88. *SBT:* September 27, and October 4, 1927. *SBN-T:* September 28, 1927.
42. Bluestone and Harrison, *The Deindustrialization of America;* Julia Leighton, Melissa R. Roderick, and Nancy Folbre, *Pick Up Your Tools and Leave, The Mill Is Down: Plant Closings in Maine, 1971-1981,* (Department of Economics, Bowdoin College, Brunswick, ME., 1981); Robert G. Sheets, Russell L. Smith, and Kenneth P. Voytek, "Corporate Disinvestment and Metropolitan Manufacturing Job Loss <Chicago>," Northern Illinois University, Center for Governmental Studies, no date (mimeo). Also see, Robert L. Aronson and Robert M. McKersie, *Economic Consequences of Plant Shutdowns in New York State,* New York State School of Industrial and Labor Relations, Cornell University, May 1980, for case studies of three plants closed by large, diversified firms.

An alternative method of interpreting plant closings is based on conventional economic theory rather than empirical case studies. It relies on the competitive market model of economic behavior. Specifically, this approach consists of postulating why business firms close plants under competitive market conditions. The answer is deduced from the assumptions made in the theory. It says, essentially, that if plants are closed, it must be because they are no longer efficient producers and therefore they should be closed. This presumes, consistent with the model, that individual firm profits are the best measure of efficient production in the market economy. It is not possible using this method to make distinctions among firms according to levels of concentration or structural diversification; these are considered irrelevant to the issue. Nor can account be taken of the social costs absorbed by displaced workers and abandoned communities; only the costs and benefits that accrue to the business firm matter. Nor is any significance attached to whether production was terminated or relocated in the closing. The leading practitioner of this method in regard to plant closings is Richard McKenzie. See, for example, Richard B. McKenzie, *Restrictions on Business Mobility: A Study in Political Rhetoric and Economic Realty* (Washington, D.C.: American Enterprise Institute, 1979).

43. Roger Schmenner, "Every Factory Has A Life Cycle," *Harvard Business Review* (March/April 1983).

44. Staughton Lynd, "The View From Steel Country," *Democracy* (Summer 1983).

Plant Closings and the Law of Collective Bargaining

Sharon Simon

Introduction

The crisis of plant closings and other forms of industrial dislocation presents the labor movement with a difficult challenge. The tremendous drain of wealth from the Northeast, Midwest and other parts of the United States means the loss of jobs, the closure of plants and businesses and the erosion of the membership base of labor unions. Labor's reaction to the crisis ranges from the implementation of short-term tactics to maintain employment, to the pursuit of long-range strategies aimed at reversing the trend of deindustrialization.

Immediate union responses include negotiating and enforcing contract language restricting a company's right to close, bargaining over an employer's decision to terminate or relocate operations, pursuing unfair labor practice charges, and taking direct action such as strikes and occupation of workplaces. Among labor's long-term strategies are the enactment of plant closing legislation, employee and/or community purchase of businesses, gaining union input into investment decisions, labor law reform and organizing previously unorganized workers.

The labor movement has made and continues to make considerable use of the law since the legal system provides one forum where challenges to plant closings and other forms of work removal may be made. Unfortunately, labor law in the United States does not adequately protect the rights of unions and their members when work removal and loss of jobs is at issue. Labor law has traditionally upheld the right of business and industry to make "investment" decisions free from "interference" by the representatives of their employees.[1] These investment decisions are at the root of employer decisions to terminate or relocate work. Decisions such as how much money to reinvest in a

Sharon Simon is Assistant Professor of Labor Education at the School for Workers at the University of Wisconsin.

plant or workplace, what rate of return on investment is acceptable, and where corporations will move their assets and locate their investments all ultimately determine whether a corporation keeps a plant at its present location, moves some or all of the work elsewhere, or completely terminates a line of production. Because labor law does not provide for worker participation in these decisions, it is not a powerful tool from which the labor movement can benefit.

Nevertheless, there are restrictions which current labor law places on employers' rights to terminate or relocate work. These restrictions need to be understood and utilized while recognizing the practical limits of the law. At its best, the law enables unions and workers to gain time in their fight against deindustrialization by slowing the pace of work removal. A lawsuit or the threat of a lawsuit is generally useful as a means to gain leverage with an employer in negotiating a better financial settlement for workers affected by the closing. However, the net result of a legal strategy is rarely to prevent or reverse the closing of a workplace.

The major restrictions on plant closings and other forms of work removal arise out of the law of collective bargaining. The National Labor Relations Act, as amended, is the statutory basis for the legal principles that have been developed and that give unions some rights and opportunities to challenge the termination or relocation of work.[2] Two major legal considerations will be discussed. The first is the obligation of employers to bargain with unions over various kinds of economically-motivated decisions to terminate or remove bargaining unit work.

The second is a restriction specifically on one form of work removal, namely relocation of unit work. This restriction prohibits relocation of bargaining unit work during the term of the contract for the purpose of avoiding paying the contractually agreed upon labor costs. Other areas to be examined are limitations placed on work removal by contract language and restrictions on closings when the closings are motivated by anti-union considerations. The last two topics will be discussed first since the governing law is relatively well established, followed by an analysis of the current major issues in the duty to bargain over work removal and the restrictions of relocations during the contract term.[3]

Contractual Limitations on the Removal of Work

It is advantageous for a union to negotiate strong contract language restricting management's right to terminate or relocate bargaining unit work. This requires anticipation of future employer interest in work removal and negotiation of restrictive language before work removal becomes an issue. Some examples of such provisions are language which promises that the plant will stay open for the term of the contract, prohibits reassignment of work elsewhere, or restricts subcontracting of bargaining unit work.[4]

While restrictions on reassignment or subcontracting of bargaining unit work may be found in some collective bargaining agreements, it is rare to find absolute prohibitions of plant closures or relocations. More common is language providing for advance notice to the union of a decision to terminate or relocate work and language requiring bargaining over such a decision. Provisions dealing with the impact of the decision on the workforce, such as severance pay, insurance benefits and transfer rights, are also common.[5] However, the reality of present day bargaining is that if a contract does not already contain provisions restricting plant closure or work relocation, such language will be quite difficult to negotiate.

If it appears that an employer is about to violate contractual limitations on work removal, the contact may be enforced through grievance arbitration. Explicit contract prohibitions usually are enforced by arbitrators. For instance, in one arbitration case the contract prohibited the company from reassigning work performed by bargaining unit employees to other personnel who were not in the unit. When the employer closed one plant and consolidated production in a second plant, the arbitrator found a violation of the contract and ordered the company to reopen the closed plant.[6]

If an employer resists arbitration, it is possible to bring a lawsuit in federal district court to "compel" arbitration under Section 301 of the National Labor Relations Act.[7] In such a suit, the union would be seeking a court order forcing the employer to arbitrate. However, the major procedural problem with grievance arbitration is not employer resistance to arbitration, but the time lag between the union's first knowledge of the contractual violation and final resolution of the dispute by the arbitrator.[8] In the interim, the employer may close the plant or begin removing the work. Therefore, a union may need to obtain a Section 301 court injunction prohibiting the employer from closing or from moving work or machinery until after the arbitrator has ruled on whether the work removal violates the contract.[9]

In deciding whether to grant an injunction requiring the employer to maintain the status quo pending the outcome of the arbitration, courts often focus on whether the employer's action will deprive the union of an otherwise effective remedy to the violation.[10] If the employer is permitted to close a plant, transfer the work to another location or sell the business before an arbitrator can decide the grievance, then the arbitrator would be presented with a *fait accompli* and the union would likely be deprived of an adequate remedy for the contract violation. For instance, it would be difficult for an arbitrator to order a plant reopened and employees reinstated after the company had closed the plant and moved the equipment elsewhere.[11]

In addition, there are other factors a court will consider when a union requests an injunction. First, is the underlying contract dispute arbitrable, i.e., is it a grievance the union and employer agreed to submit to arbitration under the terms of the collective bargaining agreement? Second, has the union demonstrated potential success in winning the grievance once it goes to arbitration? Lastly, would the union suffer more from the denial of an injunction than the employer would from its issuance?[12]

Pursuing arbitration and a status quo injunction is appropriate if the collective bargaining agreement contains a provision the union believes prohibits work removal. However, most contracts do not contain explicit restrictions on work erosion. Nevertheless, when a contract is silent concerning the employer's right to close and/or remove work, it may still be possible for a union to claim, to an arbitrator or a court, that an "implied restriction" exists on some types of work erosion. The union can argue that such a restriction should be inferred from other provisions in the contract or from a prior course of dealing between the union and the employer. For example, the union may claim that an implied prohibition against relocating or subcontracting arises from the recognition and seniority clauses of the contract; that by agreeing to this language the employer guaranteed that bargaining unit work would continue to be done by unit employees under the terms and conditions of the collective bargaining agreement.[13]

Another rationale for an implied restriction is that a collective bargaining agreement, like any other contract, creates a "covenant of good faith and fair dealing" and the employer cannot unjustly deprive the union of the value of its bargain.[14] Such a claim could arise when a union makes concessions based on the threat of a plant closing and the employer really has no intention of changing its plans to close.

A similar kind of argument was made in one case where the union agreed to substantial concessions in return for the employer's promise to spend two million dollars to modernize the plant and to use its best efforts to secure additional work to keep the facility open. Five months later the company decided to close the plant and reneged on its promise. The court refused to issue an order prohibiting the company from closing the plant because there was no clear promise in the collective bargaining agreement to keep the plant open. However, the court found that the employer was clearly in breach of its contractual promise to spend two million dollars to modernize and to seek additional work. The court therefore ordered the company to pay the union monetary damages in an amount measured by the value of the union givebacks or by the two million dollars the employer promised but failed to spend, whichever was greater. The court said, "it would be grossly unfair to permit a company, which admits it breached a three-year collective bargaining agreement within months after it had been signed, to close this facility and walk away from these workers without paying one cent in damages."[15]

In most instances it will be difficult to get an arbitrator to enforce implied restrictions since arbitrators are generally hesitant to infer these kinds of prohibitions.[16] The same problem will arise if a union seeks a status quo injunction pending arbitration based upon an implied restriction. Therefore, in order to obtain an injunction and to prevail in arbitration, it is usually necessary to have strong specific contract language restricting management's right to close or relocate work. Nevertheless, even the best possible contract language rarely empowers a union to prevent a closing. More often such language enables workers to buy time by delaying the closing and enhances the union's ability to negotiate increased benefits for workers who lose their jobs due to the work removal.

Plant Closings and Anti-Union Discrimination

Most of the legal restrictions on plant closures come from the National Labor Relations Act (NLRA). Section 8(a)3 of the NLRA makes it an unfair labor practice, a violation of the NLRA, for an employer to "discriminate in regard to hire or tenure of employment . . . to encourage or discourage membership in any labor organization." This language has been interpreted to mean that in order to violate Section 8(a)3, an employer must have acted both because of union activity and with the intent to discourage union activity. In the context of plant closings the question is, if an employer closes a plant or relocates work because of anti-union considerations, is such action a violation of Section 8(a)3?

A number of important principles have been developed concerning the application of Section 8(a)3 to a plant closing situation. An employer has the absolute right to completely terminate its business for any reason, including a desire not to be unionized.[17] This right exists only where an employer is closing its entire business (where it is not part of a larger corporate structure) and where the decision to close is permanent. In such a situation, a plant closing based on anti-union bias would not be a violation of Section 8(a)3.

However, a company with more than one plant may not close one facility if the purpose of closing is to discourage union activities in its other plants. Such a partial closing is unlawful if the following criteria are met: 1) those in control have a continuing business activity (which may or may not be the same type of business as the one that was closed) from which they will economically benefit if unionization in this other business is discouraged; 2) the plant was closed for the purpose of discouraging union activity; and 3) it was foreseeable that the closing would create fears among remaining employees that their workplace would be closed if they engaged in union activities.[18] It is only where all the above criteria are met that a closing motivated by anti-union consideration will violate Section 8(a)3.

The major hurdle to a successful Section 8(a)3 claim is proving discriminatory intent, that the employer's motivation in closing was to discourage union activity. The natural result of a plant closing is to undermine the union and by transferring work a company avoids paying wage rates and benefits negotiated in the union contract. However, this alone is not considered proof of anti-union intent and does not make a closing unlawful. A further difficulty with proving anti-union motivation is that normally in plant closings or work transfer situations an employer is able to claim some "legitimate" business reason for its actions, thereby masking its real purpose of avoiding unionization. A company may have an economic pretext available, such as a claim that it closed part of its operations because it was less profitable than other plants. Even if labor costs due to unionization were responsible for some of the decrease in profitability, as long as the employer can show that its motivation in closing was economic, a Section 8(a)3 case will be extremely difficult to establish.

If a union faced with a closing or a transfer of work believes the employer's actions violate Section 8(a)3, an unfair labor practice charge should be filed with the National Labor Relations Board (the NLRB or the Board) as soon as possible.[19] If the union prevails, the most effective remedy the Board can order is that the closed operation be reopened and the employees be given back pay. Although this remedy is the only one that completely compensates for the illegal employer action, in some situations the Board may refuse to order reopening. Even if the Board does order reopening, the courts may refuse to enforce the Board order. Such refusals usually are based on the "excessive" financial costs to the employer of reopening. Thus, the more common remedies are back pay and reinstatement rights at the new location (if there is one), including travel and relocation expenses.[20]

If there is any indication at all of anti-union motivation, it may be worthwhile to file a Section 8(a)3 charge along with any other charges, at least to get additional information about the reason for the employer's decision. It is not often that a union has a strong Section 8(a)3 case in a plant closing situation.[21] If it is not possible to prove that the work removal was undertaken because of anti-union considerations, another area to be explored is possible violation of the employer's duty to bargain over the decision to remove work.

The Employer's Duty to Bargain Over Plant Closings and Other Forms of Work Removal

Under the law of collective bargaining, employers may have the duty to bargain with unions over decisions to close plants, to relocate work, to discontinue operations, or to subcontract bargaining unit work. This obligation arises out of the NLRA's requirement that the union and the employer bargain over certain aspects of their relationship. Section 8(d) defines the duty to bargain as "the mutual obligation of the employer and the representative of the employees to . . . confer in good faith with respect to wages, hours and other terms and conditions of employment. . . ." Section 8(a)5 makes it an unfair labor practice for an employer "to refuse to bargain collectively." The issues which must be bargained, "wages, hours and other terms and conditions of employment," are called mandatory subjects of bargaining.

With work removal problems, the major legal question is whether forms of work removal motivated by economic considerations, such as plant closings, relocations and subcontracting, are mandatory subjects of bargaining. If they are, the employer must notify the union of its intention before the decision is finalized and bargain with the union over the potential work removal. If they are not mandatory subjects, the employer has no legal obligation to bargain with the union concerning its decision and may take unilateral action. A refusal to bargain generally occurs when an employer does not inform the union of its plans before implementing them, thereby barring the union from participating in meaningful negotiations about the decision.

It is clear that the "effects" or "impact" of work removal is considered a mandatory subject and thus requires bargaining. This legal duty includes the obligation of the employer to notify the union of its decision sufficiently in advance of its implementation so the union may bargain over the effects before all the details of the work removal are finalized.[22] Impact bargaining covers issues such as severance pay, seniority, insurance, pensions and transfer rights.

The issue yet to be resolved is which forms of work removal generate a duty to "decision-bargain," to bargain over the work removal "decision" itself. It is undisputed that a decision to go completely out of business is not subject to mandatory bargaining, since, as discussed earlier, an employer has the absolute right to close its business for any reason it chooses. Therefore, bargaining is not required if a company shuts down its entire operations.[23] However, in regard to other work removal situations, such as partial closures, subcontracting and relocations, the National Labor Relations Board and the federal courts have often been in conflict in their rulings.[24] Although there are certain guidelines which apply to all forms of work removal, it may not be clear in a particular situation whether an employer must bargain over an economic decision to eliminate bargaining unit work before it actually does so.[25]

Note that in the discussion which follows the term "partial closing" has a particular meaning. The Board and the courts define a total closure as when a company goes completely out of business and has no facilities left in operation. Anything less, such as when a company closes one plant but still has other facilities or plants in operation, or when a company closes part of an operation, is considered a partial closing.

Development of the Law of Decision-Bargaining

The Fibreboard Decision

The U.S. Supreme Court decision in the *Fibreboard* case established the two main principles used by the Board and the courts to evaluate when work removal requires bargaining.[26] One principle focuses on "management's rights" and does not require bargaining when an employer's decision to eliminate unit work alters the basic nature of the business or involves a major change in the capital structure of the business. The other principle, the "bargaining" principle, focuses on the union's interest in having input into the decision and requires bargaining when the decision is one which is suitable for resolution through bargaining with the union. With these imprecise guidelines as the basis for decision-making, the courts and the Board have made rulings on a case-by-case basis and have often disagreed.[27]

In general, subcontracting of bargaining unit work has required decision-bargaining. This is because it is not seen as a basic capital decision altering the nature of a business.[28] However, in order for subcontracting to create a duty to bargain, it must first be shown that the contracting out will bring about a "significant detriment" to bargaining unit employees.[29] For example, the Board has said significant detriment was present if unit employees lost all overtime, were laid off or terminated, or were transferred to lower paying jobs because of the subcontracting. On the other hand, if the subcontracting has only a minor impact on the work available for unit employees, bargaining will not be required. It has been ruled that significant detriment did not exist just because unit employees could have performed the subcontracted work, some overtime pay was lost, or because unit employees were reassigned to unskilled jobs.[30]

The *Fibreboard* principles have also been applied to plant closings. At first the NLRB applied the "bargaining" principle of the *Fibreboard* decision very broadly, seeing all partial plant closings as mandatory subjects requiring bargaining. The Board's reasoning was that workers have a right to bargain about the labor they have invested in a business and that this right is co-equal to management's right to make a change in its operations.[31] Later, however, the Board retreated and did not require decision-bargaining. During this period the Board followed the more restrictive analysis adopted by the federal courts which focused on the "management rights" principle of *Fibreboard*.[32] Using this analysis, the Board determined that if a decision involved a large outlay or withdrawal of capital which affected the ultimate direction of the business, then the decision did not require bargaining. For instance, when a large corporation sold one of its retail dealerships, the Board held that the sale could be made without bargaining because it was a basic capital decision on the scope of the enterprise.[33] In another case, where a company closed its manufacturing operation, which constituted a partial shutdown of the business, the Board again followed the same rationale and refused to find a duty to bargain.[34] However, the Board subsequently returned to requiring decision-bargaining over relocations and partial closures.

First National Maintenance

In 1981, the issue of partial closings and the obligation to bargain was presented to the U.S. Supreme Court in *First National Maintenance Corporation v. NLRB*.[35] The Court ruled that there is no duty to bargain over an economically-motivated decision to close part of a business, thereby reversing the position taken by the Board and some of the federal courts. The decision is far from a model of clarity and in some ways raises more questions than it answers, leaving unresolved the scope of labor's right to decision-bargain.

In its ruling, the Court stressed management's need to be "free from the constraints of the bargaining process to the extent essential for the running of a profitable business." To ensure that this "freedom" would be present, the Court established a "balancing test" to determine when bargaining is required: "(I)n view of an employer's need for unencumbered decision-making, bargaining over management decisions that have a substantial impact on the continued availablity of employment should be required only if the benefit, for labor-management relations and the collective bargaining process, outweighs the burden placed on the conduct of the business." In applying this vague "benefit" versus "burden" method of analysis to the situation presented, the Court concluded that bargaining was not required because the harm likely to be done to the employer by requiring it to bargain with the union over its decision would be greater than any benefit that might be gained through the union's participaton in making the decision to partially close.

The potential impact of *First National Maintenance* on decision-bargaining is far from crystal clear from the case itself. Does the case apply only to decision-bargaining in the context of partial closures, and if so, does it mean that bargaining may never be required in a partial closing situation? Moreover, what is the impact of *First National Maintenance*, if any, on other forms of work removal? One possible interpretation of the Court's decision is that partial closings will not generate an obligation to decision-bargain, but that this will not rule out a duty to bargain in other work removal situations. In *First National Maintenance*, the Court specifically stated that, "In this opinion we of course intimate no view as to other types of management decisions, such as plant relocations, sales, other kinds of subcontracting, automation, etc., which are to be considered on their particular facts."

The General Counsel's Opinion

In July 1981 and in November 1981, the General Counsel of the National Labor Relations Board issued memoranda to all the Regional NLRB offices establishing guidelines for the handling of cases related to the *First National Maintenance* decision.[36] One function of the Regional Offices is to decide whether to issue an unfair labor practice complaint and prosecute when charges are filed. Thus, if a union files a charge with a Regional Office claiming a violation of the duty to decision-bargain in a work removal situation, it is up to the Region to decide if the charge has merit, in which case it will issue a complaint and set in motion Board unfair labor practice procedures. If the Region decides the charge has no merit, it will dismiss the charge and the issues presented in the charge will not be litigated. Thus, these memoranda are important because they give direction to the Regional Offices in deciding when complaints should be issued based on charges that an employer has failed or refused to decision-bargain.

The General Counsel views a number of work removal situations as not requiring bargaining. According to the General Counsel, an employer's decision to go wholly out of business for economic reasons, an economically motivated decision to go partially out of business or to terminate a distinct line of business, and a decision to sell a business and no longer remain in that business do not require decision-bargaining. However, the General Counsel leaves some flexibility possible with partial closings as he notes it is possible that a partial closing case "could involve a fact pattern so markedly different from the facts and assumptions stated in *First National Maintenance* that a different result would be warranted."

On the other hand, it is the opinion of the General Counsel that there are certain management decisions where bargaining may be appropriate. These are decisions to relocate a plant, to subcontract bargaining unit work, to eliminate jobs through automation, and to consolidate operations. In these situations, the General Counsel says that to determine whether bargaining is in fact required, the "balancing test" established by *First National Maintenance* must be applied. This means that bargaining should be required only if the "benefit" of decision-bargaining for labor relations and the collective bargaining process outweighs the "burden" placed on the employer by having to negotiate with the union.

In explaining this balancing test, the General Counsel says the focus of the inquiry should be on whether the employer's decision is based on labor costs or other factors capable of resolution through bargaining. That is, is there a possibility the union could suggest or agree to proposals, such as concessions, which would change the employer's decision? If such is the case then it is appropriate to require bargaining.

Thus, the General Counsel limits the strict "no bargaining required" ruling of *First National Maintenance* to decisions to go out of business entirely or to sell a business, which is in accord with the law prior to *First National Maintenance*. In all other situations, including relocations, subcontracting, automation, consolidation and possibly even partial closings (if the facts are sufficiently different from those in *First National Maintenance*) it is possible that decision-bargaining will be required.

Legal Developments Since First National Maintenance

Since the Supreme Court's ruling in *First National Maintenance* there have been a number of NLRB and court decisions regarding the duty to bargain over work removal. The question of what constitutes a partial closing, as opposed to subcontracting, and whether there is a bargaining obligation in these situations has been examined. It has also been further clarified that work relocations are mandatory subjects of bargaining.

The major Board decision concerns subcontracting and partial closings.[37] The case involved Marriot Corporation and its decision to discontinue the shrimp processing portion of its food processing business and instead to purchase processed shrimp from an outside source. The Board ruled that this decision to close was a mandatory subject of bargaining. In determining whether there was a duty to bargain the Board first discussed whether the case presented a subcontracting situation or a partial closing. According to the Board, a decision to subcontract is generally within the scope of an employer's mandatory bargaining obligation. On the other hand, the Board noted that *First National Maintenance* said that an employer's decision to close part of its business is not a mandatory subject. According to the Board, "[T]he distinction between subcontracting and partial closing is not always readily apparent," and each case has to be evaluated on its particular facts to determine the true nature of the work removal.

The Board reaffirmed the basic rule that bargaining is required if the employer action is suitable for resolution through the bargaining process, but that no bargaining is required if the decision represents a significant change in operations or a decision basic to entrepreneurial control. This determination of whether bargaining is required, the Board explained, must take into account such factors as: (1) the nature of the employer's business before and after the action taken, (2) the extent of capital expenditures involved in the change, and (3) the basis for the action and the ability of the union to bargain over the decision (i.e., was the employer's concern in removing the work based on factors such as costs which could be resolved through bargaining over wages and working conditions).

Upon examining these factors, the Board concluded that the employer's action constituted subcontracting, as opposed to a partial closing. First, the employer's decision to buy shrimp from an outside source was not a major shift in the direction of the company. The nature of the business, preparing foodstuffs for its stores, remained unchanged. Second, the capital expenditures made by the employer in carrying out its action were not substantial. Finally, one of the main concerns of the employer was cost control, an issue suitable to resolution through bargaining with the union. Based on this reasoning, the Board said the employer had an obligation to bargain over its decision.

The Board's ruling in this case is important because the Board did not mechanically label the work removal as a "partial closing" and thereby foreclose mandatory bargaining under *First National Maintenance*. The Board still appears to be focusing on the traditional *Fibreboard* standard of whether the basis for the employer's decision involves factors traditionally suited to collective bargaining. This approach may give more leeway to the Board to find that negotiations are required in a given situation.

Several court cases decided since *First National Maintenance* concern relocation of bargaining unit work and uphold the obligation to bargain in a relocation situation.[38] Also significant is a report of the General Counsel which states that in the General Counsel's opinion, relocation still requires decision-bargaining after the *First National Maintenance* ruling.[39]

Application of the Right to Bargain
The Union's Right to Information

One of the most important tools a union has in bargaining over work removal is its right to information about the decision to remove work. The obligation of the employer to provide this information derives from its duty to bargain in good faith under Sections 8(d) and 8(a)5 of the National Labor Relations Act. Upon request, an employer has a duty to provide the union with information which is relevant and necessary for the union's performance of its bargaining duties on behalf of employees. Two types of information generally are relevant in a work removal situation: (1) information to assist the union in its ability to bargain over the company's decision, including the reasons for the company's plan and most importantly, information about the movement of work, and (2) information to improve bargaining over the impact of work removal on bargaining unit employees, if the final decision is to remove work.

In regard to information on movement of work, the Board and the courts have said the union is entitled to information about the movement of machines out of the plant, the relationship of the employer to its subcontractors, and the employer's customers. If the employer claims it must move its operations because of economic necessity, it must provide the union with financial information sufficient to validate this claim. A company must furnish the union information about the new location, the number and types of jobs at the new location, and the comparative costs of operation.[40]

Enforcement of the Duty to Bargain

Assuming that partial closures, relocations and other forms of work removal require decision-bargaining, what does the union need to know and do in such a situation? To begin with, the employer has a duty to notify the union of its tentative decision at an early enough point so there is sufficient time available for meaningful bargaining.[41] As soon as the union has any notice of the potential work removal, the union must request bargaining over the decision. If the union fails to request bargaining, it risks "waiving" (forfeiting) its bargaining rights.[42] The issues of timing of the notice and possible union waiver of the right to bargain also apply to "impact" bargaining (bargaining over the effects of the work removal) which is always required. Moreover, as discussed earlier, the union will need to carefully review its collective bargaining agreement to see if any provisions have a bearing on the work removal and pursue grievances as well as an injunction pending arbitration. Note that even if a union has been unable to bargain contractual restrictions on the employer's right to close or relocate, it is advantageous to negotiate language providing for advance notice of and bargaining over the management decision, especially if it appears there may not be a legal duty for the employer to bargain.

The employer's legal obligation is to "bargain in good faith" over the tentative decision, which means that an employer must meet with the union and bargain with an intent to reach an agreement.[43] However, all that is required is bargaining in good faith. The law does not require that the employer and union reach agreement or that the employer agree to any union proposals.[44] As long as the company bargains to the point of impasse (to a legitimate deadlock), it has met its legal obligation.[45] At that point, it is free to unilaterally implement its decision.[46]

If the union thinks the employer is violating or is about to violate its duty under Section 8(a)5 to bargain over the decision, to bargain over the effects of the decision, or to provide the union with information about the work removal, the appropriate course of action is to file an unfair labor practice charge with the NLRB.[47] If the Board finds merit to the charge, it will issue a complaint, which sets in motion the unfair labor practice adjudication procedure. Since the resolution of an unfair labor practice claim through Board processes may take a very long time, there is a need to attempt to prevent the employer from implementing its unilateral action in the interim.[48] The Board is empowered under Section 10(j) of the NLRA to seek an injunction in a federal district court preserving the status quo pending the outcome of the unfair labor practice adjudication process.[49] The issuance of an injunction will be crucial in decision-bargaining cases and the union should accompany its filing of the unfair labor practice charge with a request that the Board pursue a Section 10(j) injunction.[50] It is within the discretion of the Board, however, whether it will in fact seek such an injunction.[51]

A critical question for unions in cases involving refusals to decision-bargain is the nature of the available remedies. If the Board finds the employer has failed to bargain over a decision that falls within the employer's bargaining obligation, there are several possible remedies the Board may order. The strongest remedy within the Board's authority is resumption of the discontinued operations. This is the only remedy that comes close to fully compensating for the employer's wrongdoing. However, in economically-motivated work removals, this remedy is only ordered if a reinstatement of operations is "feasible" and will not place an "unnecessary burden" on the employer.[52] Often the Board and the courts find restoration is not feasible because it will be quite costly to the employer. Also, in some situations reinstitution may not be possible because a plant has been sold or gutted.

The more common remedy for these Section 8(a)5 violations is an order to bargain with the union regarding the decision and the effects of the decision and an order for back pay to laid off or terminated employees. The time period for which back pay is ordered is calculated in one of two ways. The variable is the initial date from which back pay is computed. This can either be the date the employees were initially laid off or the date of the Board order. In either case, the back pay is generally awarded until either; (1) the employer and the union reach a mutual agreement on the decision and its impact, (2) a bona fide impasse in bargaining is reached, (3) the union fails to begin bargaining with the employer shortly after the employer notifies the union it is willing to bargain, or (4) the union fails to bargain in good faith.[53] Unfortunately, if the back pay order runs only from the date of the Board's order, it will not provide much compensation for employees who have been out of work for a long period of time due to the employer's wrongdoing.

The Value of Decision-Bargaining

If an employer fails to decision-bargain it is clear that the current law does not provide solutions to the problem. Given the current legal uncertainties regarding the requirement to decision-bargain, the long time lag between filing a charge and enforcement of a National Labor Relations Board order, and the inadequacy of the usual remedy to bargain in good faith and pay back wages, most unfair practice charges will not ultimately stop a company from implementing its decision to close a plant or otherwise remove work. In fact, even if an effective restoration remedy is possible and is enforced, all the employer has to do is go through the motions of bargaining and make the decision a second time. This is possible because even if an employer complies with its obligation to decision-bargain, it is free to unilaterally implement its work removal decision after bargaining in good faith to an impasse.

Nevertheless, this does not mean that unions should not pursue their right to decision-bargain. Although it is highly unlikely that a union will stop a closing through the force of the law, there may be the rare case where a union succeeds in convincing an employer not to close a plant or remove work. A union might accomplish this not only by agreeing to concessions, but by threatening to strike or boycott the employer's remaining operations. Bargaining also provides the opportunity to verify the employer's position, since a union has the right to obtain information concerning the decision and its effects. Furthermore, the importance of obtaining back pay for employees affected by the work removal should not be underrated.

The most common function served by the right to decision-bargain however, is to delay the termination of work and to gain leverage for the union in bargaining over the effects of the work removal. A union may use unfair labor practice charges or the threat of such charges to buy time while bargaining occurs and to pressure the employer to agree to a better settlement for workers who are terminated. Thus, although the law of decision-bargaining has many limitations, there are ways in which it may be utilized.

Prohibitions on Relocation of Work During the Term of the Contract

In addition to the right to decision-bargain over various forms of work removal, a recent legal development gives unions more rights in the particular situation of relocation of bargaining unit work. The Board and the courts have examined a number of cases where the employer, for economic reasons, sought concessions from the union during the life of a collective bargaining agreement and told the union that if it did not agree to these contractual modifications the company would relocate or subcontract the bargaining unit work. When the union refused to agree, the employer relocated or subcontracted the unit work. In some cases the employer relocated the work for economic reasons without first seeking concessions. The Board and some courts have determined that these relocations of work violate the NLRA.[54]

The new doctrine enunciated in these cases prohibits relocation of work during the term of a collective bargaining agreement when relocation is undertaken to avoid paying the wages and benefits agreed to in the labor contract. In a sense, this right is stronger than the right to decision-bargain, since it is an absolute prohibition of certain work transfers during the contract term, as opposed to merely a bargaining obligation which does not assure work will not be removed.

Legal Rationale of the Prohibition

The rationale underlying this right originates from Section 8(d) which defines the duty to bargain. Section 8(d) states, among other things, that neither the union nor the employer is required "to discuss or agree to any modification of the terms and conditions contained in a contract for a fixed period." This means that if during the life of the contract, the employer seeks concessions from the union, the union may refuse to make concessions and does not even have to bargain over such proposals. The union is entitled to stand on its contract for the term agreed to. If the employer wants to modify the provisions of an existing contract, it can only do so if the union voluntarily agrees to bargain over such concessions and voluntarily agrees to the changes. Thus it is clearly established that any mid-term modification of the contract, without the consent of the union, is unlawful.[55]

Recent developments in the law concern an employer who relocates during the term of the contract to avoid paying the contractually agreed upon wages and benefits.[56] By doing so, the employer is unlawfully "modifying" the contract. It is this kind of relocation which violates Sections 8(d) and 8(a)5. Just as an employer cannot directly modify the contract during its term, it cannot avoid the contract by moving the work to another location where it will be performed at lower wage rates.[57]

This form of repudiation of the collective bargaining agreement is not excused because the employer acted in good faith or because the employer was motivated solely by economic necessity. Moreover, it is irrelevant to this type of violation that an employer bargained over, or was willing to bargain over concessions and the relocation. The violation is not based on a failure to bargain; it is based on the employer's modification of the contract and its wage rates by relocating.

Milwaukee Spring

The above principles were developed in the major NLRB decision in this area, *Milwaukee Spring Division of Illinois Coil Spring Company*.[58] In this case the collective bargaining agreement between the union and the employer ran from April 1, 1980 until March 31, 1983 and covered about 100 employees, 35 of whom worked in assembly operations. In early 1982, the employer asked the union to grant concessions, including giving up a wage increase due April 1. The company informed the union it had financial difficulties and proposed relocating its assembly operations to another facility which was not unionized.

During discussions between the company and the union, the company said it was willing to bargain over alternatives to relocation, noting that labor costs for assembly work were $8 an hour in wages and $2 an hour in fringes compared with $4.50 and $1.35 at its non-union plant. At a meeting in late March 1982, the company presented the union with a document entitled "Terms Upon Which Milwaukee Assembly Operations Will Be Retained in Milwaukee." Several days after this document was discussed, the union informed the company that the union membership rejected consideration of contract concessions. The company then went ahead with its proposal to relocate the work, planning to lay off 32 of the assembly workers and complete relocation by December 31, 1982.

At the Board, there was no dispute between the company and union over this characterization of the facts. It was further agreed that: 1) the relocation of the assembly operation was due solely to the comparatively higher labor costs under the collective bargaining agreement, 2) the relocation decision was economically motivated and was not based on anti-union considerations, 3) the failure to provide an adequate return on investment, not an inability to pay the contractual wage rates, prompted the decision to relocate, 4) the company bargained with the union over its decision, and 5) the company was willing to bargain over the effects of its decision with the union. The Board summarized the issue to be decided as:

> "[W]hether an employer, after engaging in decision bargaining and while offering to engage in further effects bargaining, may, without union consent, relocate bargaining unit work during the term of an existing collective bargaining agreement from its unionized facility to its non-unionized facility, and lay off employees, solely because of comparatively higher labor costs in the collective bargaining agreement at the unionized facility which the union declined to modify."

The Board answered this question in the negative. The Board reasoned that the employer's decision to transfer its assembly operations and lay off bargaining unit employees as a consequence was an illegal mid-term modification of the contract. However, the continued viability of the *Milwaukee Spring* doctrine is uncertain as the Board is reconsidering its decision in this case.[59]

Waiver of the Union's Right to Prevent Relocation of Work

A mid-contract relocation of bargaining unit work is permissible if made with the union's consent. It is also permissible if the union has waived its statutory right to prohibit such a relocation. Consequently in these kinds of cases, employers frequently claim the existence of a union waiver.

There are three basic ways by which waiver may occur.[60] First, contract language may specifically permit the employer to unilaterally remove unit work during the term of the contract.[61] Second, a union may waive its right through bargaining. Waiver may be established if it can be shown that during prior negotiations, the union proposed a clause limiting or prohibiting the relocation of work, but failed to obtain this provision after the matter was fully discussed.[62] Third, a waiver may be found from the failure of the union to question or object to prior work relocations. If a union acquiesced in earlier transfers which involved layoffs or terminations, this may preclude it from successfully challenging a later relocation.[63] Because a finding of waiver will be determinative of the unfair labor practice claim, waiver can often be an important issue in these cases.

Remedies for Violations

The remedies available in *Milwaukee Spring* type cases are the same as those available in failure to decision-bargain cases. The remedies are a cease and desist order (ordering the employer to cease from violating the NLRA), an order to rescind the decision and restore the discontinued operations, to reinstate laid off employees and to "make them whole" for any loss of earnings (usually involving back pay from the date of layoff to the date of recall) and benefits. *Milwaukee Spring* is an example of a case where all of the above remedies were granted.

The main question raised by a remedial order is whether it will prove to be an effective remedy. This is the same issue that arises with violations of the duty to decision-bargain. The primary corrective action needed is to restore the situation to pre-unfair labor practice conditions. This becomes more difficult if the work has already been relocated by the time of the Board's order. If the work has been relocated, the issuance of a restoration order is crucial, since otherwise the only compensation available to employees for the company's wrongdoing is back pay. As in decision-bargaining cases, even if the Board orders reinstitution, a federal court may deny enforcement of the order because it finds restoration to be "unduly burdensome" (too costly) to the employer. The Board itself sometimes may refuse to order resumption of operations for the same reason. Furthermore, in some situations it will be impossible to order restoration, such as where the plant from which work was transferred has been sold.[64]

In light of the fact that restoration orders may not be issued or enforced because it is considered unfair to compel the employer to restore work already transferred, it becomes critical to preserve the status quo pending the resolution of the unfair labor practice charges. Thus, as with decision-bargaining cases, to guarantee that the work is not relocated before the final Board order is enforced, it is necessary for the Board to seek a Section 10(j) court injunction compelling the employer to maintain the status quo. As mentioned earlier, it is within the discretion of the Board whether it will seek such an injunction.[65]

Milwaukee Spring and Collective Bargaining

Although *Milwaukee Spring* appears to benefit unions, in reality it is a mixed blessing. Its immediate practical impact has been that employers, when negotiating collective bargaining agreements, are demanding language to eliminate *Milwaukee Spring* rights. Thus, companies are insisting upon provisions which permit relocations and waive a union's right to object to mid-contract transfers of bargaining unit work. Due in large part to the depressed economy, companies often have the bargaining leverage to gain such contract language. Moreover, even if an employer is not able to obtain such a provision, it is still permissable for the employer to relocate unit work after the contract expires, as long as it has bargained in good faith to an impasse. At this point an employer has the right to transfer bargaining unit work since the *Milwaukee Spring* legal prohibition applies only during the term of the contract.

In response to an employer's mid-term relocation of work in violation of the NLRA, a union may file and pursue unfair labor practice charges, request the Board to seek a Section 10(j) status quo injunction, and hope it will eventually prevail in the Board proceedings and possible court appeal. Note that the procedures in this kind of case are the same as in a failure to decision-bargain case and that the important right to information under Section 8(a)5 also applies here.

A union needs to decide whether it will refuse to bargain in such a situation (as it has no legal obligation to bargain) and merely rest on its statutory right to object to the work relocation. If the union does this, however, it will face a long, uncertain legal fight. A union might decide that it is in its members' best interests to negotiate with the employer over the relocation while still maintaining its legal right to ultimately object to any unilateral transfer.

Conclusion

Labor's concern is its ability to protect jobs and prevent the removal of work. The foregoing discussion has focused on union challenges to work removal based on; (1) restrictions in the collective bargaining agreement, (2) the National Labor Relations Act prohibition on work removal motivated by anti-union considerations, (3) the law's requirement of decision-bargaining, and (4) the law's prohibition on relocations undertaken to escape the terms of the collective bargaining agreement.

However, there are serious shortcomings to these restrictions which make it unlikely that the legal system can adequately respond to labor's concerns. One problem is the freedom of a company to implement its decision to remove work prior to resolution of the dispute by an arbitrator, the Board or a court. Another problem is that the final remedy granted usually does not prohibit the removal of work or order the restoration of already discontinued or transferred work.

Furthermore, there is uncertainty as to the basic rights and responsibilities of unions and employers since the law is in flux. The two major issues, the parameters of mandatory bargaining and the continued viability and scope of the *Milwaukee Spring* doctrine, have yet to be resolved. However, even if the law develops in such a way as to require bargaining over all forms of work removal, the ultimate decision to close or relocate will still be in the hands of management. Similarly, even if the prohibition against mid-contract relocations is upheld and expanded, a company may still have the bargaining power to compel a union to give up this right through contract language. Therefore, even given the unlikely event that the law develops in this "pro-labor" manner, the practical impact on labor's ability to stop plant closings will not be great.

Underlying these disputes is a basic conflict. Employers want complete control over running their companies; workers, through their unions, want some control over management decisions which affect their continued employment. The law provides only minimal support for labor's efforts in this conflict. It is clear that the law does not give unions the right to participate in management decision-making nor does it empower unions to prevent closings. However, the law is useful as a defensive tool which provides unions with greater leverage in delaying a closing and in negotiating a better settlement for workers who lose their jobs.

In the long run, it will take drastic reform of the law of collective bargaining to have a significant impact on the power of unions to avert plant closings. What is entailed is a redirection of national labor policy to mandate the involvement of unions in the critical, heretofore management, decisions affecting the future of jobs.[66] Moreover, such reforms alone will have a negligible effect on the overall problem of deindustrialization unless implemented in the context of broader economic solutions.

Nevertheless, in the short run the law provides one method of defending the interest of workers in retaining their employment. As stated by one labor commentator specifically concerning the right to decision-bargain, but relevant to all union rights in this area,

"[W]e [must] view labor's effort to gain greater control of the workplace as an overall struggle with several fronts. If the right to decision-bargain is so insignificant, it is rather curious that employers have so bitterly and consistently opposed it in the Board and the courts over the last half-century. Although the right is no panacea for the overwhelming crisis of economic dislocation, it certainly enhances organized labor's relative bargaining position in the struggle against capital flight."[67]

Thus, whatever rights the law presently provides should not be ignored as it gives labor more leverage than it would otherwise have. The law should be seen as one tool among many, to be used when possible.

End Notes

1. Staughton Lynd, "Investment Decisions and the Quid Pro Quo Myth," *Case Western Reserve Law Review*, Vol. 29, 1976, pp. 396-427.

2. 29 U.S.C. Section 141 et seq.

3. Note that the scope of the discussion will be limited to restrictions placed on plant closings and other forms of work removal by the labor agreement and by the law of collective bargaining. Other laws and legal tactics are beyond the scope of this article. For legal considerations other than those arising under the National Labor Relations Act, see National Lawyers Guild, *Plant Closings and Runaway Industries: Strategies for Labor* (Washington, D.C.: National Labor Law Center, 1981), pp. 21-22.

4. For examples of contract language restricting management's right to close plants or transfer work, see Anne Lawrence and Paul Chown, *Plant Closings and Technological Change: A Guide for Union Negotiators* (Berkeley: Center for Labor Research and Education, Institute of Industrial Relations, University of California, 1983), pp. 12-15; see also *Major Collective Bargaining Agreements: Plant Movement, Interplant Transfer and Relocation Allowances* (U.S. Department of Labor, Bureau of Labor Statistics, 1981), pp. 1-18.

5. *Major Collective Bargaining Agreements*, at note 4, pp. 1-18 and *Collective Bargaining Negotiations and Contracts* (Washington, D.C.: Bureau of National Affairs, 1983), Vol. 2, pp. 65-201 to 64-204.

6. *Pabst Brewing Company*, 78 LA 772 (1982); see also National Labor Law Center of the National Lawyers Guild, *Employee and Union Member Guide to Labor Law*, (NY: Clark Boardman Company, Ltd., 1983), pp. 4-2; footnote 2, for citations to other arbitration cases where explicit contract prohibitions were found to bar plant closures and relocations.

7. Section 301(a) states: "Suits for violations of contracts between an employer and a labor organization . . . may be brought in any district court of the United States having jurisdiction of the parties."

8. The Federal Mediation and Concilation Service, in its 34th Annual Report for 1981, noted that the average time period between the filing of a grievance and the issuance of an arbitrator's award was 230 days, at 111 LRR 94 (October 4, 1982).

9. Even with strong contract language, a union faces the additional problem of having to post a substantial bond in order to get an injunction. The law requires that the union provide "adequate security in an amount to be fixed by the court" to protect the employer for any loss, expense or damage caused by an improper granting of the injunction. Section 7(e) of the Norris-LaGuardia Act, 29 U.S.C. Section 101 et seq. A union may decide not to seek an injunction because it does not want to risk the possible financial loss involved in posting a bond.

10. *IAM Local Lodge 1255 v. Panoramic*, 668 F.2d, 276, 109 LRRM 2169 (7th Cir. 1981); see also *Lever Brothers v. International Chemical Workers*, 554 F2d 115, 95 LRRM 2438 (4th Cir. 1976).

11. In a case involving the sale of a business where the union claimed the sale violated specific contract language, the court looked at what the arbitrator could do to remedy the situation if the employer were permitted to go ahead with the sale pending arbitration. The arbitrator could order monetary compensation but this would not provide sufficient relief where the permanent loss of jobs was at stake. Reinstatement, which is the traditional remedy for employees discharged in violation of the contract, would be the only remedy that would really compensate for the violation. However, if the plant were already sold by the time the arbitrator decided the grievance, the arbitrator would have to order the employer to undo the sale and offer reinstatment to terminated employees. The court did not see this as a viable alternative because an arbitrator might not have the authority to order recission of a sale and even if such authority existed, an arbitrator might be reluctant to order recission in view of the practical difficulties of implementing it. Therefore, an injunction to restrain the employer from completing the proposed sale was necessary to preserve a reinstatement remedy. *Panoramic*, at note 10.

12. See *Panoramic* at note 10, for an example of how a court resolves these issues.

13. National Labor Law Center, *Employee and Union Member Guide*, at note 6, pp. 4-4 to 4-5.

14. Ibid.

15. *Local 461 v. Singer Co.*, 54 F. Supp. 442, 110 LRRM 2407 (D.C.N.J. 1982).

16. In addition, the existence of a contractual "zipper clause" may make it difficult to claim an implied restriction. A zipper clause "zips up" the contract by stating, among other things, that the written contract contains the full and complete agreement on all bargainable issues. If such a clause is interpreted literally, the only limitations on employer actions are those stated in the contract. Therefore, a union may not be able to claim an implied restriction because it is not specifically stated in the collective bargaining agreement.

17. *Textile Workers Union of America v. Darlington Manufacturing Co.*, 380 U.S. 263, 58 LRRM 2657 (Sup. Ct. 1965).

18. Ibid. and *Midland Ross Corp. v. NLRB*, 617 F.2d 977, 103 LRRM 2908 (3rd Cir. 1980).

19. For an overview of the unfair labor practice charge procedures at the National Labor Relations Board, see Bruce Feldacker, *Labor Guide to Labor Law* (Reston, Va.: Reston Publishing Co., Inc., 1983), pp. 16-32. For a more detailed explanation see Kenneth C. McGuiness, *How to Take a Case Before the National Labor Relations Board* (Washington, D.C.: Bureau of National Affairs, 1976).

20. National Labor Law Center, *Employee and Union Member Guide*, at note 6, pp. 4-15.

21. For further discussion of Section 8(a)3 violations in the context of plant closings see National Lawyers Guild, *Plant Closings and Runaway Industries*, at note 3, pp. 3-5; see also Feldacker, *Labor Guide*, at note 19, pp. 157-159.

22. "Office of the General Counsel Memorandum 81-83, July 14, 1981," *Labor Relations Yearbook-1981*, (Washington, D.C.: Bureau of National Affairs), pp. 312 and 314, also at 107 LRR 266.

23. Ibid., p. 313.

24. Federal circuit courts of appeals are responsible for enforcing Board orders and for deciding appeals from Board decisions. NLRA, Sections 10(e) and (f). Federal district courts may issue temporary injunctions prior to unfair labor practice proceedings. NLRA, Section 10(j).

25. An additional problem is presented by the limited bargaining obligation of a "successor employer." If a new employer takes over a plant, it may not have to abide by terms of the union contract and may not even have to recognize the union. For a discussion of the successor employer issue see Feldacker, *Labor Guide*, at note 19, pp. 196-200.

26. *Fibreboard Paper Products Corp. v. NLRB*, 379 U.S. 203, 57 LRRM 2609 (1964).

27. For a detailed discussion of the historical development of the law governing an employer's duty to bargain over work removal, see Stanley A. Gacek, "The Employer's Duty to Bargain on Termination of Unit Work," *Labor Law Journal* (October 1981), pp. 659-678 and November 1981, pp. 699-724.

28. For a recent NLRB case explaining how the Board evaluates the duty to bargain over subcontracting, see *Marriot Corp.*, 264 NLRB No. 178, 111 LRRM 1354 (1982).

29. *Westinghouse Electric Corporation*, 150 NLRB 1574, 58 LRRM 1257 (1965). In addition to the "significant detriment" test, this case established a number of criteria to be examined in determining whether a particular subcontracting decision necessitates bargaining. The NLRB said bargaining is not required if all the following tests are met: (1) the subcontracting is motivated solely by economic reasons, (2) it has been past practice for the employer to subcontract various kinds of work, (3) the subcontracting does not vary significantly in kind or degree from the company's established practice, (4) there is no significant detriment to bargaining unit employees, and (5) the union has had an opportunity to bargain about changes in existing subcontracting practices at general negotiating meetings.

30. Gacek, "The Employer's Duty to Bargain," at note 27, p. 669.

31. *Ozark Trailers*, 161 NLRB 651, 63 LRRM 1264 (1966).

32. In general, the circuit court of appeals evaluated any termination of bargaining unit work as involving a major capital investment decision or a change in the basic scope of the business not requiring bargaining. In the late 1970s, however, several federal courts issued decisions which moved toward requiring bargaining over an employer's decision to shut down part of a business. These courts said there was a "presumption" that the decision to close is a mandatory subject, which made it more likely that bargaining would be required in a particular situation. *Brockway Motor Truck v. NLRB*, 582 F.2d 720, 99 LRRM 2013 (3d Cir. 1978) and *NLRB v. First National Maintenance Corp.*, 627 F.2d 596, 104 LRRM 2924 (2d Cir. 1980).

33. *General Motors Corporation*, 191 NLRB 951, 77 LRRM 1537 (1971).

34. *Summit Tooling Company*, 195 NLRB 479, 79 LRRM 1396 (1972); see also *Kingwood Mining Company*, 210 NLRB 844, 86 LRRM 1203 (1974), enforced 515 F.2d 1018, 90 LRRM 2844 (D.C. Cir. 1975).

35. 452 U.S. 666, 107 LRRM 2705 (1981). First National Maintenance (FNM) was a corporation which provided housekeeping and related services for commercial customers. Its employees were hired specifically for particular customers and the company charged its customers a set fee plus reimbursement for its labor costs. FNM contracted with a nursing home to provide cleaning services and later realized it was losing money on this contract. It therefore requested an increase in its fee and informed the customer that services would be discontinued on a specific date unless the increase was paid. The increase was not paid and FNM notified its employees at the nursing home that they were being terminated and terminated the services. Although there was no collective bargaining agreement in effect at that time, a union was certified as the representative of FNM's employees shortly before the termination and requested the company to delay the termination and bargain with the union. FNM refused and the union filed an unfair labor practice alleging that FNM unlawfully refused to bargain.

36. "General Counsel Memorandum, July 14, 1981," at note 22, p. 312; and "Office of the General Counsel Memorandum 81-57, November 30, 1981," *Labor Relations Yearbook-1981* (Washington, D.C.: Bureau of National Affairs), p. 315, also at 109 LRR 67.

37. *Marriot Corp.*, at note 28.

38. *Tocco Division of Park-Ohio Industries v. NLRB.* 257 NLRB 413, 107 LRRM 1498 (1981), affirmed 112 LRRM 3089 (6th Cir. 1983) and *Zipp v. Bohn Heat Transfer*, 110 LRRM 3013 (D.C. Ill. 1982).

39. *General Counsel's Report on Case Handling Developments at NLRB*, 112 LRR 61 (1983).

40. *NLRB v. Acme Industrial Co.*, 385 U.S. 432, 64 LRRM 2069 (1967); *Herk Elevator Maintenance*, 197 NLRB 26, 80 LRRM 1448 (1972), enforced 471 F2d 647, 82 LRRM 3091 (2d Cir. 1973); *Fawcett Printing Corp.*, 201 NLRB 964, 82 LRRM 1663 (1973); *American Needle and Novelty Co.*, 206 NLRB 534, 84 LRRM 1526 (1973); and *Royal Typewriter Co.*, 209 NLRB No. 174, 85 LRRM 1501 (1974), enforced 533 F.2d 1030, 92 LRRM 2013 (8th Cir. 1976).

41. National Labor Law Center, *Employee and Union Member Guide*, at note 6, pp. 1-9.

42. Charles J. Morris, ed., *The Developing Labor Law* (Washington, D.C.: Bureau of National Affairs, 1983), p. 647.

43. Ibid., pp. 579-606.

44. Section 8(d) of the NLRA, which defines the legal duty to bargain, states that; "Such obligation [to bargain collectively] does not compel either party to agree to a proposal or require the making of a concession."

45. For a definition of impasse and an explanation of the effect of an impasse on the duty to bargain see Morris, *Developing Labor Law*, at note 42, pp. 634-639.

46. *Ozark Trailers*, at note 31.

47. See note 19 for references to NLRB procedures.

48. It has been estimated that the time from the filing of an unfair labor practice charge to the date of a Board decision can be from one to two years. At least several additional years will be added to the process if a decision is then appealed to federal court. "The Timetable of Delay: The Unfair Labor Practice Process," *Labor Update Newsletter of the National Labor Law Center*, Vol. 2, No. 3, (March-April 1982).

49. Section 10(j) states: "The Board shall have the power upon issuance of a complaint . . . charging that any person has engaged in or is engaging in an unfair labor practice, to petition any district court of the United States . . . for appropriate temporary relief or restraining order."

50. See *Zipp v. Bohn Heat Transfer*, at note 38, where the court issued a Section 10(j) injunction ordering the employer, among other things, to bargain in good faith and to keep the operation at its present location pending final disposition of the unfair labor practice complaint at the NLRB.

51. One of the arguments employers have made in federal district court in opposition to an injunction is that the union has waived its statutory right to bargain because the collective bargaining agreement gives the employer the unilateral right to close or to relocate work. If a court finds this to be the case, it will refuse to issue a Section 10(j) injunction. The issue of waiver may also come up in the resolution of the unfair labor practice charge at the Board or in a federal circuit court appeal of Board decision. In this context, it may be argued by the employer that it did not violate Section 8(a)5 by refusing to decision-bargain since the union waived its right to bargain, thereby allowing the employer to take unilateral action. A waiver is generally established by contract language and/or other evidence showing the union agreed to permit the employer to remove work without first bargaining to a good faith impasse. See *Tocco Division*, at note 38, where the employer claimed the union had waived its right to bargain over work transfers: (1) by agreeing to contract language for severance pay in the event of work transfers, (2) in negotiations preceding the current collective bargaining agreement, and (3) by failing to object to several work transfers which occurred after the collective bargaining agreement was in effect. The court rejected the employer's contentions and found the employer in violation of its duty to decision-bargain.

52. In *Tocco Division* at note 38, where the company transferred work from one plant to another, the Board ordered the employer to restore the work to the first plant stating, "There is no evidence that this remedy creates an undue hardship on Respondent [employer]. Respondent is still in existence and presently performs many functions at the same plant facility it did in February 1979 [when it transferred the work]." On the other hand, in *Marriot Corp.*, at note 28, the Board refused to order the employer to restore the operation it had contracted out. Some of the reasons given by the Board for this refusal were that the change in operations had occurred more than two and one-half years ago and the employer had sold the machinery used exclusively in the sub-contracted operation.

53. For example, in *Marriot Corp.*, at note 28, the back pay remedy dated from the day work was discontinued by the employer. For a case where the back pay remedy ran only from the date of the Board's order, see *Royal Plating and Polishing*, 160 NLRB No. 72, 63 LRRM 1045 (1966) and *NLRB v. W.R. Grace Co.*, 571 F.2d 279, 98 LRRM 2001 (5th Cir. 1978).

54. *L.A. Marine Hardware*, 235 NLRB 720, 98 LRRM 1571 (1978), enforced 602 F.2d 1032, 102 LRRM 2498 (9th Cir. 1979); *Brown Co.*, 243 NLRB 769, 101 LRRM 1608 (1979), remanded 663 F.2d 1078, 109 LRRM 2663 (9th Cir. 1981); *Milwaukee Spring Division of Illinois Coil Spring Company*, 265 NLRB No. 28, 111 LRRM 1486 (1982).

55. *Oak Cliff-Golman Bakery Co.*, 207 NLRB 063, 85 LRRM 1035 (1973), enforced 505 F.2d 1302, 90 LRRM 2615 (5th Cir. 1974) and *C & S Industries*, 158 NLRB 454, 62 LRRM 1043 (1966).

56. Paul Bosanac, "Concession Bargaining, Work Transfers and Midcontract Modification: Los Angeles Marine Hardware Company," *Labor Law Journal*, (February 1983), pp. 72-79; Martin Klaper, "The Right to Relocate Work During the Term of an Existing Collective Bargaining Agreement," *Labor Law Journal*, (February 1983), pp. 94-103; and *General Counsel's Report*, at note 39.

57. Another way companies are attempting to avoid paying contractually agreed upon wages and benefits is by filling for reorganization under Chapter 11 of the federal Bankruptcy Code. See "Discussion of Bankruptcy Act," 114 LLR 224 (November 21, 1983); "Employers are using Bankruptcy to Force Layoffs, Wage Cuts," *AFL-CIO News*, November 5, 1983; and "Firms Using Bankruptcy to Fight Labor," *Wall Street Journal*, March 30, 1983.

58. *Milwaukee Spring*, at note 54. This case follows the reasoning of the major court decision on this topic, *L.A. Marine Hardware*, at note 54.

59. On January 23, 1984, the National Labor Relations Board issued its decision in the case of *Milwaukee Spring*, 111 LRRM 1486. The Board reversed its 1982 decision and ruled that during the term of a collective bargaining agreement, it is permissable for a company to relocate work from a union to a non-union workplace in order to escape the higher labor costs of the union contract. As a result of the Board's decision, there is no longer a legal prohibition on transferring work, without union consent, to a non-union facility where labor costs will be lower. However, the Board left open the issue of whether an employer has an obligation to *bargain* with the union over the decision to relocate.

This question was answered by the Board three months later in *Otis Elevator*, 115 LRRM 1281. In this case the Board drastically limited an employer's duty to bargain over the removal of work. The Board ruled that Otis was not obligated to bargain with the union when it transferred work from its research and development operations to another facility. The Board also ruled that since the employer was not required to bargain over its relocation decision, it was not required to provide the union with information the union had requested concerning the company's decision.

The Board's conclusion that the work relocation was not subject to a mandatory duty to bargain was unanimous, although Board members had different rationales for the decision. Members Dotson and Hunter said that an employer has a duty to bargain *only* when its decision is based on a reduction of labor costs, i.e., when the employer wishes to move work because it can have it done for less elsewhere. They say there is *no* duty to bargain if management's decision is based on a change in the basic direction or nature of the business, as was the case in *Otis Elevator*. They would apply this ruling not only to work relocations, but to a broad range of management decisions, including subcontracting, reorganization and consolidation.

The effect of this decision is to substantially restrict management's legal responsibility to bargain over various forms of work removal. *Otis Elevator* and *Milwaukee Spring* greatly narrow union rights under the National Labor Relations Act, thereby limiting the ability of unions to use the law in the face of work removal.

60. Morris, *Developing Labor Law*, at note 42, pp. 640-650.

61. For examples of waiver claims based on contract language see *L. A. Marine*, at note 54, *Milwaukee Spring*, at note 54 and *NLRB v. Marine Optical Co.*, 109 LRRM (1st Cir. 1982) (no waiver found based on preamble and recognition clauses); *Kobell v. Thorsen Tool Co.*, 112 LRRM 2397 (D.C. Pa. 1982) (no waiver found based on clause providing for preferential hiring rights in the event of relocation); *Milwaukee Spring*, at note 54 and *Kobell*, at this note (no waiver found based on management's rights clause).

62. *Tocco Division*, at note 38.

63. *Milwaukee Spring*, at note 54; *Tocco Division*, at note 38; and *Kobell*, at note 61.

64. Note that in *Milwaukee Spring*, at note 54, where restoration was ordered, the employer had just begun the transfer of work at the time of the Board's order. Also see *Brown Co.*, at note 54, where the Board ordered restoration and back pay. In *Brown*, the employer transferred its cement hauling operations to another of its divisions. The Board

noted that there was no evidence to show that the restoration remedy created an undue hardship on the employer, as the employer remained in the cement hauling business and maintained its own fleet of trucks for this purpose. On the other hand, in *L.A. Marine*, at note 54, the return of the work was not required because the company no longer owned the facility from which the work was transferred. For cases where restoration was not ordered because seen as unduly burdensome, see *NLRB v. Townhouse T.V.*, 531 F.2d 826, 91 LRRM 2636 (7th Cir. 1976); and *Jay Foods, Inc. v. NLRB*, 573 F.2d 438, 97 LRRM 3155 (7th Cir. 1978).

65. Three recent decisions where the Board sought and obtained Section 10(j) injunctions are *Gottfried v. Echlin, Inc.*, 113 LRRM 2349 (E.D. Ill. 1983); *Kobell*, at note 61; and *Zipp*, at note 38.

66. Another legal strategy presently being pursued by labor is the enactment of plant closing legislation. Proposed federal legislation, the National Employment Priorities Act, H.R. 2847, would impose minimum notice requirements and require aid for workers and communities; "House Hearing on Plant Closing Law," 113 LRR 241 (July 25, 1983).

67. Gacek, "The Employer's Duty to Bargain," at note 27, p. 722.

Worker Ownership and Reindustrialization:
A Guide for Workers

Arthur Hochner

"Employees to Buy Huge Steel Works in $66 Million Pact," *New York Times*, March 14, 1983.
"Workers to the Rescue: Can Employee Ownership Keep Factories Open?" *Christian Science Monitor*, November 11, 1982.
"Worker Ownership May Save Some A&Ps," *Business Week*, June 28, 1982.
"The Fabulous ESOP: More Companies Start Such Employee Plans," *Wall Street Journal*, August 5, 1981.

Headlines such as these have appeared in numerous newspapers and magazines for about the past decade. Workers hard pressed to save their jobs have contemplated, flirted with, or launched into takeovers or buyouts of their firms when threatened with shutdowns.

• GAF's decision to close its New England asbestos mine was met by worker and union (Local 338, United Cement Lime, Gypsum and Allied Workers International Union, AFL-CIO) blocking tactics at first. Finally, a worker buyout created the Vermont Asbestos Group (VAG). Over 175 workers thus prevented a layoff in 1975.

• Sperry Rand decided to close its Herkimer, New York, Library Bureau's furniture plant in 1976, laying off 270 workers in two International Union of Electrical Workers locals. A joint worker-community venture created the Mohawk Valley Community Corporation, which raised about $5 million and bought the Library Bureau.

Arthur Hochner is an Assistant Professor of Industrial Relations and Organizational Behavior in the School of Business Administration of Temple University. A version of this paper was presented at the Seminar on Labor Ownership and Worker Cooperatives in Grythyttan, Sweden, June 13-17, 1983. The author wishes to acknowledge a travel grant from the German Marshall Fund of the United States enabling participation in the seminar.

- The closing of Youngstown Sheet and Tube's Campbell plant by the Lykes conglomerate in 1977 and the subsequent US Steel closure there, laying off a total of over 7000 workers, prompted the formation of the Mahoning Valley Ecumenical Coalition. Together with leaders of United Steelworkers Local 1462, this group of clergymen pressed a plan, which later failed for lack of funds, for a worker-community takeover.
- In 1980, leaders of Local 46 of the United Food and Commercial Workers, AFL-CIO, proposed to save the almost bankrupt Rath Packing Company in Waterloo, Iowa. The over 2000 workers received 60 percent of Rath stock and major power on the board of directors in return for pay cuts.
- GM's Hyatt bearing plant in Clark, New Jersey, a stepping-stone in the 1920s for GM empire-builder Alfred P. Sloan, was about to be closed in 1981, laying off about 1200 workers. Attrition had cut the workforce from 2400 in 1979. Leaders and members of the Local 736 United Auto Workers negotiated to buy the plant from GM, saving almost 1000 jobs.
- In Philadelphia in 1982 Local 1357 of the UFCW sponsored the conversion of two shutdown A&P supermarkets into worker-owned-and-operated stores (known as O&O Supermarkets) in the wake of a massive shutdown of over 40 stores and 2000 layoffs.
- In 1983, 7000 members of the Independent Steel Workers Union at National Steel's Weirton, West Virginia mill decided to buy out that plant.

Introduction

These stories are only some of the most renowned examples of this job saving tactic. The National Center for Employee Ownership, a Washington-based advocacy organization, estimates that there are now about 5,000 employee ownership plans and about 500 companies where majority ownership is in the hands of workers. However, many less celebrated examples of worker interest or action exist. In the auto industry, employee stock ownership was mandated by the federal legislation bailing out Chrysler. Continental Airlines' pilots tried to push through an employee takeover in the Spring of 1981 to prevent a hostile takeover by Texas Air, a nonunion carrier. Pan Am unions agreed in late 1981 for workers to take about 15 percent of ailing Pan Am's stock in exchange for wage cuts. Other examples can be found in other industries as well; insurance (Consumers United Group), newspapers (Milwaukee Journal, New York Daily News), railroads (Chicago and North Western, Conrail), taxis (Denver, Sacramento), machine tools (South Bend Lathe), refuse collection (Sunset Scavengers and Golden Gate Disposal), plywood manufacture (in Oregon and Washington).

Not all the interest in worker or employee ownership emanates from workers or unions, however. Ford Motor pushed (unsuccessfully) worker ownership and 50 percent wage cuts for the Sheffield, Alabama, aluminum die-cast plant in October 1981 as part of the price for preventing a complete shutdown. An article in *Forbes* magazine, for instance, declared "Let Them Eat Stock," and one in the *Harvard Business Review* examined "The Uneven Record of Employee Ownership."[1] These employer-oriented journals emphasize the advantages to management of allowing employee ownership; quick capital formation, tax breaks, avoidance of pension fund obligations, union avoidance, improved worker motivation and discipline, etc. Fears of management manipulation and of lack of worker control over stock voting rights have led many unionists to be very wary of worker ownership as a solution to threatened shutdowns. Moreover, they voice fears of betting their livelihoods on rescuing management-created messes in order to save their own jobs. In a *New York Times* op-ed article Peter Pitegoff and Staughton Lynd warned workers (particularly those at Weirton) that "until they obtain sufficient information to weigh the value of those jobs against the cost of the concessions, they would do well to look very cautiously at this gift horse."[2]

Why is there such interest in worker ownership? Does it save jobs? What are the risks? What are the benefits? How does worker ownership fit into the fight against shutdowns and deindustrialization? What is the feasibility of establishing worker-owned firms? What are the differences among worker ownership, worker cooperatives, and employee stock ownership plans (ESOPs)? Does worker ownership mean that workers will run the firm? What happens to unions under worker ownership?

These are questions that will be addressed in this article. It is an attempt to introduce issues of concern to workers and unionists regarding worker ownership of industry. Readers seeking fuller details are strongly urged to consult the sources and organizations cited. Here, however, it may be appropriate to give some brief hints of answers to the questions. Workers not only in North America but also in Western Europe have increasingly turned to worker ownership as a means to save jobs, fight unemployment, and resist corporate disinvestment.

Worker ownership *can* save jobs and prevent shutdowns. But it may be risky and difficult. It should not be relied on as an exclusive strategy; neither should it be shunned. The obstacles — financial, legal, organizational — may be complex and formidable, but the benefits to workers and unions can be significant. Workers have to concentrate not simply on ownership but also on changing power relations in the firm, that is, on worker control. Unions are needed to play a strong role in fostering worker ownership and protecting worker interests. But worker ownership may require difficult changes in union behavior. For interested workers an increasing number of experiences are accumulating and organizations arising to help steer the course.

Worker Interest Present and Past

To understand the apparently growing phenomenon of worker ownership, it is necessary to look at why workers are interested and how it fits into labor strategies. The interest grows out of the circumstances of our time. These circumstances and interests are duplicated in many places, including abroad. Although worker ownership experiments in the past often failed, there is reason to believe that worker ownership can play an important part in the labor movement's economic strategies.

Generally, worker ownership has been seen as a last resort in the fight against plant closings or concessions. Only after fighting to change management's decision and failing, do workers usually begin to address alternative strategies. Most often it is already too late to accomplish the sharp turn in orientation and the mobilization of energy and resources necessary. Perhaps that is a major reason why worker takeovers or buyouts are relatively rare.

However, worker ownership seems to have moved up lately in rank order in labor's list of strategies. For instance, take the Philadelphia A&P supermarket shutdown in 1982. After suffering several massive shutdowns in previous years, notably Food Fair supermarkets and Two Guys department stores, UFCW Local 1357 was ready for the A&P challenge. In the previous negotiations with A&P, Local 1357 had won language calling for a three-week advance notice of store closings. Furthermore, leaders and organizers of the union had their ears to the ground, listening for early warning signals of a shutdown. Due to this foresight, when the closings of about 40 stores were announced, the union immediately put forth a plan for keeping the stores open under worker ownership. Eventually, A&P reopened most of the stores and even sold two stores to groups of laid-off workers. For Local 1357, worker ownership served as an offensive strategy to save jobs.

In Western Europe as well interest in worker ownership as an answer to recession and unemployment has grown. Worker-owned companies have doubled in number in both Great Britain and France since 1975. In fact, the Wales Trade Union Congress (TUC) has made worker ownership an integral part of its overall strategy for Welsh economic recovery. In Italy, the number of worker-owned firms is said to have topped 18,000, ranging in size from tiny firms with a few workers to those with thousands. Most belong to cooperative leagues affiliated with the major trade union federations.

Increasing numbers of worker cooperatives are arising in Holland, Belgium, and Denmark, too. And Spain boasts perhaps the fastest growing worker-owned sector, including the famed Mondragon cooperatives of the Basque country, employing over 17,000 in over 80 worker-owned firms. The Mondragon cooperatives are extremely well-integrated, featuring their own central bank, a technical university, and including the largest manufacturer/exporter of household appliances in Spain.[3]

In the U.S., worker ownership is not a new phenomenon, though worker and union interest in it has been dormant for perhaps 50 years. During the 19th century workers formed cooperatives during strikes, employer lockouts, and depressions. While early labor organizations such as the Knights of Labor promoted them, the AFL craft unions opposed them. Most of these worker cooperatives failed, being subject to undercapitalization, lack of business skills, weak commitment to cooperative ideals, and a hostile business environment.[4] The AFL reliance on collective bargaining strategies proved more successful in the long run. However, in times of high unemployment (the years around 1890, 1920, and 1930) new worker cooperatives popped up again.

Now in the 1970s and 1980s, with unemployment reaching post-World-War-II highs, some workers have again turned to worker ownership as an alternative strategy. The primary aim is apparently the same as in the past, namely to save jobs. Saving jobs is the bottom line of every consideration of worker ownership by workers. Unfortunately, as will be pointed out below, it is sometimes the only considered criterion, and costly concessions made to save them are disregarded until too late.

But worker ownership is also being increasingly looked at in broader strategic focus. First of all, it can be promoted as a collective bargaining tactic. UFCW Local 1357 sees it as part of a job security insurance plan. That is, successful worker buyouts and takeovers show both management and workers that workers have alternatives in the face of management threats. They can pressure management to reconsider shutdowns both to save face and to prevent new competition. And they can infuse workers with more confidence that they do not have to take shutdowns lying down.

Secondly, worker ownership involves local control of jobs, which can be linked to attempts to stop or slowdown runaway captial, such as through plant closing legislation. It is no secret and no surprise that plant shutdowns are not simply the result of the deepest recession since the 1930s and record numbers of business failures. Structural shifts in the industry mix, automation, foreign competition, and union avoidance are to blame as well. However, Barry Bluestone and Bennett Harrison convincingly demonstrate the role played by excessive capital mobility and corporate growth policies. Shutdowns are fostered through conglomerate mergers, multinational investments, and inter-regional competition.[5]

Plant closing legislation aims to control or case the effects of these disinvestment policies. Such legislation has long been a priority of the AFL-CIO and the entire labor movement. Furthermore, volumes of Congressional testimony have documented that profitable plants are being shutdown. Many such plants might be kept open under worker ownership. The major plant closing bills introduced in Congress and at least eight state legislatures (with union support) include provisions to assist worker buyouts.[6]

Despite the interest by some workers, local unions, and legislators in worker ownership to fight shutdowns and to save jobs, it does not really seem to form part of labor's official strategy for reindustrialization. The AFL-CIO's "Economic Program for Jobs and Fairness"[7] calls for a national industrial policy, including a new Reconstruction Finance Corporation, massive jobs programs, expanded social programs, and equitable tax reform. The program further asks for joint business and labor involvement in the setting of national industrial policy. In addition, it calls for aid to workers hit by plant closings and major layoffs. However, mostly government and private sector actions are requested. There is no mention of aiding worker ownership as a means of job saving and bringing labor's voice into investment decisions.

The failures of 19th century worker cooperatives and the American tradition of collective bargaining incline many unionists to serious skepticism concerning worker ownership. They feel it is a management trap and an anachronistic strategy, when unions should be firm and forward-looking.

So why are some workers still choosing this path? First of all, workers in this country have always been subject to the attractions of independence and entrepreneurship, that is, being one's own boss. Secondly, however, there are some new circumstances compared to the past. There has been an increasing interest among workers not only in participation but greater control over management decisions.[8] There has been a growing awareness of the immense powers of corporate manipulation they have been subject to.' But traditional solutions through normal collective bargaining have recently been weakened by employer offensives (e.g., the defeat of Labor Law Reform in 1978) and widespread disinvestment by corporations out of unionized areas. Add into this current situation all of the calls for labor-management cooperation and a "new industrial relations."[9] How is this to be achieved? Some workers seem to feel that worker ownership provides direct action to save jobs, direct control over management, direct resistance to corporate deindustrialization, and a proper test of labor-management cooperation.

Furthermore, the appeal of worker ownership has attracted many exponents besides workers faced with shutdowns. Bluestone and Harrison's analysis of the patterns of deindustrialization ends up advocating worker ownership to be part of labor's strategy.[10] Dan Luria and Jack Russell, respectively UAW staffer and Michigan legislative consultant, in their plan for "rational reindustrialization" recommend the use of worker ownership to insure a strong worker voice in enterprise governance.[11] The Conference on Alternative State and Local Policies, which has done extensive lobbying on plant closing legislation, includes worker ownership on its list of solutions to the problem.[12] Of course, these are aside from the legislators who have joined in the chorus.

Is worker ownership *the* strategy to meet the goals of job security, control, resistance, and cooperation, as well as overall re-industrialization? No, though it makes sense as part of a larger stategy. Is it an anachronistic dead end? No, but if not carefully used, it can create more problems than solutions. The current interest by workers in this job saving method reflects the changed circumstances of the 1970s and 1980s. Is it worth labor's efforts? The answer should be an enthusiastic maybe. Worker ownership can become a productive part of labor strategies in collective bargaining and industrial policy. However, its success depends on the forms of ownership chosen and the way it is carried out.

Pitfalls, Promises, and Practices of Worker Ownership

Much of the disregard of worker ownership, confusion about it, and skepticism for it by union members and leaders stems from the complexities of the issues involved. These complexities include theoretical, legal, motivational, financial, organizational, and operational facets. That is, what worker ownership means depends on:

A. How it is understood in abstract terms, such as ideological, political, or moral terms.

B. What legal forms it takes and what legal implications it has.

C. Who initiates it and why.

D. What its feasibility and viability are in particular circumstances.

E. How it runs, including worker involvement in management and the union role.

Theory

Advocates for worker ownership are many, but often there is great variation in how they conceive it. There are conservative capitalists, liberal reformers, radicals, socialists, and a few other shades of the spectrum among them. Some ideological capitalists consider it a way of giving "everyone a chance to be a capitalist."[13] They want to make capitalism consistent with democracy by broadening the ownership of capital. Along the way they hope to make workers more loyal to the current system.[14] Other pro-management pragmatists see worker ownership as a practical tool corporations can use to take advantage of tax breaks, to raise capital, to take care of pension benefits, and to motivate workers.

Some liberals see it as a way to use the "free enterprise system to create a more equitable distribution of rewards."[15] They see it as an alternative to government transfer payments, training programs, and job creation efforts. Moreover, pro-union liberals see it as a flexible tool unions and workers should be able to choose or reject in particular fights against plant closings.[16]

More radical interpretations explain worker ownership as the melding of the labor theory of property and the democratic theory of government.[17] That is, the labor theory is based on the principle that workers should have the right to the fruits of their labor. The democratic theory involves the principle of rule by the governed. Thus, in this view the workers should share in the profits and the management of wherever they work.

Finally, those interested in extensive but decentralized social reform, including some democratic socialists, call for worker ownership to be part of the framework of "economic democracy."[18] That is, worker ownership should be part of a political program to restructure the American political economy, reducing corporate dominance and increasing the power of workers and the public. These advocates of worker ownership find precedents in Scandinavian social democratic plans for economic democracy, which specifically means there the transfer of industrial ownership from private hands to workers and unions.

Worker ownership can appeal to many political philosophies. But that does not mean it should be all things to all people. In a labor strategy for reindustrialization, arguments for greater democracy and control over corporate behavior will probably carry weight. Worker ownership has some potential to help achieve these goals at the same time as saving jobs and distributing wealth. However, it also has some potential to drive a wedge between worker owners and nonowners by encouraging the perception of common interests between worker owners and other capital owners. How and whether these potentials are realized depends a great deal on the way the labor movement conceptualizes worker ownership. By looking at it as a tool of reform rather than of status quo maintenance, labor has a better chance of wresting from it advantages for workers.

Legal Forms

Although there are two predominant forms of worker ownership in the U.S. — worker cooperatives and employee stock ownership plans (ESOPs) — there are numerous variants and hybrids even within these categories. The diversity of types is often highly confusing and causes much miscommunication. Different advocates use the same labels to mean rather different things. However, many of the distinctions among the types are extremely important to grasp. Different legal structures establish not only the financial basis but also the internal governance of rights, responsibilities, and rules. What follows is a brief sketch of the major forms and their implications. For a more thorough treatment, the reader should consult Olson's article, as well as other sources and handbooks.[19]

Of the two major forms, worker cooperatives are the oldest. Despite current strong advocacy of them by the Industrial Cooperative Association (ICA), the best known of the few cooperative consulting companies, few worker-owned companies arising from shutdowns are cooperatives. True worker cooperatives are characterized by (1) shareownership by members, (2) one member one vote, and (3) equal responsibility by members for work in the cooperative. Thus, these firms are set up as worker-controlled egalitarian democracies. True worker cooperatives are rarely found, however. In fact, most 19th century cooperatives seem to have fallen far short of the goal of equal shareownership.[20] This shortcoming, perhaps, was a major reason for their failure.

In traditional worker cooperatives each member invests an equal amount of money, which forms the basis of the firms' capital. However, recently, a new model of worker cooperative has been developed by ICA to deal with some of the problems of the traditional model. For instance, as the value of the company rises, the value of the individual shares rises too. In traditional worker cooperatives, therefore, after a while success is a golden handcuff. Share values are too high for potential new members to afford. This may lead to hiring of non-owning workers or selling out to a larger, capitalist firm. These problems have occurred in the San Francisco Bay area scavenger cooperatives and also in the plywood cooperatives of the Pacific Northwest. ICA's model of worker cooperatives gets around this problem by drastically lowering the cost to be a member (to about $100). Members have equal voting rights, and they share in the profits. But the members' profit shares are distributed, not in the form of stock, but to what are called "internal savings accounts" which operate like internal pension funds.

The worker cooperative form would not be difficult to structure were it not for a lack of standard state or federal worker cooperative law. Most recently, Massachusetts became the first state to pass a law providing a specific legal framework for worker cooperatives.[21] Generally, to set up a worker cooperative requires jockeying around various laws. However, the advantages of worker cooperatives' commitment to equality and democracy have greatly influenced recent creations of ESOPs in plant closing situations. Olson calls these new hybrids "cooperative ESOPs." Before describing these, we will go over the basics of ESOPs.

Employee stock ownership plans (ESOPs) are newer than the idea of worker cooperatives, but were advocated as far back as the 1920s.[22] They did not really catch on until the early 1970s, when changes in tax and pension laws clarified them and expanded their benefits. The Employee Retirement Income Security Act of 1974 (ERISA) and other changes in the tax codes popularized ESOPs by defining them as qualified stock bonus plans — that is, qualified for tax breaks. Employers who establish ESOTs (employee stock ownership trusts) for their employees give or sell stock in their own company to employees as a benefit, somewhat similar to a pension fund.

Tax breaks to the employer issue from this transaction; for instance, no FICA or social security tax must be paid on contributions to the trust, and employer contributions may be entirely tax deductible. Employees get a tax exempt benefit and receive vested stock when they leave the firm. The ESOT can borrow money to purchase stock and use the employer's contributions to pay off the loan. The ESOP particularly attracts employers because of its usefulness for (1) corporate finance, i.e., using the ESOT to raise investment capital; (2) corporate divestment, i.e., to pass a company on to employees; and (3) pension finding, i.e., to provide a special type of pension plan, exempt from several important ERISA protections. For workers the ESOP is generally not a suitable substitute for a fully protected pension plan.

So far, the ESOP sounds like an employer bonanza. What does it have to do with worker ownership and shutdowns? ESOPs have been the most common legal and financial structures for worker buyouts to save jobs. Furthermore, it is the typical method used by corporations to give workers some ownership in return for wage cuts and other concessions. (There may be other names used for these plans, such as TRASOPs and PAYSOPs).[23] The ESOP form provides a clear legal model of worker ownership which also gives substantial incentives to employers for agreeing to a worker buyout. This contrasts with the situation for worker cooperatives.

Probably the major advantage of the ESOP form for workers, especially when compared to the typical cooperative, is as many writers put it, its flexibility. However, unless the flexibility is managed correctly, it can have some serious consequences negating its pro-worker, pro-union potentials. This flexibility involves several important issues; who buys stock; the distribution of ownership; the degree of overall worker ownership in the firm; how worker ownership is paid for; and the rights and privileges of worker ownership, including voting rights and control.

(1) Who buys stock — ESOPs may involve worker purchase options or employer-conferred benefits to all employees. Voluntary purchase plans mean that some workers will buy stock and others will not. Such a situation will undermine the solidarity of the union and may even threaten the unity of the worker buyout effort. An example of this occurred in the purchase of GM's Hyatt bearing plant by members of UAW Local 736. Despite a defeat (by 16 votes out of over 1500 cast) in a rank-and-file referendum to support a union-funded feasibility study of worker ownership, Local 736 leaders went ahead anyway with voluntary contributions. When the ESOP was created to take full ownership, internal union conflicts erupted. Charges were filed by a group of dissident union members charging the union with breach of fair representation duties. They claimed that the defeat of the feasibility study was the will of the members, which was not carried out. Furthermore, they claimed that those who voluntarily contributed to the study were promised preferential hiring status in the new worker owned firm. An ESOP which confers ownership as a benefit to all, or an ICA cooperative, will probably be less controversial.

(2) The distribution of ownership — ESOPs may distribute stock ownership not only to workers, but also to managers. Managers may be useful to the organizing effort and even to the continuity of the

firm's operations. However, often stock is distributed according to the income of plan participants or is sold on the basis of ability to pay. Thus, higher paid workers can buy more, and managers can maintain or achieve control. This occurred at the Mohawk Valley Community Corporation, which was bought out from Sperry Rand in 1976. Top and middle managers had an average of over 1600 shares of stock, while the average unionized blue-collar and white-collar worker had less than 690. Within a few years, the company's board of directors issued new stock which allowed managers to gain a definite controlling interest.[24] Equal shareownership or equal voting power for all members, as in worker cooperatives, will insure against this type of management domination.

(3) The degree of overall worker ownership in the firm — ESOPs enjoy the flexibility of no set limits on how much of the company is owned by workers. That is, worker ownership can vary from zero to 100 percent. Worker cooperatives require 100 percent worker ownership. When attempting a worker buyout, this flexibility of an ESOP can be a big advantage. A minority interest, if structured properly and voted as a bloc, may be useful to place "watchdog" worker directors on the board to provide information crucial to job security, such as plant closing and investment decisions. Pan Am unionized workers agreed to an ESOP in the hopes of eventually controlling several director positions. A minority interest can even become a controlling interest if the ESOP is the largest single stockholder.

A majority, though not 100 percent, interest will not only virtually guarantee a controlling interest, but will also make financing easier. That is, workers have to finance less by themselves. Besides, sometimes it is just plain impossible to buy up every share. The ESOP does not have to.

It should not be forgotten, however, that worker directors on the board or majority ownership do not insure worker control or democracy. William Winpisinger, President of the International Association of Machinists, AFL-CIO, predicted that workers on the board would lose their identity as workers.[25] At VAG, the worker directors were accused of forgetting their roots and selling out to management. Workers eventually sold their shares to a businessman who took control of the company. At South Bend Lathe, stock voting rights were not passed through the ESOT to the workers. Thus, the workers could not even appoint trustees to the ESOT, which held stock they supposedly owned. Owing to this and other causes, workers struck against their own company in 1980 for nine weeks.

(4) How worker ownership is paid for — Along with the flexibility in the degree of ownership, ESOPs allow for flexibility in financing. The typical ESOP is called a "leveraged ESOP." That is, the ESOT borrows money from a lender to buy company stock. The company repays the loan — through the ESOT, so that payments of both principal and

interest are tax deductible. But in the meantime the ESOT accumulates stock with little outlay of workers' own funds. Workers also are not taking a personal risk through the ESOP in case loans are not repaid. Cooperatives do not have this advantage. Finding finance is tricky, for conventional lenders are skeptical. But there are some federal and state funds available. In addition, some recently incorporated private investment funds have been targeted to worker-owned firms, specifically cooperatives; the ICA revolving loan fund in Massachusetts and the O&O Investment Fund in Philadelphia.

(5) The rights and privileges of worker ownership — This topic is perhaps the most important of all in discussing the legal forms of worker ownership. The key rights are voting rights. As hinted at above, worker ownership does not automatically convey worker control. In a plant closing situation, where the priority is to save jobs, worker control may not impress workers as a very salient or important issue. That is how the workers at South Bend Lathe felt in setting up their ESOP. Swift action was important, and previous experience with ESOPs was minimal. Not only did this lead to lack of worker representation on the board of directors or even on the ESOT board of trustees, but it also meant management could destroy the pension plan and use the ESOP as a substitute.

When it comes to control rights and internal governance of the firm, the flexibility of the ESOP really signifies its vagueness. There are no specified rights and management structure in the ESOP, as there is in the cooperative which at least mandates one member one vote. There might be a few advantages to such ESOP flexibility, but it leaves things open to management manipulations that are not in workers' interests.

To protect worker rights, it is essential, no matter how many shares of stock each worker-owner has, that control rights in the worker-owned company be distributed democratically. That is, each worker should get an equal vote on stockholder issues. Furthermore, stock voting rights must pass through to the worker-owners and not sit with the trustees of the ESOT. The trustees have to be accountable to and representative of the worker-owners.

In partially worker-owned companies, these rights must also be protected from the very beginning of the ESOP. Moreover, the right of ESOP to be voted in a bloc should be protected, for that insures the strongest and most unified expression by worker-owners rather than the dilution of worker control through individual voting.

As several writers point out there has been a trend, as workers and unions gain experience, to combine many of the advantages of the two main forms of worker ownership into a hybrid form. Olson calls these the cooperative ESOPs.[26] These hybrids take the major feature of worker cooperatives, commitment to democratic control, and join it to the major feature of ESOPs, flexibility in financing and taxation. Creatively structured cooperative ESOPs have been initiated by both Rath Packing and Hyatt Clark Industries. These large worker-owned firms provide for worker control over management through democratically structured, one-member-one-vote ESOPs. The cooperative ESOP owes its genesis mainly to the active involvement of the local unions, which fought to protect worker interests and to avoid serious pitfalls of previous efforts, such as South Bend Lathe and VAG.

Initiation

Probably the most vigorous criticism of worker ownership comes from unionists who see it as a pro-management scheme foisted on vulnerable workers. To them worker ownership connotes concessions, cutbacks, and intra-union competition. They find support for this view in many experiences. For example, worker ownership at South Bend Lathe involved loss of pension rights and guarantees. The plan put forth by Ford Motor at the Sheffield plant called for 50 percent wage cuts. The conversion to worker ownership of GM's Hyatt plant through UAW Local 736 is perceived as a ploy by GM to force future wage reductions in negotiations with the international UAW. Other cases could easily be cited as well.

Certainly advantages to employers can be numerous. Corporations can use ESOPs to obtain refinancing and investment capital, create a market for their stocks, facilitate divestiture, limit pension obligations, bust unions, and provide employee incentive plans to raise productivity, among other reasons. Furthermore, offering ownership to workers in a failing company can be used to spread the blame for failure, allow management to give only seeming concessions for those it receives, and manipulate public opinion. For these reasons and more corporate managements have been not only receptive to the idea of worker ownership but have become aggressive promoters of it. Many unionists wonder, if it is so good for corporate employers, how good can it be for workers?

For a long time, the only answer unionists could come up with was that worker ownership saves jobs. Workers get involved in buyouts for defensive purposes primarily. This defensiveness implies vulnerability and reactive responses. In such a situation management takes the lead and exploits workers' weaknesses. Workers may find themselves continually on the defensive, though with worker ownership it may appear that they keep demanding sacrifices of themselves to keep the firm alive. They wonder whether it is worth it to save jobs this way.

In most plant closing situations workers and unions may have to concede some things. But recently groups of them realize that to preserve job security and living standards, they have to be aggressive about getting what they want through worker ownership. Union-led worker buyouts at Rath Packing, Hyatt Clark, and O&O Supermarkets exemplify this role. In each case workers have used the buyout situation to structure the ESOP in as favorable a way as possible, given the fact they were buying facilities unwanted by the parent corporation. At Rath Packing Local 46 UFCW tried hard to follow the worker cooper ative model using the ESOP form. Furthermore, they made strong and mostly successful efforts to maintain the standards of the national UFCW collective bargaining agreements. A similiar pattern was followed at Hyatt Clark.

In the 1982 A&P shutdown in Philadelphia, UFCW Local 1357 went even further in pressing the plan for worker ownership. The union used worker ownership as a bargaining chip in continuing negotiations with management after the shutdown announcement, leading to the reopening of many of the stores by A&P. The worker ownership plan and its enthusiastic reception by many A&P workers not only got corporate management's attention but also led to the inclusion in the reopening agreement of three virtually unique provisions; (1) establishing worker participation in store management through a QWL program; (2) granting of the right of first refusal to purchase stores shutdown in the future; and (3) establishing a fund from one percent of the reopened stores' gross sales revenues, a portion of which is set aside for funding future worker buyouts. This investment fund is considered by local leaders as a job security insurance plan. It has the potential to save jobs not only in the future through new worker-owned firms, but also in the present by making corporate management think at least twice before shutting down stores.

The three cases cited here demonstrate only some of the advantages to workers and unions of taking an aggressive, initiating role in worker ownership. Workers do not have to take the backseat. Nevertheless, even in the cases most beneficial for workers, costly concessions and sacrifices have been made. In the Rath case, after two hard years resulting from depressed product markets, the union agreed to terminate the union pension plan in order to keep the company alive. As Pitegoff and Lynd warn, workers must carefully weigh the costs and benefits in deciding whether to pursue worker ownership at all.[27] But once they decide to try it, an initiating role demanding that worker interests are met is essential.

Feasibility

The real bottom line of worker ownership is whether or not it works. Is it a feasible way to save jobs? Or, as some critics claim, are plant closure buyouts examples of "lemon captialism?" If the corporate owner cannot make it, why should anyone expect the worker-owners, lacking entrepreneurial experience and expertise, to revive dead firms? Questions about the viability of worker-owned firms worry even those predisposed to favor them. This section attempts to address the feasibility of worker buyouts and what factors affect their success or failure.

The "lemon capitalism" argument implies a view of plant closings as caused by the inescapable, invisible hand of market forces. That is, competition, technological change, population shifts, educational expansion, cultural upheaval, and other such seemingly impersonal forces make the plant close. And if workers buy it out to save jobs, they are just swimming against the tide.

However, this conventional wisdom of yesterday has been over-turned by observation of companies closing down profitable plants. As scholars like Bluestone and Harrison and Whyte have tirelessly pointed out, capital mobility and the search for overall corporate growth (despite particular plants' performance) have destroyed thou-sands of jobs in the name of better profit-and-loss statements. Absen-tee ownership and conglomerate organization make it easier for cor-porations to milk "cash cows," acquire, merge, and divest with little concern for the effects on employment. Some of the plants or firms suffering the effects of such corporate policies may be candidates for worker ownership.

Certainly such was the case for the O&O Supermarkets in Philadel-phia. A&P unloaded them (and many others) to satisfy its corporate goals, not because they were unprofitable. Despite lack of purchasing and marketing advantages of a large chain, the two O&O stores are succeeding quite well.

Furthermore, there are numerous plants that could be profitable if some of their operating procedures changed. Corporate management may extract tribute — i.e., corporate overhead — to pay for executive headquarters or for subsidization of other parts of the business. Man-agement may enforce bureaucratic practices which hamper effec-tiveness and efficiency. For example, the Mohawk Valley Community Corporation bought out the Herkimer Library Bureau from the Sperry Rand conglomerate. Under Sperry, the Library Bureau salesmen had to go through corporate level salesmen if they were entering corporate territory, i.e., corporate clients. MVCC found much greater efficiency in being able to skip this corporate step.[28]

No one should get the impression that every plant closing is an appropriate target for worker ownership, however. Consultants in the field warn that feasibility depends on the particulars of each case. For instance, despite the massive mobilization in Youngstown around a worker-community ownership plan for reopening the Campbell works, the practicability of accomplishing that goal was limited. Among other obstacles, enormous debts would have had to be in-curred to raise the necessary capital, leading to a very high debt/equity ratio.[29] Moreover, the former conglomerate owner, Lykes corporation, had milked the plant's cash flow and had run the capital equipment into the ground by not reinvesting. Concerning another case, the Industrial Cooperative Association (ICA) cites a company at which they recommended against a worker buyout. Local 1665 of the United Paper Workers had asked ICA in 1980 for assistance in the shutdown of Stevens Paper Mill in Westfield, Massachusetts. After an extensive feasibilty study ICA concluded that the buyout had no real chance of success and that workers should not risk their savings.

If not all plant closings are ripe for worker ownership, how do you know which ones are likely to succeed? Several studies and excellent handbooks tell those interested just what is needed; timing, planning, resources, technical assistance, and organization, as well as luck. The key element is an objective feasibility study, or as Woodworth puts it, "a cold, hard look at the facts." Virtually all of the successful worker buyouts involved one or several feasibility studies.[30]

In fact, the California State Office of Economic Policy, Planning and Research's handbook, *Buyout: A Guide for Workers Facing Plant Closings*, suggests a preliminary study to assess whether worker ownership is an option at all, and an in-depth study to investigate projected projects, markets, capital sources, and detailed business plans.[31] The preliminary feasibility study uses readily available sources of data to answer the following major issues and questions:

(1) *Time:* Is there enough time to pull all of the pieces together before the plant closes and before key customers and suppliers are lost? Generally, it is thought to take about six months or more to put things together.

(2) *Negotiating with the Corporate Owner:* Are the present owners amenable to an employee buyout? Will they cooperate and share information?

(3) *Transition:* Is the firm organized so that a smooth transition to worker ownership is possible? Will there be leadership, management, all of the other functions needed to run the business?

(4) *Product Market:* Are the products produced at the plant facing stable, growing, or declining markets?

(5) *Competitiveness:* Is it possible for the plant to be an efficient producer in the industry? Is capital equipment in good shape? How do costs compare with other firms?

The in-depth feasibility study should be done by technical assistance professionals who are objective, but who are also knowledgeable about worker ownership and who reflect the values and perceptions of workers and the union. For instance, the feasibility study at Rath, paid for by the corporate owners, recommended severe wage and benefit cuts, dismantling the pension program, and moving to new, nonunion facilities. Local 46 UFCW, needless to say, disagreed and had to order another study.[32]

In addition to the elements outlined above, successful worker buyouts must have sources of finance, a governance structure involving workers in decisions, and of course union support. Adequate financing is crucial, for many failures of worker-owned firms, particularly of the 19th century cooperatives, have been traced to undercapitalization. The governance structure may assume greater importance well after the buyout is established, but the time to set it up is in the earliest stages. Nevertheless, as Pitegoff and Lynd caution, "Maximum control is crucial to retain and expand the benefits of worker ownership. But control alone will not make up for other deficiencies."[33] Finally, the union's support is usually the key to mobilizing the tremendous energies needed to accomplish this collective event and, ultimately, to safeguard worker interests.

Disregarding the claim that feasibility is a case-by-case matter, not subject to easy generalization, can workers really afford the costs of time, energy, conflicts, and (most often) financial sacrifices? That is, is it really worth the effort? A look at the record of worker ownership is in order.

James O'Toole in the *Harvard Business Review* called the record of worker ownership uneven.[34] However, his generalization mixed weak minority ESOPs with strong worker cooperatives. Even so, worker ownership can be called a success. The California State Office of Economic Policy, Planning, and Research estimates that worker ownership has saved at least 50,000 jobs directly.[35] There are about 5000 ESOPs and about 500 majority worker-owned companies according to the National Center for Employee Ownership.[36] Yet, as the California handbook states, "What is more impressive is that to the best of our knowledge only four employee buyouts, involving 300 employees, have failed." A University of Michigan study of the effect of worker ownership on profitability found worker-owned companies 1.5 times as profitable as their conventional counterparts and that profitability was higher the more ownership workers had.[37] Finally, a recent study by the NCEO of 130 majority worker-owned firms showed that they create jobs (that is, grow in employment) about three percent faster than conventional firms in their industries.[38] In the durable goods sector, job creation is about 4.5 percent faster.

These average figures are impressive. The costs workers may have to pay to achieve a particular worker buyout may also be impressive. In the National Steel worker buyout plan for the Weirton, West Virginia, plant, the proposal calls for 32 percent wage cuts, reduced employment levels, and the spending of over $1 billion over the next ten years on capital investment. Huge cases like Weirton get huge publicity. Nevertheless, the average of numerous cases, many unpublicized in the national news media, shows a more favorable balance between benefits and costs. Worker ownership may be very risky but the advantages are substantial too. It is not an outright raw deal. And even skeptics about the Weirton deal, such as Pitegoff and Lynd do not denounce the plan; they just want all the facts to be considered.[39]

Operations

Even if worker-owned companies do save jobs, skeptics want to know, "What then?" Once the euphoric glow of reversing a plant closing has worn off, are they any different? Do firms in which workers have ownership, from minority ESOPs to fully worker-owned cooperatives, translate that ownership into worker say or control over management? Moreover, as businesses, are they efficient and productive? For unions, especially, there are questions concerning their place in worker ownership and the consequences — legally, organizationally, and in negotiations — for them.

There are differing viewpoints on these questions. Nevertheless, the evidence as a whole tends to find worker ownership, especially when combined with worker control or participation in decision making, to perform quite well, though differently from conventional ownership.

That is, the cooperative ESOP described above seems to combine the best operational features, but other forms of worker ownership have advantages as well. In the first part of this section, we will examine the operation of the firm. Later on, we will discuss the implications for unions.

Some commentators expect that worker-owned companies and worker-managed ones will be inherently inefficient. That is, they argue, worker-owned companies suffer from certain inevitable defects: (1) A lack of management expertise, especially in activities concerning the world outside the firm, such as marketing and finance, is predicted. Especially in cooperatives, the emphasis on equality, particularly in wages, may make difficult the recruitment of managers. (2) Commentators expect that worker-owned firms will thus foster an erosion of internal discipline and control, without competent management. In fact, many follow the judgments of Sidney and Beatrice Webb, the famous early 20th century British historians and labor activists, that the managerial job is impossible where workers are owners. (3) A sizeable body of commentators and researchers try to show that worker-owned firms tend inevitably to degenerate, that is, over time to die out or change over to conventional capitalist firms due to internal flaws. For instance, worker-owners will tend, it is predicted, not to reinvest in the company, preferring to take higher wages, thus endangering its long-term viability.

Contrary to these pessimistic prognostications, others believe that worker-owned companies have tremendous operational advantages over conventional companies: (1) They do not have to seek the same profit targets set by corporate managements, hence are more flexible. (2) They tap resources unrealized in conventional firms, such as greater teamwork, decision consensus, worker commitment, involvement, creativity, fulfillment, and more open communication between workers and managers. Moreover, they require less supervision, it is argued, than conventional firms. (3) Furthermore, some advocates of worker ownership expect that given sufficient capital, suitable markets, and a supportive environment, firms will survive and grow.

Evidence on these issues does not exist in great quantities for American and Canadian worker-owned firms, partly because of few cases and partly because of the sparseness of research. On some issues there is much information, on others very little. However, the evidence does allow us to settle some questions of operations easily.

Discipline, control, and productivity have not been problems. Most studies done on the currently operating set of worker-owned firms find on the contrary that workers express more commitment and are less prone (or no more prone) to turnover and absenteeism. Studies done by Michael Conte and Arnold Tannenbaum indicate that worker ownership, even of a minority share in the firm, has a positive effect on both productivity and profitability. Moreover, the larger the workers' share of ownership, the greater the effect.[40]

Managerial expertise *can* be a problem but is not an inevitable one. Most researchers agree that managerial expertise is crucial, and sometimes is hard to recruit or keep. However, as Richard Long reported concerning a worker-owned Canadian trucking firm, managers were more likely to cite advantages than disadvantages for themselves under worker ownership. Advantages included greater worker input in decisions, greater worker interest in doing a good job, and better cooperation between workers and managers. Disadvantages for managers included workers overrating their importance and demanding too much say, loss of some authority, and that managers will need to work harder and perform better. To take account of these managerial realities Carl Bellas, who studied the plywood cooperatives of the Northwest, prescribed careful selection of managers for worker-owned firms: "The manager must be an educator and a motivator, knowing full well that his autonomy will diminish as he increases the capability of his employees."[41]

Concerning issues such as reinvestment and long run viability or degeneration, there is more controversy over the conclusions to be drawn. The fact is that worker ownership has historically been a rare phenomenon, and compared to conventional firms there are few long-lived worker-owned ones. The causes are still in dispute. In the past researchers placed most of the responsibility on internal factors, such as discipline and management. However, recent research studies have shifted much of the cause (though not all) to the conditions outside the firms, such as hostility from banks and lack of support (moral, economic, and political) from the labor movement.

Nevertheless, the basic operational issue which distinguishes between less effective and more effective firms is the difference between having only worker ownership versus having ownership *and* worker control. Those worker-owned firms which do not allow much worker participation in management decisions, worker representation on board of directors, or worker input into operating methods, may miss out on the long-term operational advantages of worker ownership. William Foote Whyte of Cornell University's School of Industrial and Labor Relations and his colleagues point out that there are often three stages in the development of these ownership-only firms:

(1) Before ownership conversion — worker, union, and management cooperation;
(2) Right after conversion — euphoria, harmony, and trust for several months;
(3) About one year after conversion — disillusionment, reinforcement of conventional managerial hierarchies, and conventional labor relations.[42]

Several cases follow this pattern. In fact, it may be suspected that the degeneration and loss of viability by worker-owned firms is traceable to their frequent failure to link worker ownership with worker participation, if not control. Examples of these firms include Vermont Asbestos Group (VAG), South Bend Lathe (SBL), and the Mohawk Valley Community Corporation (MVCC). As pointed out above, VAG was eventually sold by the worker-owners to a private capitalist and at SBL worker frustrations led to a strike. Even such firms may show some significant positive effects of worker ownership: Lower profit margins are necessary than corporations require. Flatter organizational structures may be used. Many costs are saved due to lack of corporate overhead. Greater local control means better decisions are made to suit actual conditions. But as the sale of VAG, the strike at SBL, and the disillusionment of workers at MVCC demonstrate, the effects on workers' attitude are not positive. Many studies of worker ownership without participation tend to confirm this seeming contradiction.

In contrast, William F. Whyte and his colleagues describe the process at Rath Packing which became worker-owned in 1980. The shift in ownership involved a shift in internal operations from top to bottom, from the board of directors to the shop floor:

> In all of these activities, workers not only voiced complaints and suggestions but were actively involved in working out solutions. No problems were declared out of bounds. For example, the program to revive the company involved major investments in new machines. Salespeople, who were accustomed to meeting with executives in top-management offices, were surprised to find themselves talking also with rank-and-file workers in the departments where the new machines were to be installed. The workers did not hold back from raising questions and expressing opinions based on their long years of experience in production and processing operations. These discussions were educational for all parties. At times, the salespeople found workers' questions more difficult than management questions, and the management people came to recognize that workers were alerting them to problems that would inevitably arise in the installation and operation of the machines.[43]

A similar process occurred at Hyatt Clark Industries where worker ownership led to what researcher and consultant Warner Woodworth has described as a changing "organizational culture."[44] Not only were there changes in the openness and flexibility of collective bargaining by both labor and management, such as opening management's books, wage concessions, changed job classifications, and union representation on the board, there were also a number of participative practices and structures, such as worker action research teams, established. A level of supervision was eliminated, and worker-manager relations became less formal and status-ridden. For example, supervisors no longer wear ties and the parking lot no longer segregates workers from managers. Owing to greater cooperation, the scrap rate declined, and quality improved as did productivity.

Experiences with genuine worker-owned-and-controlled firms are relatively rare and fairly new in buyout situations. However, there are signs that these firms truly change operationally; in methods of decision making; in worker introduced innovations in work methods; and in new product development. Donald Nightingale in a study of 10 participative Canadian firms including some worker-owned companies, found that participative decision making methods change the nature of work. They provide the average job with more autonomy, allow more use of a worker's skills, encourage more social interactions, and create more interdependence among jobs.[45]

Despite the general upbeat evidence about worker ownership combined with participation, it is not a paradise, by any means. As Nightingale's study points out, there is also more on-the-job conflict experienced by the worker in participative firms. Why? Daniel Zwerdling, journalist and researcher on worker ownership points toward an answer. Most people, he says, "have never learned how to work together and make decisions in an efficient, egalitarian, cooperative, and democratic way." Even at the long-established plywood cooperatives, Zwerdling found that participation was often a problem.

> Moving the worker-and-community-owned corporation toward democracy requires nothing less than a resocializing process: workers who have been taught for a lifetime to perform isolated tasks, taking orders from a boss, must learn to acquire the confidence, responsibility, and autonomy to make decisions on their own — yet they must also learn to feel responsible to the entire corporation. Employees who have never before seen their corporation's annual report must become familiar with management-level information. Managers, meanwhile, must learn to give up their privileged positions and to begin sharing information with the rank and file, delegating power as much as possible, inspiring and motivating workers rather than giving orders. Perhaps most important, they must perceive their roles as working on behalf of the workers, not over them. And both employees and managers alike must learn new democratic skills — trivial sounding but crucial skills such as running efficient meetings, analyzing problems, and making decisions effectively in groups. Attitudes and skills like this don't come easily in a matter of weeks or even months.[46]

To reap the benefits of worker ownership and make it viable, it seems necessary to take the risks of worker participation and control, hence to change the organizational culture. While participation does not guarantee success financially, a lack of participation may be associated with failure to satisfy workers' goals and to the eventual decline of the firm.

Thus, education for workers and worker directors on management and participation is required. As the cases of Rath and Hyatt Clark show, education can come from consultants with experience in area-wide labor-management committees and from academics with skills and knowledge about worker ownership. The establishment of the O&O stores in Philadelphia points further to the educational role played by local consulting and advocacy groups such as the Philadelphia Association for Cooperative Enterprise (PACE). Similarly, as noted earlier, the Industrial Cooperative Association (ICA) in Somerville, Mass., provides not only services such as business planning, but also operational consulting and educational materials to help in the installation of worker participation and control.

The Role of Unions

Unions have been understandably skeptical about worker ownership. Some commentators on worker ownership see no role for a union once workers are owners and point to the absence of unions at the plywood cooperatives of the Northwest. However, others believe the role of the union will be preserved and made easier through reduced grievance rates, fewer strikes, and more cooperative contract negotiations. Unionists are particularly concerned about: (1) potential negative effects on collective bargaining, (2) legal conflicts over the union's role and responsibilities to members, and (3) conflicts between the local union and the national union.

The impact on collective bargaining seems somewhat mixed, but not nearly as negative as some unionists seem to expect. Most studies of the issue have found basically no change in the union's traditional roles in the firm. Richard Long's studies even found some cases of long-term improvements in labor-management relations in ESOPs. There is some evidence that worker-owners may gradually lose some of their commitment to the union, but they seem also to feel a continued need to keep it and use it.[47]

So far, there appear to be very few cases of worker rejection of the union and decertification in the face of worker ownership. In a typical case, for instance, the workers at Jeanette Sheet Glass decertified their union in response to lack of support and active hostility from the International Glass and Ceramic Workers. At SBL a decertificaton election was held and narrowly won by the United Steelworkers, after the international had tried to block the ownership plan. The problem seems to arise when a union throws obstacles in the path of workers determined to buy out the company.

There is still a significant and necessary role for the union at worker-owned companies. Where the union has taken a leading role to facilitate conversion to worker ownership, it often acts to push for participative changes in management and the oganizational culture. In negotiations, unions have held the line on worker sacrifices, though they have given in when convinced by evidence or by bank pressures. Moreover, they have fought to retain benefits, such as pension plans. At Rath, for instance, the union fought from 1980-1982 to save the pension plan. It only consented to liquidating it when the company was under immense difficulties in the competitive meat packing business and when the former union president was chairman of the board.

Legal conflicts over the roles and responsibilities of unions and their officials potentially can arise in three primary areas: (1) between roles as representatives for employees and as representatives for management on the board of directors; (2) in protecting employee benefits; and (3) as possible anti-competitive agents, in violation of anti-monopoly law and the Landrum-Griffin Act. As Deborah Groban Olsen points out in her excellent review of these and other legal issues in worker ownership, such conflicts are resolvable, especially if the union itself is not involved in ownership, but is only the facilitator and advisor to its members. In general, the best way to prevent these conflicts is to design the worker ownership plan correctly.[48]

Conflicts between the local and the national are possibly the thorniest area. As William F. Whyte and his colleagues point out, local union officers and national officers have some differences in interests and perspectives. National leaders want to maintain standards established over time and put into national agreements. They are concerned about the potential for local arrangements to drive a wedge between workers in the same industry who work in different places. Some national union leaders have been cited as saying that worker ownership would be a catastrophe for the union and would, in addition, make workers responsible for business failures. Local leaders may be more interested in maintaining jobs and working conditions. They may favor worker ownership, even at the cost of sacrifices, if it saves jobs.

Therefore, locals and nationals may clash. For instance, at SBL, regional and international officers of the United Steelworkers union actively worked to block the ESOP. Warner Woodworth gives this account of what happened at Hyatt Clark (HCI):

> UAW headquarters had a long history of dissatisfaction with Local 736. Like GM, it viewed the union as militant, perhaps even leftist beyond the political stance of the international. In a sense, Local 736 had been on the bad side of the international for years as a kind of troublesome maverick local.
>
> The worker-buyout idea seemed preposterous. Union officers in Detroit were not prepared to cope with the concept, nor had they any in-house expertise to evaluate what was occuring in New Jersey. In addition they were fearful that concessions at HCI would set a precedent for upcoming industry-wide contract talks. Thus, the international officially took a position that Local 736 efforts were simply a regional experiment about which Detroit had no opinion.
>
> Union leaders in Clark interpreted this as a rejection of the idea, and in subsequent discussions clearly felt criticized for attempting the buyout. However, their response tended to be one of asking what else should be done. If ownership were not the best answer, what else could be?[49]

More recently, there are indications in the UAW of a changed attitude in Detroit. Woodworth reported that the international began to seek Local 736's advice on an official union position regarding worker ownership in plant closing situations. And in the November, 1983, issue of the UAW's magazine *Solidarity*, a story called "Taking Over" describes how members of UAW Local 271 in West Pittston, PA, bought out the closing Renold Power Transmission Co.[50] They established a worker-owned firm they named Atlas Chain. Moreover, they had the financial, technical, and political help of the regional and international UAW. Perhaps other internationals will adopt similar attitudes as they work out their policies on reindustrialization.

Of course, unions may have to go through some changes to take on worker ownership. They may have to take on new roles and question some traditional values of adversarism. They may need to take an initiating role to insure that worker ownership is beneficial to workers and not a management ploy. They need to learn how businesses are run and financed. They need to develop open communication with worker-owner managers and with their own members (to educate and protect them). They have to learn how to cooperate with management without being co-opted. These new roles require serious education. But there are certainly benefits to be had. Unions can add to collective bargaining roles and tactics by using worker ownership properly. They can learn more about the expansion of collective bargaining into management rights and management decisions. And they can expand their role in moving the economy in a more worker-oriented and job-protective direction.

Conclusion

The apparently rising trend of worker ownership can save jobs and be effective. However, it is a complex issue with many facets to understand. As experience with worker ownership is gained, valuable lessons from past experience are being learned that can be used to advantage in the future. A large network of advocacy, educational, and technical assistance groups can be called upon by unions and workers to aid them in the face of plant shutdowns and in considering worker ownership.

Worker ownership can be part of a labor strategy for reindustrialization, even if it is a minor role. It fits into the defense of jobs, the expansion of collective bargaining power, increased worker information and control vis-a-vis management in the use of watchdog directors and QWL programs, and an overall changed role for labor in the development of the economy. However, worker ownership will thrive as a labor strategy only within the context of a broader strategy involving; more job creation through government action (public works and fiscal policies) to reduce unemployment; controls on corporate investment and disinvestment (e.g., through plant closing legislation and possibly some kind of reconstruction finance agency); the use of pension funds for further control over job creation; further encroachment on "management rights;" and the overall aim of more worker and public control and influence over corporate decision making. This does not mean mere labor-management cooperation, but more of a joint control. Worker ownership is one way of achieving some of these aims.

End Notes

1. *Forbes*, "Let Them Eat Stock," November 22, 1982; and James O'Toole, *Harvard Business Review*, "The Uneven Record of Employee Ownership" (November-December 1979).

2. Peter Pitegoff and Staughton Lynd, "Workers Can Be Choosers," *New York Times*, October 27, 1982.

3. *Prospects for Workers Cooperatives in Western Europe* (Brussels, Belgium: European Economic Commission, 3 vols., 1982).

4. A. Shirom, "The Industrial Relations System of Industrial Cooperatives in the US 1880-1935," *Labor History* (Fall 1982), pp. 533-551; and H. Aldrich and R.N. Stern, "Resource Mobilization and the Creation of U.S. Producer's Cooperatives, 1835-1935," *Industrial and Economic Democracy*, 4, No. 3 (August 1983), pp. 371-406.

5. Barry Bluestone and Bennett Harrison, *The Deindustrialization of America* (New York: Basic Books, 1982).

6. *Conglomerate Mergers, Their Effect on Small Business and Restraint of Trade* (U.S. House of Representatives, Committee on Small Business, 1982).

7. *American Federationist* (Washington, D.C.: AFL-CIO, March 1983).

8. *Labor Relations in an Economic Recession: Job Losses and Concession Bargaining,* (Washington, D.C.: Bureau of National Affairs, 1982).

9. *Business Week,* May 11, 1981.

10. Bluestone and Harrison, *Deindustrialization.*

11. Dan Luria and Jack Russell, *Rational Reindustrialization* (Detroit: Widgetripper Press, 1981).

12. W. Schweke, *Plant Closings: Issues, Resources, and Legislation* (Washington, D.C.: Conference on Alternative State and Local Policies, 1980).

13. S. Speiser, *A Piece of the Action: A Plan to Provide Every Family With a $100,000 Stake in the Economy* (New York: Van Nostrand, 1977).

14. C. Rosen, *Employee Ownership: Issues, Resources, and Legislation* (Arlington, VA: National Center for Employer Ownership, 1982).

15. Ibid.

16. Deborah Groban Olson, "Union Experience with Worker Ownership: Legal and Practical Issues Raised by ESOPs, TRASOPs, Stock Purchases, and Co-operatives," *Wisconsin Law Review,* 5 (1982), pp. 729-823.

17. D. Ellerman, "What is a Worker Cooperative?" (Somerville, MA: Industrial Cooperative America, 1980).

18. M. Carnoy and D. Shearer, *Economic Democracy* (New York: Sharpe, 1980).

19. Olson, "Union Experience."

20. Shirom, "Industrial Cooperatives."

21. *Issues of Employee Ownership* (Arlington, VA: National Center for Employer Ownership, 1982 and 1983 Newsletter).

22. R. Russell, *Sharing Ownership in the Workplace* (Harvard University: Unpublished PhD. dissertation, 1979).

23. Olson, "Union Experience."

24. Daniel Zwerdling, "Employee Ownership: How Well Is It Working?" *Working Papers* (May-June 1979), pp. 15-27.

25. Olson, "Union Experience."

26. Ibid.

27. Pitegoff and Lynd, "Workers Can Be Choosers."

28. R. Stern, H. Wood, and T. Hammer, *Employee Ownership in Plant Closings: Prospects for Employment Stability* (Kalamazoo, Michigan: Upjohn Institute, 1979).

29. Ibid.

30. W. Woodworth, "Worker Takeover of a General Motors Plant: Toward A Robin Hood Theory of Change." Paper presented at Third International Conference of the International Association for the Economics of Self-Management, Mexico City, August 23-25, 1982.

31. J. Parzen, C. Squire and M. Kieschnick, *Buyout: A Guide for Workers Facing Plant Closures* (San Francisco: California Office of Economic Policy, Planning and Research, 1982).

32. Ibid.

33. Pitegoff and Lynd, "Workers Can Be Choosers."

34. James O'Toole, "Uneven Record."

35. Parzen, et al., *Buyout.*

36. *Issues of Employee Ownership,* NCEO.

37. R.J. Long, "The Effects of Employee Ownership on Organizational Identification, Employee Job Attitudes, and Organizational Performance; A Tentative Framework and Empirical Findings," *Human Relations,* 31 (1978), pp. 29-48.

38. Carl Bellas, *Industrial Democracy and the Worker Owned Firm* (New York: Praezer, 1972).

39. Pitegoff and Lynd, "Workers Can Be Choosers."

40. Michael Conte and Arnold Tannenbaum, "Employee Owned Companies: Is the Difference Measurable?" *Monthly Labor Review,* 101 (July 1978), pp. 23-28.

41. Carl Bellas, *Industrial Democracy.*
42. William Foote Whyte, T.H. Hammer, C.B. Meek, R. Nelson, and R.N. Stern, *Worker Participation and Ownership: Cooperative Strategies for Strengthening Local Economies* (Ithaca, N.Y.: ILR Press, 1982).
43. Ibid.
44. Warner Woodworth, "Worker Takeover."
45. Donald Nightingale, "Work, Formal Participation, and Employee Outcomes," *Sociology of Work and Occupations*, Vol. 8 (August 1981), pp. 277-196.
46. Daniel Zwerdling, *Workplace Democracy*, (New York: Harper and Row, 1980).
47. R.J. Long, "Employee Ownership and Attitudes Toward the Unions," *Relations Industrielles*, 33 (1977), pp. 237-253.
48. Olson, "Union Experiences."
49. Warner Woodworth, "Worker Takeover of a General Motors Plant."
50. *Solidarity*, November, 1983.

Resource Organizations

California Economic Adjustment Team
State of California
Dept. of Economic & Business Development
1030 13th Street, Suite 200
Sacramento, CA 95814

Center for Community Self-Help
P.O. Box 3259
West Durham, NC 27705

Industrial Cooperative Association
249 Elm St.
Somerville, MA 02144

National Center for Employee Ownership
1611 S. Walter Reed Drive, #109
Arlington, VA 22204

Philadelphia Association for Cooperative Enterprise
133 S. 18th Street
Philadelphia, PA 19103

Prof. Warner Woodworth
Dept. of Organizational Behavior
Brigham Young University
Provo, UT 84602

Prof. William Foote Whyte, Director
New Systems of Work and Participation Program
368 Ives Hall
Cornell University
Ithaca, NY 14853

The Role of "Enterprise Zones" in Reindustrialization

Bruce Nissen

Introduction

In the past 30 years the economies of America's largest cities changed dramatically. Among these economic changes were the relocation of manufacturing firms to areas away from the inner city, tax write-offs and investment incentives which encouraged the deindustrialization of urban centers, the movement of middle and upper income residents to the suburbs and a host of other developments which created urban blight. Center city areas lost much of their business activity and created a low income population largely dependent on government support, while buildings and the physical surroundings deteriorated. A vicious cycle set in as worsening conditions drove productive enterprise and middle and upper income residents away, furthering the economic decline.

Numerous government programs were implemented in the 1960s and 1970s to combat the economic decline of the nation's inner cities. These programs changed names and approaches frequently; the most important ones remaining by 1980 were those administered by the Small Business Administration (SBA), the Comprehensive Employment and Training Act (CETA), and the Urban Development Action Grant (UDAG) programs administered by the Department of Housing and Urban Development (HUD). The degree of success or failure of these programs is a matter of dispute — clearly, they alleviated many problems for inner city residents and just as clearly they failed to overcome the underlying changes which created urban blight.

On top of the economic distress which inner city areas experienced even in the best of times, the U.S. economy in the 1970s slipped into a state of chronic stagnation coupled with inflation. Furthermore, the industrial firms that many inner city residents depended on for jobs

Bruce Nissen is an Assistant Professor of Labor Studies at Indiana University.

left, deindustrializing the cities and entire parts of the United States. When a large scale recession occurred in the early 1980s, the plight of the inner cities became acute.

Enterprise Zones: A New Approach

Against this background, policy makers searched for alternative strategies of inner city economic development in the late 1970s and early 1980s. The alternative which the Reagan administration, many conservative lawmakers and a surprising number of congressional liberals opted for is labelled a free market approach. Following the lead of the Conservative government of Margaret Thatcher in England, legislation has been proposed to create enterprise zones. Thirteen such enterprise zones have been in operation in Great Britain since the second half of 1981. The individual most responsible for introducing the idea to the United States is Stuart M. Butler, an economist affiliated with the ultra-conservative Heritage Foundation in Washington, D.C.[1]

The earliest bill at the national level was introduced into the House of Representatives by the conservative Congressman from upstate New York, Jack Kemp (Republican) and a liberal inner city Congressman from the Bronx, Robert Garcia (Democrat). The original Kemp/Garcia bill was slightly altered and reintroduced as Kemp/Garcia II; meanwhile the Reagan administration introduced its own slightly modified version, the Enterprise Zone Tax Act of 1982. At the state level numerous bills of a similar nature have been introduced, and by 1983 over 12 states had passed enterprise zone legislation.

The bills introduced and/or passed to date show a great variety in specifics, and not all supporters of the enterprise zone concept agree on all details. However, they all have a common core:

(1) picking economically depressed geographic areas of urban cities and designating them special zones (enterprise zones) for purposes of tax policy, government regulations, and possible other government treatment;
(2) providing tax breaks and less government regulation, primarily for businesses operating within the zone; and
(3) eventually phasing out the tax breaks and regulatory relaxation, after a number of years (between 10 and 25 years, depending on the particular bill).

In many of the state bills there are provisions for at least nominal community participation in running these zones; however control is almost always left in the hands of business interests and government officials.

Therefore, stripped of superfluous rhetoric, enterprise zones reduce to corporate tax havens and opportunities for corporations to evade normal government regulations. While the details of different state and national proposals vary considerably, they all make it likely that an enterprise zone firm could avoid taxation entirely for some period of time. Easing government regulations usually would be at the discretion of the responsible agency; the extent of regulatory evasion thus would depend on the predisposition of the relevant agency.

Although enterprise zones are touted as a free market approach to economic development, it is easy to see that they actually entail considerable governmental intervention and planning. Tax burdens and the negative side effects of regulatory relaxation will be transferred to the rest of the community, while the favored enterprise zone firms will be given special treatment. All of this will occur through conscious government policy, a tacit admission that the free market alone won't do it.

What are enterprise zones expected to accomplish? Proponents give many answers. They will create jobs for the chronically unemployed; they will generate investment in decaying urban areas; they will stabilize low income areas of our cities and improve their quality of life; they will encourage small business enterprises (especially new ones), etc. Above all, they will revitalize the economics of urban America, and therefore will contribute to the reindustrialization of the United States.

Enterprise zone proponents especially emphasize how useful the zones will be to small businesses. This is a persistent theme of Butler's many writings — in fact, Butler argues that the success or failure of enterprise zones will be determined by their effect on new small businesses. State officials pushing enterprise zone legislation use terms like "cottage industries" to describe what they expect to flourish within the zones. While terms like "sweatshops" or "industrial homework" are carefully avoided, these unregulated and marginal labor-intensive enterprises appear to be at the heart of the enterprise zone vision of urban reindustrialization.

The Reagan administration has made enterprise zone legislation the centerpiece of its program for urban renewal. All other programs are either being curtailed or cut back. The theory behind this free market solution to the U.S.'s urban ills is similar to the supply-side theory underlying Reagan's 1981 tax cuts. It is claimed that taxes — especially business taxes — are driving firms either away or out of business. So are overly stringent government regulations. The solution; reduce business taxes and regulations.

This theory and its implementation have potentially grave consequences for the labor movement. In the remainder of this article I will evaluate enterprise zones from both the criteria used by its proponents and from a labor perspective.

Enterprise Zones and Economic Development

One way to evaluate the enterprise zone approach is to take the claims of its backers seriously and see if they are supported by the present evidence. Proponents argue that enterprise zones will

(1) promote new small businesses,
(2) generate new investment in depressed urban areas (and thus new jobs, especially for the hardcore unemployed), and
(3) improve the quality of life in and around the zone.

Each of these claims merits careful scrutiny.

Will Enterprise Zones Aid Small Business?
In an influential study, David Birch claims that small businesses employing 20 or fewer workers generate the majority of net new jobs in the United States.[2] His results have been criticized, both on the grounds that improper methods led to mistaken conclusions and on the grounds that jobs for small employers are not the kind of desirable, well-paying jobs with pensions and other fringes that should be at the center of any jobs-creation strategy. While one or both of these objections may be correct, inner city residents desperate for jobs — any jobs — might very well welcome a program that significantly aids small business in their area. Genuine aid to small businesses should generate substantial new employment. The question is: Will enterprise zones aid small businesses, especially new ones, as is claimed?

The evidence indicates that they will not. Taxes and regulations — the centerpiece of enterprise zone legislation — are relatively unimportant and marginal concerns for new small businesses. The National Federation of Independent Business (NFIB) released a study which indicated that taxes are one of the least important obstacles to success.[3] The most important problems were; managerial incompetence, insufficient initial markets, and inadequate financial support. They concluded that start-up capital and capital to operate the first few years were crucial; taxes were irrelevant to new firms who made little profit to tax in the first place. In fact the NFIB has repeatedly rejected the enterprise zone idea as an aid to small business.

The Council for Northeast Economic Action held a roundtable discussion by small businessmen in 1981 on enterprise zone proposals.[4] The participants concluded that access to capital is the fundamental issue for small businesses; regulations are not a central consideration and taxes are not key. Enterprise zones thus ignore small business' real problems and address imaginary ones. As urban development consultant Edward Humberger puts it:

> If no start-up capital is to be provided, what types of new small business would, in fact, be created? Are we talking about "mom and pop" stores, sweatshops, and delivery/repair services that can be started with minimal capital from savings of family and friends? If the ultimate benefit of the Enterprise Zone proposal . . . lies in exempting the corner candy store from taxes and the minimum wage, then we have come a long way from any vision of long-term economic development in distressed areas.[5]

From the evidence above it seems clear that if the U.S. urban redevelopment policy is organized around the concept of enterprise zones, with its focus on suspending taxes and regulations for business, its stated goal of aiding new small business will not be achieved.

Will Enterprise Zones Create New Jobs?
Whatever the cost in eroding the local tax base and in eroding protective regulatory measures, many desperate mayors would welcome enterprise zones if they were convinced that a net increase of jobs for their hardcore unemployed would result. So the question is rele-

vant: Will new investment be generated to create a net gain in jobs for the inner city unemployed?

Again, the evidence points to an answer of "no." Business relocation and initial investment decisions have been studied intensively in recent years. And the studies are virtually unanimous: Taxes are not a critical variable. The degree of regulation is a more difficult variable to capture, but it is so peripheral that it is not considered important in most studies. I will cite here only two of the most recent and best conceived studies. Dr. Roger J. Vaughan, in a 1979 book on the subject, concludes:

> There is a popular myth that a reduction in the level of state business taxes will produce a flood of new development. The truth is very different. The level of business taxes has very little impact on the local growth rate or on interstate location decisions of firms . . . States have devoted considerable manpower and resources to devising tax breaks for firms that move in, firms that threaten to move out, and firms that promise to expand. There is little evidence that these costly programs had much influence on either investment or location decisions. . . . States should concern themselves with the overall economic climate, not on bribing a few footloose firms.[6]

Michael Kieschnik, after exhaustively reviewing previous literature on the subject and conducting new research of his own,[7] concludes:

> — In most industries, the level of business taxation has an undetectable effect on investment patterns. And even where some effect can be seen, it is quite small.
> — Overall business tax reductions, even if targeted to "sensitive" industries, are likely to be entirely ineffective in stimulating new investment.
> — Most firms making new investments never consider investing in any state other than their final choice, seldom know about available incentives, and where they do, rarely attribute any importance to them.
> — And finally, the states are foregoing a substantial amount of revenue through tax loopholes that are clearly useless in creating or retaining jobs. At a time when an increasing number of states are under severe fiscal restraint, when federal tax changes are certain to depress the states' own revenues by billions of dollars, and when federal budget cuts are placing a growing pressure on the states to fund basic human service programs of all kinds, these departures from an equitable administered tax system are simply indefensible.

Numerous other studies arrive at similar conclusions; the evidence is so overwhelming that enterprise zone advocates are forced to concede the point, even though it undermines their main argument.

If enterprise zones are combined with free trade zones (envisioned in many proposals), some businesses likely would relocate into the zones to enjoy tariff exemptions. Such firms are generally either warehousing operations or high technology firms. Neither would provide jobs for unskilled hardcore urban unemployed. Warehouses hire few workers at all, while high-tech firms need a few skilled and small numbers of unskilled workers.

In short, while the tax losses to cities and states in the state enterprise zones (and to the federal government in national enterprise zones) could be substantial over the long run, enterprise zones will create few net new jobs. Damage to the tax base is certain; benefits in the form of new jobs that would not have been created without the zones are dubious at best.

Will Enterprise Zones Improve the Quality of Life?
Enterprise zone advocates claim they will improve community life in and around the zone. Economic growth and its accompanying social and community benefits will stabilize low income areas, thus setting the stage for long term revitalization, it is argued. What is the evidence surrounding this claim?

First, it bears repeating the evidence just cited that few net new jobs are likely beyond what would have occurred anyway. If the government overseers of the zone are determined to bring jobs into a zone at all costs, it is likely that they can do so. However, the jobs are likely to be at the expense of jobs elsewhere, as footloose firms "jump site" to take advantage of the tax breaks. This is exactly what William Barnes, Senior Policy Analyst for the National League of Cities, found in his preliminary analysis of England's new enterprise zones. Finding that enormous resources of the British government were being utilized to provide almost unlimited funds and auxiliary services to zones, Barnes notes that the zones will "work" although they will probably be "unsuccessful" in creating net new jobs:

> Any experiment that attracts that kind of attention and support from the highest levels of the government does not really have the option of not working. Moreover, in several cases, zones were designated in areas where significant development work was already underway, thus, further ensuring that these zones will produce the desired results.
>
> Businesses are moving into the zones . . . Few are new. The local authorities are marketing their zones vigorously and are getting numerous inquiries. It is too early to reach any conclusion, but what I saw and was told promises neither a flowering of new enterpreneurship nor a harvest of the fruits of net new investment. . . . the program will "work" in that the zones will fill up with businesses, but . . . will not be significantly "successful" in creating net new jobs and investment for the British economy.[8]

In good times, when the economy is expanding rapidly, enterprise zones will likely attract some investment, as will many areas which are not zones. But what type of investments do the zones attract? Do they attract stable investments by companies providing decent jobs and wages, or do they attract unstable investments at low wages and poor working conditions?

Fortunately, we have some historical experience to help us answer this question. Puerto Rico has had a program known as "Operation Bootstrap" operating since shortly after World War II. Operation Bootstrap is virtually identical to enterprise zone programs. Companies investing in Puerto Rico get total exemption from all U.S. and Puerto Rican taxes for a period of 10-30 years (longer exemptions if the investment is in areas of higher unemployment). Furthermore, regulatory relaxation is granted; environmental, minimum wage, worker safety, and other regulations are often loosened. In other words, Puerto Rico is the United States' enterprise zone of the past 30 years.[9]

What kind of investment did Operation Bootstrap attract? Most were minimum wage (or less) operations with little initial capital investment. Ladies garment firms, marginally profitable and therefore dependent on low wages and favored government treatment like tax exemptions, were typical. Thousands of such firms moved to Puerto Rico (which can export to and import from the U.S. free of tariff barriers), then closed up shop when the local tax breaks ended. Others moved on to Haiti or elsewhere when the breaks stopped. In no sense was the investment of the type which would generate stable long-term development for the island's economy.

Some investment was more capital intensive; petrochemicals, petroleum, and pharmaceutical are examples. Pharmaceutical companies relocated some of their highest profit lines on the island to avoid taxes; petroleum and petrochemical firms were attracted by lax environmental regulations and cheap water and space. Yet none of these industries have produced the hoped for flow of "good jobs." The pharmaceutical firms employ mostly skilled technicians imported from the U.S., while the petroleum and petrochemical industries set up huge complexes manned by few workers. In fact, they have delivered less than 8% of the jobs they promised when they began to invest.[10] Wages in Puerto Rico are notoriously low; the island advertises this fact plus the high productivity of Puerto Rican workers in the business press such as the *Wall Street Journal* to attract U.S. industry.

All of this hardly promises an improved quality of life for inner city residents. "Fly-by-night" operations setting up sweatshops and then leaving when the tax holiday ends do not provide a quality community environment. Puerto Rico's economy has lost all self-reliant features; unemployment far exceeds 20% (well over 30% by some estimates), the gap between rich and poor is enormous, the government is unable to finance itself without huge subsidies from Washington, D.C. because of tax exemptions, well over 50% of the population qualifies for food stamps (some estimates say over 70%), etc. Crime, drug addiction, and a host of other negative side effects of poverty are rampant on the island. Skeptics may question the relevance of Puerto Rico to our inner cities, yet they share precisely the relevant characteristics; geographically distinct areas with low income (often minority) residents, out-migration, high unemployment, high business failure, lack of internal capital and other resources, high welfare dependency, etc. In most respects there is greater comparability than is usually recognized.

And surely Great Britain is not all that different from the U.S., William Barnes found that English enterprise zones are creating a "blighted halo" around their boundaries, have set up noticeable warehousing districts in the zones, and primarily benefit absentee and other landlords through higher rents. None of this promises an improved quality of life for zone residents or neighbors.

And finally, the hard question has to be asked: Who will pay the taxes to support all the essential facilities and services necessary for zone success in attracting business? Businesses will demand sewers, water lines, streets and transportation, police protection, and a number of like services if they are to invest in the zones. Who pays? Not the businesses benefiting from tax breaks. The burden is shifted onto taxpayers not receiving the tax holiday. Once again, this is hard to sell as an improvement in the local quality of life.

Implications of Enterprise Zones for Labor

Most of organized labor has opposed the idea of enterprise zones. The national AFL-CIO testified on numerous occasions against federal legislation in 1982, and on the state level labor movements have also opposed them.[11] The basis for the opposition has centered on four points:

(1) tax losses and the erosion of the tax base,

(2) the incentive for firms to "jump site" or "run away" from existing plants into the zone,

(3) the potential for zones to be an opening wedge to roll back protective legislation, and

(4) the inequity of the "trickle down" tax breaks to big business while shifting the tax base onto other taxpayers.

All of these are valid objections. The labor movement and workers in general will be negatively affected in all four respects. The existing evidence shows that the tax base will be eroded; that footloose firms will go "site-hopping" if offered enough incentives; that many zone advocates do view them as only the beginning of a concerted effort to rid industry of "burdensome" regulations protecting workers; and that the tax breaks are inequitable. Organized labor should be advertising these disadvantages widely.

However, these objections may appear to be narrow "special interest" concerns on the part of organized labor if they are the only ones raised. I remember sitting next to a representative of the liberal black mayor of a large midwestern city at an enterprise zone hearing in 1982. When labor representatives raised the above concerns, this representative began cursing and muttering to himself. In his own subsequent testimony, he made it plain that his city would gladly forego the taxes, the regulations, or the apparent inequity if it could attract jobs — almost any jobs — to its depressed areas. While this probably represents a regrettable retreat from liberal principles of justice and equity, it also demonstrates how desperate many municipalities have become.

Under these circumstances, any arguments that might be construed (however contorted the logic) as "special interest" claims by organized labor should be supplemented by more general "public policy" arguments such as those raised in the preceding section. For, if the labor movement does its homework, it can demonstrate that the enterprise zone proposal will fail to achieve its triple goal of helping new small business, creating new jobs, and improving inner city community life. There is no way such arguments can be seen as narrowly self-serving on the part of organized labor. Also, opposition to enterprise zones will probably be more effective if it is based on a thorough understanding of the context within which zones are being proposed. Once this historical context is understood, it becomes apparent that enterprise zones are a logical step in a long-term assault on the wages and working conditions of all workers in the U.S.

The economy within which the U.S. labor movement operates has changed enormously since World War II. Especially since the 1960s, large U.S. companies have been going "multinational." They are moving increasing percentages of their capital and investment abroad:

> The largest U.S.-based global firms, such as Ford, ITT, Chrysler, Kodak, and Proctor & Gamble, employ more than one-third of their workforce outside the United States. As of 1966, U.S.-based global corporations employed overseas 3,324,321 non-Americans, approximately 30 percent of their total payrolls. The figure is unquestionably much higher today.[12]

These multinational U.S. conglomerates no longer think or operate within national boundaries. They now have the resources and capabilities to relocate enterprises throughout the world very rapidly; tax write-offs and investment tax credits actually encourage them to do so.

This changing global economy has a negative impact on the labor movement's ability to protect its members. Capital mobility gives management inordinate power in its relations with labor:

> Nothing is better calculated to weaken the bargaining power of labor than management's prerogative to divide and shift tasks at will on a global scale . . . Corporate organization on a global scale is a highly effective weapon for undercutting the power of organized labor everywhere. Capital, technology, and marketplace ideology, the bases of corporate power, are mobile; workers, by and large, are not. The ability of corporations to open and close plants rapidly and to shift their investment from one country to another erodes the basis of organized labor's bargaining leverage, the strike . . . Management finds that its power to close an entire operation in a community and to transfer everything but the workers out of the country produces a marvelously obliging labor force.[13]

While the labor movement's bargaining power declines, corporations close down aging industrial operations in the Midwest and Northeast, creating effective "disinvestment" in these regions.[14] The urban blight of our nation's inner cities is at least partially a consequence of this disinvestment. Low wages, raw materials, less regulations, a non-unionized labor force, and tariff avoidance are some of the lures attracting industries overseas. Why pay U.S. wages or accept regulated U.S. working conditions when teenage girls in Singapore can be worked 12 hours a day at a fraction of the cost?

Keeping these global labor markets in view, American businesses and their allies in government are trying to get the various states and regions in the U.S. to compete with each other for jobs. They are to go backwards in the direction of the underdeveloped Third World. Similar attractions — lowest wages, least unionized workforce, least protective regulations, greatest tax breaks, etc. — should be offered to create a better "business climate." If they don't, the threat is to move away. Such corporate blackmail is highly effective, whether the companies seriously intend to leave or not.[15]

Here is where enterprise zones enter in. They may be a major component of the attempt by corporate America and its allies to depress wages, weaken unions, and worsen working conditions in the United States and localities will compete for zone status to provide the best "business climate" and worst working conditions, just as Third World countries now do to attract investment. Compare enterprise zone provisions with the following statement:

> Avoiding taxes, circumventing tariffs, and steering clear of stringent antipollution controls are all reasons why global corporations build factories abroad.[16]

Obviously, enterprise zones are attempts to compete with the Third World. No wonder critics claim that enterprise zones are nothing more than bringing the Third World within the borders of the U.S. "Mini-Puerto Ricos" are to be created in small zones dotted across the U.S. landscape.

The implications of this for organized labor are obvious and ominous. If zones are not contained, they may begin to "spill over" into the surrounding community. And in any case, the labor movement is not looking to lower standards of living or worsen working conditions through corporate "perks;" it is seeking the exact opposite — protection and improvement in living standards and working conditions. The logic of enterprise zone proposals is anti-labor through and through.

Alternatives to Enterprise Zones: A Labor Perspective

Although it is not the intent of this article to fully explore alternative strategies for reindustrialization, brief mention of different approaches can be made here. No attempt at completeness or comprehensiveness is claimed; rather, this is a very brief look at several options now being considered.

First, as a preliminary to reindustrialization, the labor movement can take some steps to prevent further deindustrialization. Changes can be made in collective bargaining structures so that a more united front — regionally and even worldwide — is maintained against multinational companies. Bargaining solidarity must be extended well beyond present union and national boundaries. Difficult as it probably will be to achieve, coordinated bargaining for all workers of a multinational corporation in all countries is one way to match its economic strength and prevent further runaways. Political controls over corporate behavior also are necessary — national and state plant closing legislation is one example. Neither of these changes will be easy, but they are necessary if the disinvestment tide is to be stemmed.

Regarding reindustrialization, a wide variety of proposals have been put forward. Here I will not address the role of QWL, worker ownership, or collective bargaining in reindustrialization plans since these questions are dealt with elsewhere in this book. Current proposals fall into four basic frameworks:

(1) Pension fund power
(2) Sunrise-Sunset industrial development policy
(3) Industrial development planning through a Reconstruction Finance Corporation (RFC), an Industrial Development Bank, and/or other planned government interventions
(4) Industrial development planning through a mixture of public ownership, worker control, and other labor oriented government interventions controlling corporate power.

The "pension power" strategy begins by noting that enormous sums of capital in the U.S. economy are held in pension funds for union and government workers. If the unions in the private and public sector achieved half of the vote in bodies controlling investment of their pension funds (which is legal), unions would suddenly have considerable power to control major investments in our economy (between ¼ and ½ of all investments made). This power could be used to redirect investments into this country, into union firms, into a union local's community, into socially desirable projects, and into the areas and industries needed to reindustrialize our country. Therefore, it is argued, unions should do what capitalists failed to do — reindustrialize our country in socially beneficial ways — through control of their pension funds. There are a number of legal, technical, and economic controversies surrounding this approach to reindustrialization which I cannot enter into here.[17] The approach does seem to have definite possibilities, although the larger claims of a total redistribution of economic power in our economy being put forward by some pension power adherents is unlikely to happen by this means alone.

The "sunrise-sunset" approach to reindustrialization is most closely associated with MIT economist Lester Thurow and *Newsweek* magazine.[18] Thurow argues that the government should hasten the decline of industries with outmoded faciles ("sunset" industries) while encouraging new ("sunrise" industries) high-tech firms, computer chips, etc. Democratic Party politicians agreeing with this perspective have acquired the label "Atari Democrats." The thinking behind this proposal is much influenced by Japan's planned industrial policy, which ruthlessly eliminates uncompetitive firms and industries while pouring enormous funds into new competitive fields. Whatever the merits of this proposal from a purely abstract economic point of view (debatable in the American context), it would be disastrous for existing unions and thousands of industrialized cities. Even coupled with job retraining and relocation assistance, the "sunrise-sunset" strategy would bring enormous suffering on the industrial Northeast and Midwest, not to mention the industrial unions.

The third approach to reindustrialization is most closely associated with Wall Street investment banker Felix Rohatyn.[19] Rohatyn and others propose a Reconstruction Finance Corporation, a quasi-public agency that would use public funds to bail out and restructure bankrupt firms like Chrysler in 1979. Similar proposals envision an Industrial Development Bank to channel capital into key sectors of the economy under circumstances where private banks won't. Rohatyn also has proposed a major government bail-out of ailing banks. In all cases, proposals of this type call for extensive government intervention in the economy to aid business, often coupled with job retraining programs, government funding of research and development, limited protectionist trade policies, and the like.

While the labor movement may find a number of these features to be positive, several aspects are worrisome. First, Rohatyn is adamant that the standard of living of U.S. workers must be cut, so that business can have a larger share of national income. Second, he proposes to by-pass democratic political control over government policy by creating business-dominated agencies with token labor and public representation to institute policy. Even though public money will be used, there will not be public control.

In addition, Rohatyn's role in the bail-out of New York City in 1975 is not reassuring. There he engineered the creation of bank-controlled quasi-public agencies which stripped elected officials of all power over the budget, forced a real wage cut on all city workers, permanently laid off thousands, and reduced services and aid to the city's residents, especially its poor.

The final approach to reindustrialization calls for a much more thorough reorganization of the functioning of our economic system. The premise is that corporate power and corporate dominance of the economy are at the root of our economic troubles; the solution is a transfer of political and economic power to workers and the public. Specific plans within this framework vary;[20] here I will give the general outlines of various proposals. In general, a mixture of private and public ownership, selected public subsidies with specified public returns in the form of controls and economic gains, greater worker control through a variety of mechanisms, massive jobs programs and increases for the social services "safety net," and the like are advocated. While some proposals are more modest and others more ambitious, all challenge the accustomed way of "doing business" in the U.S. to a larger degree than does Rohatyn's RFC proposal. Unlike Rohatyn's version, all emphasize democracy and have a labor orientation.

An "industrial policy," or reindustrialization program, has also been developing rapidly into a political idea with major support. The Democrats in both the House and the Senate came up with major industrial policy proposals in late 1983. Both were basically in the Rohatyn mold, with the major difference being that the Senate version did not include an industrial development bank as a major component.[21] Clearly, an industrial policy to reindustrialize the country is becoming a national political issue.

Conclusion

The concept of enterprise zones is not the only proposal to reindustrialize urban America. There are alternative plans for reindustrialization which the labor movement can consider and act upon. All of these approaches contrast markedly with the enterprise zone attempt. The "free market" rhetoric is totally absent in all cases; there is a clear admission that conscious planned intervention in the market behavior of firms is necessary if we are to reindustrialize the United States.

Enterprise zones will not aid reindustrialization in this country. They will fail to achieve their stated goals, even when evaluated by the rationales put forward by their advocates. Furthermore, they have definite anti-labor implications; the labor movement has good cause to view them with alarm.[22]

If the labor movement is to have any impact on reindustrialization attempts, it will have to debate the alternatives and develop plans to intervene in the upcoming political struggle over the shape of economic development policy in the United States for the 1980s. To some degree it has already begun that task.[23]

End Notes

1. For samples of Butler's work, see Stuart M. Butler, *Enterprise Zones: Greenlining the Inner Cities* (New York: Universe Books, 1981); and "The Enterprise Zones as an Urban Frontier," in *Community Action* (September-October 1981). For a shorter piece, see his Op-Ed article in the *New York Times*, June 13, 1980.

2. David Birch, *The Job Generation Process* (Cambridge, Mass.: MIT Program on Neighborhood and Regional Change, 1979).

3. National Federation of Independent Business Study, 1981.

4. *The Urban Jobs and Enterprise Zone Act: Recommendations from the Small Business Community* (Boston: Council for Northeast Economic Action, 1981).

5. Edward Humberger, "The Enterprise Zone Fallacy," *Community Action* (September/October 1981), p. 25.

6. Roger J. Vaughan, *State Taxation and Economic Development* (Washington, D.C.: Council of State Planning Agencies, 1979), pp. 6-7.

7. Michael Kieschnik, *Taxes and Growth* (Washington, D.C.: Council of State Planning Agencies, 1981).

8. William Barnes, "Cautions From Britain: The EZ Answer Proves Elusive," *Urban Innovation Abroad* (Washington, D.C.: Council for International Urban Liaison, May 1982), pp. 2,3.

9. For information on Puerto Rico, see *Latin American Perspectives* (Summer, 1976) which is entirely devoted to the island. See also Sidney Lens, "Puerto Rico: Trouble in the 'Showcase' " *The Progressive* (August, 1977).

10. James Dietz, "The Puerto Rican Political Economy," *Latin American Perspectives* (Summer, 1976), p. 10.

11. For reports on AFL-CIO testimony against enterprise zones, see the *AFL-CIO News*, February 6, 1982, April 3, 1982, April 24, 1982, and May 8, 1982. Also the newspapers of many international unions carried articles against the concept. Also see

the A. Phillip Randolph Institute press release "Urban Enterprise Zones: No Answer to Black Plight," March 25, 1982.

12. Richard Barnet and Ronald Muller, *Global Reach: The Power of the Multinational Corporations* (New York: Simon and Schuster, 1974), p. 303.

13. Ibid., pp. 304, 308, 309.

14. For a pathbreaking analysis of this phenomenon, see Barry Bluestone and Bennett Harrison, *The Deindustrialization of America* (New York: Basic Books, 1982). Also see Bluestone, Harrison, and Lawrence Butler, *Corporate Flight: the Causes and Consequences of Economic Dislocation* (Washington, D.C.: The Progressive Alliance, 1981).

15. The best study of this is Robert Goodman, *The Last Entrepreneurs: America's Regional Wars for Jobs and Dollars* (New York: Simon and Schuster, 1979, and reprinted, Boston: South End Press, 1982).

16. Barnet and Muller, *Global Reach*, pp. 306-307.

17. The two most important places to begin looking at the issue are: Jeremy Rifkin and Randy Barber, *The North Will Rise Again: Pensions, Politics and Power in the 1980s* (Boston: Beacon Press, 1978), and the AFL-CIO's August 1980 report Investment of Union Pension Funds. Also see the AFL-CIO Industrial Union Department periodical *Labor and Investments*.

18. Lester Thurow, *The Zero-Sum Society* (New York: Basic Books, 1980), *Newsweek*, June 30, 1980.

19. See Felix Rohatyn, "A New RFC is Proposed for Business," *New York Times*, December 1, 1974. See also Rohatyn's articles in the *New York Review of Books:* "The Disaster Facing the North" (January 22, 1981); "Reconstructing America" (February 5, 1981); "The State of the Banks" (November 4, 1982); and "Time for a Change" (August 18, 1983); Somewhat similar to Rohatyn in many of his proposals is Robert Reich of Harvard University. Reich's thoughts on the topic can be found in "A U.S. Industrial Policy?" *Industry Week* (Nov. 14, 1983), pp. 38-44, and in longer form in his book, *The Next American Frontier* (New York: Times Books, 1983). For a brief, and very clear, summation of his thinking, see "Industrial Evolution" in *Democracy* magazine, Vol. 3, No. 3 (Summer 1983), pp. 10-20. Both Rohatyn and Reich offer industrial policy proposals from a corporate perspective which is acceptable to a limited but influential group of business leaders.

20. For examples, see Samuel Bowles, David Gordon and Thomas Weisskopf, *Beyond the Waste Land: A Democratic Alternative to Economic Decline* (New York: Anchor-Doubleday Press, 1983); the final chapter of Barry Bluestone and Bennett Harrison's *The Deindustrialization of America;* and "An Interview with Bennett Harrison and Barry Bluestone" in the January-February 1983 *Working Papers*. David Kotz, "A Jobs Program to Rebuild U.S. and Expand Democracy," *In These Times* (March 9-22, 1983), is in a similar vein; Martin Carnoy, Derek Shearer, and Russell Rumberger, *A New Social Contract* (New York: Harper and Row, 1983) is somewhat within this mold, although it makes many compromises with a Rohatyn version of industrial policy. Finally, UAW economist Dan Luria and policy analyst Jack Russell develop a concrete plan along these lines for Detroit in *Rational Reindustrialization: An Economic Development Agenda for Detroit* (Detroit: Widge-tripper Press, 1981).

21. For an interesting analysis, see Robert W. Merry, " 'Industrial Policy' Divides Democrats, But Is Seen as a Cornerstone for Election", *Wall Street Journal*, January 9, 1984. Also see *Our Jobs, Our Future: Questions for the Candidates about America's Industry and Economy*, an undated publication of the Project on Industrial Policy and Democrcy (2000 P St., N.W., Wash., D.C. 20036).

22. A particularly reactionary bill was the original 1981 proposal in the state of Illinois. It would have "called for suspending all zoning and building codes, eliminating minimum wages, initially abolishing property taxes, prohibiting any state aid not provided in the act itself, weakening unions (through right-to-work laws), and eliminating all environmental regulations and health and safety laws." (William Goldsmith, "Bringing the Third World Home," in the March-April 1982 *Working Papers*). This law was vetoed by the governor; the veto barely was sustained after extensive labor and community lobbying against the bill. Illinois presently has enterprise zone legislation, but it is not as

reactionary as the original bill in its provisions

23. Three proposals have recently come out of the labor movement on reindustrialization. The AFL-CIO published "Rebuilding America: A National Industrial Policy" in the *AFL-CIO American Federationist*, Vol. 90, no. 5 (October 22, 1983). The UAW published its "Blueprint for a Working America" as its May 16-31, 1983 edition of *Solidarity* magazine. The International Association of Machinists published *Let's Rebuild America*, an undated 263-page book offering a comprehensive restructuring of U.S. industry. There are some major differences of approach in these three plans; all three deserve close scrutiny. Also, it should not be assumed that the labor movement is unanimously in favor of the current reindustrialization approaches. An outspoken critique by Tony Mazzochi, a long-time activist and leader in the Oil, Chemical, and Atomic Workers Union, is contained in: "Toward a Workers Party" *Democracy* magazine (Summer 1983), pp. 34-40. Further criticisms are contained in Kim Moody's "Going Public: In Search of an Economy that Works" in *The Progressive* (July 1983), p. 18-21; Moody's three-part series on industrial policy in *Labor Notes* (in the July 27, August 23, and September 27, 1983 issues); and John Russo, "Strategies for a New Economy" *The Nation* (October 22, 1983), pp. 365-367.

Technological Change and Reindustrialization: Implications for Organized Labor

Carol J. Haddad

Introduction

A radio advertisement for a Michigan bank depicts the following scene:

A customer languishes helplessly in a long line behind people engaging in complicated transactions. A woman wants the interest on her account computed over a forty-year period; a man requests two thousand dollars worth of traveller's checks — "in small denominations." Finally our helpless hero reveals in exasperation, "I just wanted to cash a twenty-dollar check!" The narrator sympathizes and tells us that salvation rests in the form of "fast teller" — an electronic banking machine capable of performing simple transactions expeditiously. The advertisement ends by inviting us to "get out of the slow lane, and into the fast lane — with fast teller."

The critical listener may wonder: is it not possible to offer the same level of efficiency by establishing a "fast lane" for simple transactions that is serviced by a *human* teller? What happens to the "fast lane" when the "fast teller" machine malfunctions? These questions are neither asked nor answered. The advertisement creates a single impression: speed and efficiency can only be achieved through the use of electronic technology.

High Technology and Reindustrialization

Variations of the "fast lane" theme have surfaced with increasing frequency in the writings and speeches of business and political leaders, economists and policy makers. We are told that in order to rebuild American industry, in order to maintain economic competitiveness with other industrialized nations, we *must* embrace high technology. Inherent in this drive are three assumptions: first, states plagued by declining industries and severe unemployment can realize prosperity and jobs by attracting high technology firms. Second, in

---

Carol Haddad is an Assistant Professor in the School of Labor and Industrial Relations at Michigan State University.

order to maximize efficiency and productivity, American workplaces must "modernize" their operations by installing robots, computers and other forms of microelectronic-based technology. Third, the success of such workplace transformation depends on the setting aside of traditionally adversarial relationships between labor and management, in favor of a "new social contract" characterized by "cooperation," "problem solving," and "team work."[1] In this paper, I will evaluate the validity of these three assumptions, and will analyze two related questions; first, how should organized labor view the promise that high technology firms will provide jobs for the unemployed and for new entrants to the labor market? Second, what can labor do in the immediate future as employers introduce new technology into the workplace on a broad scale?

Many economically depressed states have accepted the notion that embracing high technology is the key to recovery. With its heavy reliance on the troubled automotive industry and its depression-level unemployment, Michigan has been regarded by business and political leaders as fertile ground for economic "diversification" in the direction of high technology. In 1981, then Governor William Milliken began to preach the high-tech gospel. Apostles were chosen from among the state's most prominent private and public sector leaders to constitute a "High Technology Task Force." Its members included such notables as industrialist Max Fisher, Burroughs Corporation President and former U.S. Treasury Secretary W. Michael Blumenthal, Dow Chemical Company Secretary Herbert Dow, Upjohn Corporation President Dr. William Hubbard, former Bendix Corporation Chairman William Agee, Irwin International Corporation President and Chairman Samuel Irwin, University of Michigan President Harold Shapiro, and former Michigan Lieutenant Governor James Brickley. Noticeably absent from the starting lineup were representatives of organized labor.

As the High Technology Task Force went about its business of mapping out an economic development agenda based on robotics and molecular biology, the Governor, assisted by the media kept the issue alive: "If advances in robotics technology are researched, engineered, developed, manufactured and maintained in Michigan, we will have still more jobs — and a wider range of them — in the robotics industry itself."[2] A generous State grant of $25 million was targeted to support this effort, with $158,000 earmarked to finance an "Innovation Center" at the University of Michigan, and $500,000 to establish a "Robotics Center" at the same institution.[3]

Governor Milliken's Task Force spawned the Industrial Technology Institute, an Ann Arbor-based non-profit corporation dedicated to manufacturing process technology research and technical assistance to Michigan industry. It currently employs thirty part-time engineers and scientists.[4] A Democrat, James Blanchard, succeeded Milliken as Governor of Michigan, and appears to be headed down the same high-tech highway.

Michigan is not the only state entering the "fast lane." Massachusetts and California have had a significant head start in the high technology race, North Carolina with its billion dollar "Research Triangle" is not far behind, and other states are scrambling at the starting line. To be sure, a state can benefit from playing host to high technology firms. They provide jobs for engineers, scientists, and technicians and, perhaps more importantly, bring prestige and hope to economically embattled states. But is this enough to base a reindustrialization policy on? Some experts think not.

High Technology and Employment Growth
  Stanford University researchers Henry Levin and Russell Rumberger have discovered that contrary to popular belief, high technology will account for very little of the new job growth in the coming years.[5] Levin and Rumberger examined the impact of high technology on projected employment growth (i.e.; new jobs added to the economy rather than job openings) between 1978-1990. Using Bureau of Labor Statistics data and assuming modest growth rates, they have projected an overall employment increase of 22 million or 23 percent by 1990.[6]
  In examining *relative* job growth (percentage change within a particular job category over a period of time), they found that high technology occupations figured prominently, with data processing machine mechanics increasing by 148 percent, computer systems analysts by 108 percent and computer operators by 88 percent between 1978 and 1990.[7] However, as the authors indicate, these figures are misleading. In terms of *absolute* job growth (actual numbers of jobs created over a period of time), high technology "will account for only 7 percent of all new jobs between 1980 and 1990."[8] The five job classifications expected to account for greatest numbers of new jobs between 1978 and 1990 are: janitors, nurses' aides, sales clerks, cashiers, waitresses and waiters.[9] Levin and Rumberger further project that approximately 150,000 new jobs for computer programmers will open up during this twelve-year period, compared to 800,000 new jobs for fast-food workers and kitchen helpers, and that clerical and service occupations will account for 40 percent of all employment growth between 1978-1990, with professional and managerial occupations accounting for only 28 percent of such growth.[10]
  Other analysts have made similar projections. Michigan economic development specialist Jack Russell predicts that at best Michigan, a state with 641,000 residents counted as unemployed, may realize 20,000 robotics-based production jobs by 1990, if the state is "very aggressive, very generous, and very lucky."[11] He adds that many of the newly-created production jobs will go to "people living in the secondary cities and towns of the state where non-UAW wages are the rule," and that most of the technical, scientific, and managerial positions will be held by those who "live in Ann Arbor, drive BMWs, sip Chablis, and eat quiche."[12]

Russell's technology-based job projections are affirmed by researchers H. Allen Hunt and Timothy L. Hunt. They predict that under the most favorable conditions, robotics will account for 17,737 new jobs in Michigan by 1990.[13] According to the Hunts, the two largest occupational categories created by robotics will be robotics technicians — those who program, install, test and maintain industrial robots — and engineers, providing (at best) 4,469 and 3,537 jobs respectively.[14]

Even the pages of *Business Week* reflect skepticism about high technology's ability to create jobs: ". . . the number of jobs that will be created in high-technology industries in the next ten years is disappointing . . . in fact, . . . the number of high-technology jobs created over the next decade will be less than half of the two million jobs lost in manufacturing in the past three years."[15]

Unlike the Hunts' study, *Business Week* predicts that ". . . most of those [jobs] will be in traditional occupations, not technical ones. Fewer than one-third will be for engineers and technicians, according to DRI [Data Resources, Inc.], and the remainder will be managers, clerical workers, operators, and other factory workers."[16] Moreover, high technology industries provide no guarantee of job security; Atari, Inc. dashed the hopes of many by announcing the permanent layoff of 1,700 of its 7,000 workers, and the shifting of much of its production from California to Hong Kong and Taiwan.[17]

High Technology And Job Elimination

While the ability of high technology industries to create jobs is dubious, high technology's capacity to eliminate jobs in other industries is clear. Despite industry assurances that "robots are ugly, dumb and don't want your job, so stop worrying,"[18] it is clear that microelectronic technology creates the potential for displacing many workers in a vast range of industries and occupations. A Carnegie-Mellon University study predicts: "By 2025, it is conceivable that more sophisticated robots will replace almost all operative jobs in manufacturing (about eight percent of today's workforce), as well as a number of routine non-manufacturing jobs. . . . Over half of all unskilled and semi-skilled operative workers — the types of jobs which could be replaced by robots — are concentrated in the four major metal-working sectors. Almost one-half of all production workers in these four industries are geographically concentrated in the five Great Lakes States — Indiana, Illinois, Michigan, Ohio and Wisconsin — plus New York and California."[19]

Within the metalworking sector, the automotive and steel industries will be the hardest hit. According to the Congressional Budget Office, new technology will eliminate 200,000 auto production jobs by 1985, and 2-3% of the steel industry workforce by 1990.[20] In the automobile industry, robots are currently being used to perform such functions as materials handling, inspection, welding, painting and assembly. And as robot vision and sensing systems improve, utilization will undoubtedly broaden. General Motors estimates that by 1987, 90 percent of the new machines it buys will be computer controlled.[21] And the nation's number two automaker, the Ford Motor Company, recently announced plans to purchase 4,000 robots by 1990, adding to the 1,000 already in operation.[22] If each robot replaces three workers on a multi-shift basis, that adds up to 15,000 jobs at Ford alone. Overall, it is expected that the auto industry will introduce as many as 25,000 robots, plus other computer-operated equipment, by the 1990s.[23]

Although the manufacturing sector's adoption of new technology often receives the most attention from industry analysts, media sources, political leaders and even unions, it is in fact the office sector that is being most dramatically impacted by microelectronics. Word processors, minicomputers, electronic mail and filing, and tele-conferencing make it possible to operate "paperless" offices — with substantially fewer employees. The West German technology firm Siemens has determined that forty percent of that country's clerical jobs could be standardized, and 25-30 percent of such jobs could subsequently be fully automated by 1990. In public sector offices these figures increase to 75 percent standardization and 38 percent auto-mation.[24]

It is expected that high technology will enter offices in industrialized countries far more quickly than it enters factories. There are several reasons for this. First, the office sector has a much lower degree of capital investment than the manufacturing sector; about $2,000 worth of equipment per office employee, compared with $30,000-$40,000 per factory employee.[25] A second reason cited for the rapid introduction of office technology is its ability to boost office productivity. It is claimed that microelectronic technology is capable of boosting office pro-ductivity by up to 200 percent and reliability by up to 500 percent.[26] Of course, productivity measurement in this sector is a variable and subjective practice. A third incentive for management introduction of new office technology is increased unionization among office workers.[27] The office sector has become a sort of last frontier for labor unions faced with dwindling membership. Furthermore, organi-zations like 9 to 5, National Association of Working Women and District 925 of the Service Employees International Union have been effective in bringing the concerns of office workers into the limelight.

Microelectronic technology will continue to threaten employment in a number of other service sector industries as well. Electronic banking, computerized inventory control in retail stores, microprocessor-controlled sewing machines, electronic switching, traffic and storage systems in the telephone industry, electronic sorting machines in the postal service and computerized diagnostic and monitoring systems in health care all add up to reduced employment prospects in what has traditionally been a growing sector of our economy.

Disparate Impact On Women And Minorities
The most vulnerable members of our labor force — particularly women and minorities — stand to suffer the most as a result of technological job displacement. Historic patterns of sex and race discrimination have resulted in a disproportionate concentration of women of all races and minority men into lower-paying service and manufacturing jobs.

Table I
Occupational Distribution of Women in the U.S. Labor Force

Occupation	% Female in 1981
Total Workforce	42.8
Private household workers	96.5
Typists	96.3
Bank tellers	93.5
Telephone operators	92.9
Nursing aides, orderlies, attendants	86.6
Clerical workers	80.5
Sales clerks-retail trade	71.2
Service workers (except private household)	59.2
Professional & technical (includes teachers and registered nurses)	42.8
Operatives (except transport)	39.8
Postal clerks	37.9
Public administration	36.0
Managers	27.5
Lawyers and judges	14.1
Craft workers	6.3
Engineers	4.4

SOURCE: *Labor Force Statistics Derived From The Current Population Survey: A Databook*, Vol. I. (Washington, D.C.: U.S. Dept. of Labor, Bureau of Labor Statistics, Sept. 1982) pp. 664-681.

As Table I illustrates, women are highly concentrated in occupations that have already experienced significant job erosion due to the introduction of new technology. For some occupations, the job loss is particularly alarming when measured over a period of time; for example, between 1970 and 1981, computer technology in telecommunications resulted in a thirty percent decline in the number of women employed as telephone operators.[28] These losses are not being offset by increased employment of women as computer operators, programmers and systems analysts.

Minority workers tend to be concentrated in occupations that are not as likely to be directly affected by technological change. (See Table II). However, new technology, combined with our current economic "recession," threatens to erase the gains that minorities have recently made in industries and occupations that have traditionally excluded them. In 1981, minorities constituted 17.1 percent of all assemblers and 9.2 percent of all telephone installers and repairers, compared to 1972 percentages of 13.2 and 4.2 respectively[29] As new technology eliminates jobs such as these, formal seniority systems and the prevalence of the "last hired, first fired" principle will result in disproportionate layoffs of minorities and women alike.

Table II
Occupational Distribution of Minorities in the U.S. Labor Force

Occupation	% Minority in 1981
Total Workforce	11.6
Cleaners and servants	51.5
Garbage collectors	42.7
Housekeepers	40.6
Clothing ironers and pressers	39.8
Lodging quarters cleaners	38.3
Welfare service aides	31.8
Cement and concrete finishers	31.3
Building interior cleaners	30.4
Textile operatives (spinners, twisters and winders only)	29.4
Nursing aides, orderlies & attendants	29.0
Taxicab drivers & chauffeurs	28.7
Laundry & dry cleaning operatives	28.4
Postal clerks	26.4
Assemblers	17.1
Professional and technical	11.6
Clerical workers	11.6
Craft workers	8.5
Managers	5.8
Sales workers	5.4
Lawyers and judges	4.6

SOURCE: *Labor Force Statistics Derived From The Current Population Survey: A Databook*, Vol. I. (Washington, D.C.: U.S. Dept. of Labor, Bureau of Labor Statistics, Sept. 1982) pp. 664-681.

Perhaps the most significant impact of high technology on vulnerable members of the labor force is not job displacement *per se*, but rather reduction of employment prospects. Because new technology often results in job de-skilling (as will be discussed in more detail later), promotional opportunities for those in low paying, relatively unskilled or "dead end" jobs become limited.[30] Additionally, as high technology permeates service industries, those who have traditionally looked to this sector for deliverance from higher-than-average rates of unemployment will find little salvation. A study by the International Labour Organization predicts:

> . . . what scope there is for employment creation lies in the service sector, especially in clerical and managerial work. It is precisely this sector, however, which will be most severely affected by information technology and its offspring, office automation. It is also within this sector that much of the female labour force is concentrated in developed countries, and increasingly in developing countries. . . . The poor prospects for job creation have important social consequences; particularly for the young. . . . Not only are there more young people unemployed, but the duration of their unemployment is increasing . . . the situation looks grim. To absorb the net increase in the labour force in the 1980s, eleven million jobs will need to be created in the United States on the assumption that the decade begins with an unemployment level of six million.[31]

International Competition

Proponents of high technology dismiss projections of massive technological job displacement as "alarmist" on a number of grounds. First, it is claimed that the introduction of workplace technology is vital if American industry intends to "stay in the race" alongside West Germany and Japan.

American industry has indeed lost some competitive ground to West Germany, Japan and other industrialized nations. This is not, however, the result of any inherent inability on the part of American companies or workers to operate efficiently and produce high quality goods. Rather, the problem stems from what two authors refer to as "competitive myopia" — the pursuit of short-sighted investment, marketing and managerial strategies designed to yield high margins of profit.[32] Despite federal tax credits and other incentives, it has been common practice for companies to shun capital reinvestment in favor of high profit investments (e.g. — real estate speculation) unrelated to their operations. Mobil Oil's purchase of Montgomery Ward stores and Container (box) Corporation for $1.8 billion, Gulf Oil's purchase of Ringling Brothers' Circus and U.S. Steel Corporation's investment in Disney World hotels serve as testimony to this fact. As Barry Bluestone has stated: "While Japan was adapting basic oxygen furnace technology, which had been developed in Austria, U.S. Steel was quite literally making Mickey Mouse investments."[33] A U.S. House Small Business Antitrust Subcommittee similarly noted: "What we found is a sad pattern of corporate management concentrating on short-term profit maximization to the detriment of the broader interests of the national economy and public interest."[34]

The stubborn refusal of the automobile industry to retool and shift to fuel efficient car production even after the 1973-74 gasoline price hikes (falsely attributed to the Arab oil embargo)[35] is further evidence of such shortsightedness. As one automotive executive put it: "Big cars yield big profits." Even more stunning was the industry's recent announcement — after losing a significant share of its market to fuel-efficient foreign autos — that with the dip in gasoline prices it is planning a return to the production of large cars.

Compounding all of this is the fact that American industries enjoyed virtual hegemony over the rest of the world for a period of thirty years following World War II. Europe and Japan rebuilt their devastated factories and have simply caught up with us. And many Third World countries, such as the oil producing nations, have come to understand the value of their resources, and after years of exploitation are demanding their "fair share."

Clearly, the causes of American deindustrialization are complex, and warrant greater discussion than this paper can offer. No doubt this debate will continue to fill the pages of economics journals for years to come. In fact, it is the very complexity of this issue that calls into question the simplistic assumption that high technology will cure our nation's economic ills. The "high technology" placebo appeases those seeking a "quick fix," but it is no substitute for a comprehensive reindustrialization policy.

The Productivity Debate

A second and related argument advanced by proponents of high technology is that it will improve the productivity of American workplaces and the quality of American products, and, in the long run, actually *save* jobs. In fact, the argument continues, there is no firm evidence that workplace technology creates unemployment; rather, it eliminates jobs that are "dirty, dull, and hazardous," thereby freeing workers to perform jobs that are more skilled and more humane.

Machines that are allegedly able to work twenty-four hours a day, seven days a week — without taking coffee breaks, going on strike or demanding wages clearly have appeal to those who regard workers as the cause of declines in United States productivity rates. But productivity is itself a complex phenomenon, and is influenced by a multitude of factors: capital investment, research and development, skill of the workforce, safety of the work process and overall economic conditions. This latter factor is very significant; current declines in U.S. productivity can be attributed to "substantial reductions in manufacturing output and in employment and hours."[36] The AFL-CIO states the issue more bluntly: "Avoiding recessions is the most important step we can take to increase U.S. productivity growth."[37]

Undeniably, productivity gains can be realized through the introduction of high technology. There is, of course a price tag attached — one that is often hidden from the eager customer. In addition to the actual purchase price of the equipment are tooling costs, installation costs, engineering costs and operating costs (labor, energy, supplies, depreciation).[38] Other variables in the productivity equation are; the appropriateness of the new technology to the task it is expected to perform, the congruence of the new technology with other machinery and with the physical attributes and skill levels of human operators, and acceptance by managers, employees and unions.

Moreover, the "trickle down" promise that productivity benefits derived from high technology will be passed on to workers in the form of employment opportunity is highly suspect. As has been noted, there is a correlation between the introduction of new workplace technologies and job displacement. Advocates of technology dispute the causality of this correlation, and there is a strand of truth in this presumption. New technologies in the workplace are often accompanied by other labor-saving changes; in the manufacturing sector these may be corporate reorganization or consolidation, transfer of certain operations to other plants (within or outside of the U.S.), subcontracting, or any number of "systems rationalizations." In the service and public sectors, high technology enables a shift from "service" to "self-service" operations. In these contexts, it is difficult to isolate the degree of job displacement due to high technology *per se;* yet, the sum total equals job reduction no matter which way the numbers are added together.

In fact, worker elimination is often the principal incentive in the introduction of workplace technology. In a survey of its members regarding the factors that influenced their decision to install robots, the Robot Institute of America found that "respondents *overwhelmingly* ranked efforts to reduce labor cost as their main motivation."[39] As one corporate executive admits: "Will the robotics industry create more jobs than robots displace? The answer, in net terms, is no. Otherwise, robots will not have improved productivity on a national or global scale."[40]

This particular executive goes on to state a commonly held view; that while technology may eliminate many "menial" jobs, it will also create jobs in new areas. Presumably, then, the status of workers will be elevated as they attain higher levels of skill and job satisfaction. This viewpoint is accurate insofar as technology provides the *potential* for such advancement. But there is little evidence to suggest that the push for workplace technology is motivated by this noble goal. To the contrary, as worker skill and knowledge is transferred to computerized machines, the remaining work becomes monotonous, routine, less challenging and sometimes more lowly paid. A report by 9 to 5 describes what happened to a worker in the insurance industry:

> I used to be a keypunch operator. The company wanted to downgrade the keypunch operators, so they announced that they are calling the job 'data entry processing' so that the people who work it will become 'data entry technicians.' In this way, they could get around the job classification. They take clerks, train them on the data entry machines and thus eliminate the keypunch operators. Because they're making keyboards that look like adding machines, you don't have to have that much knowledge to do the work. They still need some keypunching, though, so they budgeted the keypunch operators at 7½ hours a week.[41]

Automation, New Technology and Shifts in the U.S. Economy

There is a final myth about new technology and employment that must be put to rest; "new" technology is merely the latest phase of industrial innovation, and since our workforce survived the "Industrial Revolution" and later automation of the 1940s and 1950s, it will withstand workplace introduction of microelectronic technology without major consequence. This premise is founded on a number of faulty assumptions. The first is that there is no difference between today's technology and yesterday's mechanization and automation. To the contrary, new technology differs from its predecessors in two basic ways; the breadth of its application and the rapidity of its development. Mechanization represented the substitution of human strength with operated machinery. Automation took this process a step further by integrating machines into automatic, standardized, repetitive and in some cases self-regulating production systems.

Today's technologies — because of the rapid development of microelectronics — are multifunctional, reprogrammable and possess an unprecedented degree of sophistication. Advances in microelectronics are based upon silicon-integrated circuits. Today's silicon chip, which is smaller than a fingernail, holds more information than did the first commercially available computer, which filled an entire room.

Microelectronic technology was developed and refined in the 1960s primarily for American military and space programs. Today's generation of technology is seemingly limitless in its versatility. Since microcomputers can be programmed to perform a variety of functions, application goes well beyond performance of production processes to include such operations as storage and transmittal of data, inspection and monitoring. Hardly an industry or occupation will remain untouched by technology. And as citizens and consumers we've witnessed even more of its applications — from government and private surveillance to highly sophisticated military hardware to digital clocks, microwave ovens and PAC-Man.

A second faulty assumption about industrialization and automation of the past is that workers affected by these phenomena suffered no significantly adverse consequences. Labor history tells us otherwise. Sweatshop conditions, child labor, assembly line speed-up, and high industrial accident rates were by-products of the transformation from an agricultural to an industrial economy. Moreover, both men and women experienced a lowering of their economic status and control over the work process. Problems resulting from the use of labor-saving machinery were discussed at an 1878 meeting of the American Social Science Association:

> . . . It has broken up and destroyed our whole system of household and family manufactures, as done by our mothers, when all took part in the labor and shared in the product, to the comfort of all; and has compelled the daughters of our country and towns to factory operations for 10 to 12 hours a day in the manufacture of cloth they may not wear. . . .
>
> It has broken up and destroyed our whole system of individual and independent action in production and manufacture . . . and has compelled all working men and women to a system of communal work, where . . . they are forced to labor . . . with no

voice, no right, no interest in the product of their hands and brains, but subject to the uncontrollable interest and caprice of those who too often know no other motive than that of avarice. . . .

It has thrown out of employment substantially one-half of the working classes. . . .[42]

Furthermore, workers of the 1940s and 1950s *were* displaced from certain jobs. In testimony before a Congressional Subcommittee, Walter Reuther — then President of the UAW — described the plight of a 61-year-old male auto worker who, after 27 years as a job-setter at the Ford foundry machine shop, was transferred to a new automated engine plant. In the words of the employee: "The machine had about 80 drills and 22 blocks going through. You had to watch all the time. . . . And the machines had so many lights and switches — about 90 lights. It is sure hard on your mind."[43] In the end, this man could not keep up with the machine, and was downgraded. But, as Reuther pointed out, this individual was one of the luckier workers. Others were displaced altogether.

James Carey, then President of the International Union of Electrical, Radio and Machine Workers, spoke at a 1955 Conference on the devastating consequences of automation in his industry:

The introduction of the "printed circuit" at the Philco plant in Sandusky, Ohio, resulted in elimination of 25% of employees on the soldering and wiring assembly line. G.E., which makes printed circuits for other industries, boasts that these circuits will reduce a company's labor force by 50%. Another change in method whereby the entire bottom of a radio is now soldered all at once in a soldering bath has resulted in only three solderers being employed by Philco instead of the previous 40.[44]

Still, when workers were displaced from one occupation or industry during this period, they generally found employment in another. By the 1960s, this was already beginning to change. Economist Charles Killingworth noted the reasons for this change:

I think when a major labor-saving invention is introduced in an industry which is in its rapid growth stage — its adolescence — the invention may help to spur further rapid growth, especially through price cuts, and total employment in the industry may increase substantially. This is the historical pattern which prompts many people to argue "machines make jobs." But the fact is that when an industry has reached maturity — for example, when there is already one car for each three people — it just is not possible to achieve further dramatic increases in sales, even with the largest price cuts within the realm of reason. The improved productivity made possible by labor saving machines simply enables the industry to keep up with the normal growth of the market while employing fewer production workers. This is what happened in a number of our major industries in the 1950s

The doctrine that "machines make jobs," to the extent that it rests on research rather than faith, is drawn primarily from studies of the periods 1899-1937 and 1899-1953. These were mainly years when the growth potential of most markets for goods was still very great. I think that it is a major source of error to assume that the markets of great mass-production industries will grow at the same prodigious rate in the second half of the 20th Century that they achieved in the first half. Without that kind of growth rate, the doctrine that "machines make jobs" will surely be as obsolete as the Model T.

We can get some perspective on our present situation by considering the basic causes for the booming prosperity which most of Western Europe and Japan are now enjoying. Those countries are in the early growth stages of the mass-consumption society. Their ratios of automobiles to population, electric refrigerators to houses, and so on, are generally comparable to our ratios in the 1920s (or earlier). At their present rates of growth, it will be several decades before they achieve our degree of saturation of markets. So automation is having a different impact there.[45]

Compounding the problem described by Killingsworth is the impact that double digit inflation and unemployment have had on American consumers' purchasing power in recent years. As Walter Reuther, once observed; while robots can build cars, they cannot buy them.

Furthermore, high technology's invasion of the service sector of our economy raises serious questions about the assumption that workers displaced by manufacturing jobs will find employment elsewhere. In the absence of a national job creation strategy, they may very well find their career choices limited to part-time, non-union work at the local fast-food chain — or enlistment in the military.

The "New Social Contract"

The introduction of new technology into the workplace is often accompanied or preceded by management-inspired programs designed to soften adversarial relationships between unions and employers. These programs exist in a variety of forms, but they all share a universal goal — substitution of conflict with cooperation, in the hope that " . . . labor and management will see where their interests coincide and put the energy they employ as adversaries to work solving mutual problems."[46]

The presumption that adversarial relationships preclude cooperation is a curious one. The U.S. labor movement has, throughout its history, repeatedly demonstrated a willingness to cooperate with employers in a number of ways such as, workplace labor-management committees, wage freezes, "no-strike" pledges (particularly during wartime), community philanthropic activities and most recently concession bargaining. In light of this, one must wonder why employers are currently pushing cooperation schemes so strongly. AFL-CIO Secretary-Treasurer Thomas Donahue recently observed, ". . . a trade unionist has to be struck by the correlation between the timing of the growing problems of U.S. industry and the coincidental growth of interest on the part of employers in the quality of their employees worklife."[47]

What *is* clear about employer goals is that the type of participation and cooperation they advocate generally extends only as far as the shop floor. Union representatives are not invited to participate in decision-making concerning such areas as manpower planning, qualifications of directors and senior management, research and investment plans, plant location, product line or pricing and profit structures.[48]

Even at the shop floor level, it is easy to question whether job enrichment and participation programs are simply the latest phase in management's traditional struggle for greater control over the work process.[49] To the extent that they represent an attempt to subvert the collective bargaining process and shop steward system, organized labor has cause for concern. Two British labor educators have formulated a list of questions that may serve as useful yardsticks to unions wishing to measure the value of worker participation programs.

- Firstly, are we accepting new patterns of negotiation at the expense of our previous positions of strength which we have built up?
- Are our representatives on the new types of committees held strictly accountable to the shop floor?
- Are reporting-back procedures adequate to ensure accountability?
- Are we accepting 'responsibilities without powers'?
- Are we being placed in a position where management can hold us responsible for 'unpopular decisions'?
- Is management using us as sounding-boards to obtain information about the situation on the shop floor?
- Are they using us as messenger boys to carry their communications to the shop floor?
- Are we in danger of becoming part of management's supervision network?
- How much information is management really giving us, and how much are they still concealing?[50]

By setting forth its own agenda, organized labor is in a better position to insist that workplace cooperation schemes incorporate principles of industrial democracy.

New Technology and Organized Labor

While the search continues for a balanced reindustrialization policy, new technology continues to enter a broad spectrum of workplaces. Its introduction poses new challenges to organized labor. One of the most serious problems that unions face around the issue of high technology is membership erosion. As jobs are eliminated, downgraded (or "reclassified") and transferred to non-union plants and workplaces, union treasuries — and bargaining power — will continue to decline. And to the extent that Silicon Valley serves as an example, union organizing will be a steep uphill battle within the high technology industry itself.

Companies regularly assist each other in combating union drives. The American Electronics Association sponsors an ongoing series of seminars on the techniques of union-busting and serves as a clearinghouse for information on union activities at individual plants. More subtly, antiunionism is also built in to the very structure of the Silicon Valley life-style. When the corporation isn't only a place of work but also an arena for *individual* self-fulfillment and "growth," then the option of *collective* action to resolve workplace problems becomes almost impossible to imagine.[51]

Another challenge to unions posed by new technology is the unprecedented degree of control over the work process that it affords to managers and employers. Electronic cash registers (known as "scanners") and word processors are capable of recording the speed of the operator, the number of errors and the frequency and duration of pauses and rest periods. This amounts to twenty-four-hour-a-day, seven-day-a-week time-and-motion study — an expansion of "scientific management" that undoubtedly would have delighted Frederick Winslow Taylor.

In a Michigan discount department store chain, individual stores post, on a weekly basis, charts revealing the production and error rates of each cashier — by name. Store managers then add comments beside employees' names, such as "Very good!," or "Come And See Me Immediately." Not only is this a source of humiliation and job stress for the cashiers, but the data may be used (although it has not yet been) against those who consistently fail to meet production standards. The collection of such data has serious implications for organized labor. Stewards will have a much harder time arguing grievances and arbitration cases against computerized data than against the word of the supervisor. While unions do not dispute the right of management to set production standards, measuring performance in such a restrictive way disregards the value of human interaction, and penalizes employees who exhibit anything but robot-like behavior.

Employee monitoring of this nature has implications for consumers as well. Clerks operating under this type of pressure may be less likely to engage in friendly conversation or answer customer questions. Furthermore, as the use of scanners increases, consumers will need to guard legislation requiring "item pricing" alongside the "Universal Product Code."[52]

Computer-facilitated control over the work process extends far beyond the checkout lane. When new technology is combined with multiplant and multinational production, labor's bargaining power is severely weakened. Robotized plants programmed by long-distance telecommunications enable companies to produce at whatever levels and locations they deem necessary at any given point in time, thus rendering the strike weapon virtually meaningless. This situation was discussed at a 1982 International Metalworkers' Federation Conference in Munich:

> The power of multinational corporations has grown enormously with the introduction of new technology and worldwide data processing systems in the view of IG Metall, the German metalworkers union. Extensive automation projects and worldwide production transfers could hardly be imagined without comprehensive information planning and control systems based on computers, nor would they be nearly so effective, declared Lutz Dieckerhoff, IG Metal Executive member responsible for white collar affairs in the German union. Among the examples, said Dieckerhoff, was the U.S. company, Texaco, which had developed a worldwide finance reporting system with the help of which a daily world balance sheet which was drawn up by the use of a satellite and by which the whole worldwide company was directed. Similar systems were being developed in the automobile industry. The worldwide transmission of data and its central analysis in top management had extremely negative consequences for workers. Individual workshops or branches of the company are transferred or sacrificed like chess pieces from headquarters. The fate of human beings weighs as little on the scale as regional labor markets and the interests of regional or national governments.
>
> Company managements also attempted to play plant-level representatives and national trade union organizations off against each other through the knowledge only obtainable by them. Data processing gave management the possibility to institute productivity and cost comparisons for individual groups of workers in plants of the company worldwide. The consequences were an increased pressure

through the continual menace of transfers of production to a country where costs were lower. In addition, the exact surveillance of production processes in all the individual plants of the company gave management the possibility of short-term switches to other plants whenever a strike was threatened. Against a background of massive unemployment, it was sufficient to threaten transfers to production to prevent even the listing of demands.[53]

Such activity by multinational corporations exacerbates existing economic, racial and national tensions among nations, thus hindering effective international union solidarity.

Unions are not powerless in the face of the high technology invasion; indeed many unions in this country and abroad have already developed and implemented effective strategies for dealing with new technology. But for effective responses to be developed, the problems surrounding high technology must be acknowledged. One study suggests that some unions have been slow to do so. Following interviews with 100 labor relations practitioners (union leaders, management representatives, and neutrals) and a survey of available literature, researcher Doris McLaughlin concluded that the most common union response to the introduction of new technology was "willing acceptance."[54] Where unions opposed the technology initially, their responses generally turned to acceptance if "the employer made acceptance of the new technology more palatable by offering some sort of *quid pro quo* . . . or because it became clear that the union would have to adjust to the change to remain a viable organization."[55] In any event, union opposition, where it occurred, only impeded the *rate* at which the technological change was introduced, not its introduction *per se*.

That union resistance to technological change may be lacking is also suggested by the results of an AFL-CIO analysis of labor-management contract clauses.[56] It found technological change provisions in "fewer than 20% of current agreements."[57] Advance notice clauses and retraining clauses were the two most common provisions in these agreements.

Still, many unions *are* aware of the pitfalls of high technology and their responses have taken a variety of forms; negotiated agreements, convention resolutions, policy statements, conferences and training programs and, in a few cases, strikes.

Contractual Responses

A union's first line of defense regarding the new technology is collective bargaining. The AFL-CIO study discusses the different forms that technology contract clauses have taken.[58] The strongest option is language that limits management's ability to introduce new technology. This may take the form of modification of the "management rights" clause, provisions for advance notice of impending technological change, and the right to consult about or to negotiate over such change.

A second category is contract langauge that regulates job changes that may result from the introduction of new technology. Some contracts provide for negotiation over any potential changes in job classification, wages and work conditions. Other contracts establish union jurisdictional control over any new jobs created as a result of technological change. This is an important protection, given the reorganization and deskilling that often accompanies new technology.

A third category of technological change in contract language deals with displacement of workers. Some clauses prevent layoffs that directly or indirectly result from technological change and require that reductions in force be accomplished by attrition. Other clauses provide for retraining of workers whose skills or jobs become obsolete as a result of the new technology. In some cases the employer pays for the retraining, and as a trade-off, retains discretion over who is eligible for it. The employee is generally free to accept or to reject such retraining, but rejection may relieve the employer of future responsibility toward that employee.

A fourth category of contract language involves various protections for workers who do in fact lose their jobs as a result of new technology. These protections range from transfer and relocation rights to severance pay to preferential rehiring rights. A less common option is to negotiate a provision for work sharing or increased vacation time in lieu of employee layoffs. One group of U.A.W. rank-and-file workers in Michigan has developed a program along these lines called "C.E.R.P." The program seeks three benefits in return for the productivity gains achieved through the introduction of new technology; cost-of-living adjustments for retirees, earlier retirement and paid personal holidays.

Other categories of contract language not mentioned in the AFL-CIO survey are those that provide protection against computerized monitoring of employee performance or output and those which deal with the impact of new technology on employee health and safety.

Regardless of the type of contractual protection sought, it is advisable for the union to define what is meant by "new technology" and to negotiate this definition into its collective bargaining agreement. A contractual definition of new technology provides a basis for other clauses that may be negotiated in this area. The I.A.M. has developed a model definition that offers wide latitude:

> Technological change shall be defined as any alteration in equipment, material, methods, and/or changes in work design. This should also include any change in product line.[59]

Two British unions have developed equally broad definitions of new technology. The Association of Scientific, Managerial and Technical Staffs (A.S.M.T.S.) offers the following model; " . . . any changes in equipment or other physical capital (including additions in both) which may affect working arrangements, skills required, the amount of work needed, or changed workforce levels or systems."[60] Similarly, the General and Municipal Workers' Union (G.M.W.U.) defines new technology as ". . . all changes or proposed changes in materials, processes or products and all changes or proposed changes in working practices or conditions associated therewith."[61]

Even more inclusive is the definition of new technology arrived at by the Norwegian Federation of Trade Unions (L.O.) and the Norwegian Confederation of Employers (N.A.F.):

> In this agreement the term technology shall cover technology attached to production (including automation), administration and systems of management. This agreement covers technology and systems that are used in the planning and carrying out of the work, as well as systems for data storage and use of personal data. By personal data is meant all data which either by name or by other identifying code may be traced back to concrete persons employed by the individual undertaking."[62]

This Norwegian agreement is far-reaching in a number of other respects as well. It states that ". . . it is important that new technology is evaluated not only from technical and economic conditions but also from social angles."[63] It requires management to provide to employees, through their shop stewards, all the information necessary for them to evaluate potential new technologies before they are introduced. Furthermore, such information must be provided ". . . clearly and in a language easily understood by persons without special knowledge of the area concerned."[64] The agreement prevents the "collection, storage, processing and use of personal data" not specifically related to the needs of the employer. Disagreements about this are settled through local negotiations, and if no agreement is reached there, the matter is resolved at the national level.

Perhaps the most unusual protection afforded by this agreement is the union's right to select "data stewards." These are special union representatives who are responsible for monitoring the potential introduction of new technology and the ongoing impact on employees of any existing technology. The system of data stewards has existed in Norway since 1975 and is beginning to spread to unions in other countries. The British union A.S.M.T.S. and the American I.A.M. have each encouraged their locals to adopt such a system.

Legislative — Job Protection

In pursuing legislative goals, organized labor in the United States is somewhat handicapped in comparison to its counterparts in other Western industrialized nations. In the United States, government involvement or regulation is generally viewed as "intervention" or interference in the free market private enterprise system. A bill introduced into the Michigan legislature in 1979 (HB 5104) that would have required companies to provide advance notification to local communities before closing a facility was termed "The Industrial Hostage Act" by the President of the Michigan Manufacturers Association. The legislation was in fact modeled after existing laws and practices in several European countries.

This philosophy contrasts with that of a number of European countries, which regard governments as social welfare agents, operating to improve the living and working standards of their citizens. The Security of Employment Act in Sweden and the Employment Protection Act in Britain, which prohibit "unfair dismissals" of workers irrespective of any union affiliation are examples of laws that have no counterpart in the United States.

Another difficulty faced by the American labor movement is its relative lack of political clout. Labor unions in a number of other industrialized nations have their own political parties and have much higher percentages of their workforces organized into unions. American union membership on average has been steadily declining since the 1950s.

Despite these encumbrances, American labor must pursue its new technology objectives on all fronts if it intends to become a full partner in policy planning. The four most logical areas to pursue legislatively are: 1) protection of workers from technological job displacement and de-skilling; 2) protection against computerized monitoring and data storage; 3) health and safety standards pertaining to specific forms of new technology; 4) worker education and training. Advances made by foreign unions in some of these areas may provide inspiration and guidance to American unionists.

Protection of workers from technological job displacement may take several forms. One is advance notification to workers or their unions of impending technological change and/or of impending layoffs. This may include the right to negotiate over these changes or layoffs. Sweden has three different laws relating to this concept. The Act on Safety and Hygiene requires that employers inform unions of planned changes relating to work methods, the purchase of new machinery and tools, and technical or organizational changes (short and long-term). Again, the unions have the right to bargain over these changes before they are implemented. The Law on Employees' Representation on the Board of Directors in medium-and-large size enterprises also provides unions with advance information on company decisions and an opportunity to influence these decisions.[65]

West Germany has a legislative-based system of co-determination that provides unions with advance notification (usually one year) of any proposed workplace changes and allows for continuous labor-management bargaining on a wide range of issues, including new technology. German workers are further protected by comprehensive social insurance systems.[66]

In Britain, labor laws passed since 1974 provide employees with protections such as written notice of terms and conditions of work, including advance notice of termination, severance payments and the right of unions to consult with management before "redundancies" (layoffs). On the other side of the Atlantic, Canadian workers covered by the Canada Labour Code are entitled to ninety days notice of proposed technological change, providing that a "significant number" of employees will be affected by the change. After receiving notice, the

employees' designated bargaining agent may apply to the Canada Labour Relations Board for authorization to commence negotiations.[67]
Other forms of legislative job protection are relocation assistance for workers displaced by new technology, increased paid vacation and educational leave and earlier retirement. Many of these benefits are provided for by law in a number of European countries.

Other Legislative Protections
The same laws that guarantee workers in a number of countries the right to prior notification of technological change also afford them an opportunity for input into the selection and sometimes even the design of new equipment and work processes. This frequently results in negotiated agreements that may prohibit job displacement, job de-skilling, computerized monitoring and data storage, and that may place limitations on the amount of time employees can be required to work with certain types of equipment.

A case in point involved Sweden's social insurance workers — primarily women — who used that country's 1976 Co-determination at Work Act and researchers and computer specialists from the Swedish Center of Working Life to do an extensive study of the impact of computerization in their industry. The result was a massive training program for its members, and an agreement that protected skilled jobs from computerization, provided for the maintenance of employees' professional job knowledge and ability to provide quality service which limited video display terminal work to one-hour periods, with a maximum of two such periods per day.[68]

A similar situation occurred in Norway, and two American researchers contrast the response of the Norwegian workers to that of their industrial counterparts in the United States:

> . . . metal workers at an aircraft parts plant in Kongsberg, Norway, have had far more success in coping with the introduction of computer-based machine tools than have workers at a similar plant in Lynn, Massachusetts.
> At Kongsberg, the trained union technology committee received complete information before the computerized machine tools were installed. On the basis of this information, the committee insisted that machinists' skills were broadened rather than narrowed by the technological change.
> In contrast, at Lynn, the equipment was installed without consultation with the union. Now supervisors or nonunion programmers handle the computer work, thereby reducing many skilled machinists to "machine tenders" or "button pushers" with less interesting work and lower pay. Job losses for union members are possible and any future job action by the union will be less effective.[69]

Unions outside of the United States have also been able to use existing laws to bolster their bargaining clout in the area of computerized monitoring. Relying on a provision of the Workers' Statute of 1970, Italian workers affiliated with the Federation of Metalworkers, recently won an agreement with IBM of Italy that prohibits the use of data-processing systems for monitoring of the performance of individual workers.[70]

Of course even in countries where unions have legislative protection and greater political and numerical clout, their ability to influence the introduction of new technology is not guaranteed. Although they may be under a legal obligation to "consult" or even to negotiate with unions, in many cases management retains final determination over how its operations will be conducted, and what equipment and processes will be utilized. In Sweden, the Electronics Division of a company named ASEA has gradually introduced new office technology that enables management to monitor productivity rates of individual employees. According to one observer, "Consultation with union representatives was said to have been minimal — no more than that required by the various pieces of labor legislation in effect."[71] Moreover, even in relatively prosperous countries like Sweden, unions may find themselves forced to choose between short-term job preservation and new technology. When the A.C. Machine Division of ASEA introduced numerically controlled machines and robots:

> This decision was at first resisted by the union. However, the machinery became accepted when it seemed that without it, the facility in question might have had to close because of its lack of ability to compete in both the domestic and international markets. Without the automation that had thus far occurred, this plant would have employed about twice as many people as the nearly 700 it does now. As it is, production doubled in ten years, with a stable workforce.[72]

Still, it should be clear from the foregoing discussion that unions have much to gain by pursuing a political agenda around the issue of new technology. In so doing, American unions might wish to refer to the three guiding principles of the I.A.M.'s "Technology Bill of Rights":

1. New technology must be used in a way that creates or maintains jobs.
2. New technology must be used to improve the conditions of work.
3. New technology must be used to develop the industrial base and improve the environment.[73]

A comprehensive model for legislation regulating workplace microelectronic technology has been developed by Canada's National Union of Provincial Government Employees. It includes the following elements:

1. a broad definition of technological change that includes work processes as well as equipment;
2. a requirement of "immediate disclosure" by employers to unions of any planned technological change;
3. a prohibition on the introduction of new technology until there is agreement between the union and the employer on the method of introduction;
4. the legal right to reopen collective bargaining agreements to negotiate over technological change and related provisions (eg. classification) as legal subjects of bargaining;
5. a dispute settlement mechanism in the event of deadlocked negotiations regarding technological change, providing that the union retains the right to strike;
6. a requirement that employers justify layoffs and that they implement procedures to minimize the extent of layoffs required (eg., retraining, relocation, shorter hours);

7. employer-provided retraining on company time (with no loss of pay or benefits to employees, with training geared to marketable skills); also, employer-provided relocation;
8. minimum health and safety standards pertaining to new technology;
9. options on early retirement for older employees, not wishing retraining or relocation;
10. portable pensions and immediate vesting;
11. protection of unemployment insurance legislation;
12. removal of legal barriers regarding union organizing and negotiation of a first contract;
13. protection against abuses in the collection, coordination, access and use of personal data banks;
14. mandatory affirmative action programs to encourge the mobility of women beyond sex-segregated occupations and which involve workers and their unions in planning, implementation and monitoring.[74]

Training, Retraining and Education

A third area of union response to high technology is that of training, retraining and education. The important connection between education and jobs in an age of technological development has long been recognized. In 1963 Charles Killingsworth testified:

> The most fundamental conclusion that emerges from my analysis is that automation and the changing pattern of consumer wants have greatly increased the importance of investment in human beings as a factor in economic growth. More investment in plant and equipment, without very large increases in our investment in human beings, seems certain to enlarge the surplus of underdeveloped manpower and to create a shortage of the highly developed manpower needed to design, install and man modern production facilities. . . . And we don't have all the time in the world. Human history has been described as a race between education and catastrophe. In the past dozen years, education has been falling behind in that race.[75]

The passage of some twenty years has done little to improve the situation. Ayres and Miller observe:

> Even though robot manufacturing, programming and maintenance itself will provide some new jobs, it appears that most new jobs will not be in manufacturing. Yet, we have no idea of how many of these displaced workers and new workers can be expected to be absorbed in other sectors. This issue must be addressed if we are to go beyond identifying vulnerable workers and actually prepare them — as well as the entering workforce — for the likely changes to come. . . . There has been little serious discussion to date of how to cope with the hard reality of developing needed work skills on the one hand and how to deal with people who have obsolescent skills, on the other.[76]

The job skills of a wide range of population groups will be affected by our nation's current infatuation with high technology; those currently employed whose skills will become obsolete as a direct or indirect result of the technology; those who are underemployed; women and minorities who face job discrimination and occupational segregation; the chronically unemployed, teenagers, the elderly, displaced homemakers; workforce re-entrants; and school-age children preparing themselves for the world of work. Yet despite the compelling need for a comprehensive program embracing *all* of these groups, job training and education is currently carried out in piecemeal fashion and the response falls far short of the need.

Labor unions in search of training programs for members facing technological job displacement can look to three sources; government-sponsored programs, industry-sponsored programs, and union-sponsored programs. Regardless of the source, the following questions may serve as useful criteria by which to evaluate job training and retraining programs:

1. Who will be eligible for the training or retraining? How will eligibility be determined? Are stipulations or conditions attached?
2. What occupations will people be trained or retrained for? What mechanisms exist to forecast future job needs and interface existing workforce skills with the changing requirements of a technologically advancing economy?
3. How will training or retraining programs redress historic patterns of sex and race based job segregation?
4. Who will finance the training or retraining?
5. What institutions will conduct the training or retraining? Are they equipped to do so?
6. Will trainees receive compensation? At what rates?
7. What mechanisms are in place to assist people who have completed the training or retraining in finding work? Will relocation assistance be offered? Who will finance this?

Government-sponsored job training and retraining programs exist at both the national and state levels. But close examination of this potpourri exposes a common theme: there are too few programs, operating with too little funding and training too few of our nation's. unemployed and underemployed. Over the years, our country's leaders have abandoned even modest full-employment goals, and job training has fared no better as a national priority. Federal funding for job training programs has plunged from $9.5 billion in fiscal year 1978 to $3.6 billion in fiscal year 1983.[77]

Despite enactment of the Job Training Partnership Act of 1982 (J.T.P.A.) at the federal level with its proposed budget of $2.8 billion for fiscal year 1984, it is clear that much of the burden for job training and retraining will fall on the shoulders of states, private industry, unions and the workers themselves. In Michigan, for example, although the state will receive a higher allocation of J.T.P.A. funds than most other states, the amount of money available to local service delivery areas will actually be *less* than was available under J.T.P.A.'s predecessor — the Comprehensive Employment and Training Act (C.E.T.A.).

There are other signs that J.T.P.A. will do little to relieve workers suffering from chronic unemployment and technological displacement. Most of the Act's funding is targeted to Title II, which covers economically disadvantaged adults and youths, and those who have encountered barriers to employment (e.g., school drop-outs, teenage parents, displaced homemakers, the handicapped, those with limited English proficiency, veterans, older workers). A far smaller proportion of the money finances Title III, which is the dislocated workers program; the Act limits eligibility to those who:

(1) have been terminated or laid-off or who have received a notice of termination or lay-off from employment, are eligible for or have exhausted their entitlement to unemployment compensation, and are unlikely to return to their previous industry or occupation;

(2) have been terminated or have received a notice of termination of employment, as a result of any permanent closures of a plant or facility; or

(3) are long-term unemployed and have limited opportunities for employment or reemployment in the same or a similar occupation in the area in which such individuals reside, including any older individuals who may have substantial barriers to employment by reason of age.[78]

While those covered with Title II are every bit as deserving of training opportunities, it is clear that retraining programs for dislocated workers are seriously underfunded. A truly rational program would prepare people *before* the catastrophe stage.

Secondly, funds are administered to local service delivery areas through local government units and "private industry councils" (PICs). Section 102(a) of the Act requires that private sector members, nominated by business organizations, constitute "a majority of the membership." The rest of the PIC seats are reserved for representatives of "educational agencies, organized labor, rehabilitation agencies, community-based organizations, economic development agencies and the public employment service." Clearly, organized labor's ability to influence the PIC will be tempered by its numerical disadvantage.

Third, J.T.P.A. is neither a jobs creation nor an income maintenance program. Those trainees who are not already receiving some sort of public assistance or unemployment compensation, or who are not fortunate enough to qualify for "needs-based payments" (less than 15% of the Act's funding is earmarked for such purpose) will have to find some other way of paying their bills.

Finally, J.T.P.A. lacks strong and meaningful affirmative action guidelines. Although section 102(c)(1)(A) encourages PICs to seek out representatives of "small business, including minority business" (women-owned businesses are not mentioned in the Act), and although the Act includes a general non-discrimination statement, evidence of implementation to date suggests that white and minority women and minority men are underrepresented in both the composition of local PICs and selection of trainees.

Given the inadequacy of existing federal job training and retraining programs, a number of states have established programs of their own. In 1981, Massachusetts established the Bay State Skills Corporation (BSSC) in an attempt to promote greater intersection between the skills of workers and the job needs of an economy moving rapidly toward high technology. The BSSC funnels money to educational and training institutions, which must also rely upon matching private sector grants. These institutions are then encouraged to provide training relevant to "high growth sectors" of the state's economy. One positive feature of the program is its commitment to special groups; in 1982, $260,000 was allocated to set up three regional centers for displaced homemakers.[79] Given the BSSC's goal of training 2000-2500 people in a two-year period,[80] it is clear that the program falls far short of the needs of thousands of the state's unemployed. But it is a start.

Another interesting Massachusetts initiative — unrelated to the BSSC — is a tuition-waiver program for eligible unemployed workers taking business, data-processing and computer courses at community colleges and state universities and colleges.[81] Of course, the program's bias toward high technology-related courses is distressing. As has been noted earlier, the ability of high technology industries to provide significant numbers of jobs is questionable at best. Additionally, a displaced worker might benefit more by taking courses that relate directly to his or her level of formal education, existing skills and qualifications, and career interests.

Although bold state initiatives deserve some applause, we cannot — as neo-conservatives would have us believe — expect beleaguered states to assume primary responsibility for funding massive retraining efforts and other education and social service programs. Greater amounts of our federal tax dollars can — and should — be spent on retraining, education and job creation. Organized labor must use its lobbying and voting power to insure that these issues become national priorities. It is indeed a tragic irony that while our national leaders pour billions of dollars into the defense budget, and while educational institutions at all levels are facing unprecedented fiscal crises, the National Commission on Excellence in Education reports: "If an un-friendly foreign power had attempted to impose on America the mediocre educational performance that exists today, we might well have viewed it as an act of war."

Some observers feel that government has a role to play in fostering human resource development:

> . . . [one] of the government's key roles should be to provide incentives which would induce industry to take positive action on upgrading its human resources now. For example, the government could give tax incentives to partially reimburse industry for education and training investments in their employees. It could provide more favor-able tax treatment for individuals who undertake formal retraining programs in mid-career. And, of course, it could provide inducements (financial and other) to educational institutions to induce them to redirect their efforts into new areas.[82]

A second source of training, retraining and education for workers facing technological displacement is private industry. Unionized workers have an advantage over their non-union counterparts, in that instead of waiting patiently for benevolent employers to bestow job training or retraining upon them, they can negotiate these provisions into collective bargaining agreements. A number of unions have done just that.

The 1982 Agreement between the U.A.W. and Ford Motor Company provided for the creation of an Employee Development and Training Program. The program is funded by a company contribution of five cents for every hour worked by employees. It is expected that this will produce an annual budget of $12-15 million.[83] The program consists of three elements: 1) vocational retraining and job placement assistance for laid-off workers seeking employment both in and out of the auto industry; 2) tuition assistance for workers seeking new skills; 3) in-plant career counseling, upgrading and retraining for those who are still employed.[84] An important feature of the program is that the union retains equal influence with the company in decisions regarding over-all policy and program expenditures. The center is based at the Henry Ford Community College in Dearborn.

The UAW is involved in a similar program with the General Motors Corporation and the State of California. This tripartite effort aims to provide job counseling, retraining and job placement for employees who have faced dislocation as a result of G.M. plant closings in California.[85]

A third source of training programs for trade unionists facing work-place technological change is the unions themselves. Union-sponsored training in this area is usually based upon one or more of the following objectives:

1) to better understand the various forms of new technology entering the industry or industries under its jurisdiction for the purpose of developing appropriate stra-tegies and responses;
2) to promote awareness of which job skills will be rendered obsolete by the new technology for the purpose of developing, negotiating and/or promoting worker education, retraining and upgrading programs;
3) to "de-mystify" new technology for the purpose of exploring and/or promoting potential uses of technology for union administration, education, organizing and political action purposes.

An example of the first type of technology training was the Com-munications Workers of America's (C.W.A.) "Conference on Tech-nological Change" that was held in November 1979. The conference was elaborately organized; sessions were videotaped, and the tapes were immediately made available to conference participants for pur-poses of feedback and analysis. Additionally, an excellent summary of 368 participant responses was prepared in which union leaders de-scribed in great detail how new technology had affected them to date, and how they viewed the future.[86]

Another example of this type of training is the collaborative effort that has taken place between unions and university or college-based labor education programs. These training sessions offer a rich blend of practical and theoretical information that enable participants to under-stand the broader implications of the changes they are witnessing in their own workplaces.[87]

The second category of union training programs revolves around skills assessment and exploration of career options. This may result in any number of union responses, including on-the-job training and upgrading programs; tuition reimbursement for those enrolled in degree programs; union-sponsored classes in math and language proficiency.

In order for unionists to take maximum advantage of either category of programs, it is helpful for them to be eligible for paid release time to attend union-sponsored (or college or university sponsored) educational classes. In the United States, it is often only officers of large local unions, or Regional and International full-time staff members who qualify for this benefit. This type of leave is a negotiable item. Unionists in Britian have managed to obtain it in another way: Section 57 of that country's Employment Protection Act allows employees "reasonable time off during working hours" for "relevant" union education.

With respect to the last category — training to explore or to promote union utilization of high technology — there are a number of examples already in place. For years, many unions have utilized computer technology to compile membership records, produce mailings and store and locate research, legal and financial data. The AFL-CIO's George Meany Center For Labor Studies course entitled "Computers for Local Unions" serves as testimony to this fact. Unions are beginning to develop new uses of high technology as well. Utilizing videotape and cable television, they are producing their own broadcasts for purposes of union education, organizing and political action. These technological developments are providing unions with unprecedented media access — to their members and to the general public as well.

Conclusion

In conclusion, it should be evident that the problems that have been described on these pages are not the result of high technology itself. Rather, they are the result of uncontrolled technological development and implementation, without regard to the social consequences. Several years ago, two scholars observed:

> . . . it advances our understanding very little to say that technology wears two faces, as though one were comedy and the other were tragedy. Technology, in a sense is nothing more than the area of interaction between ourselves, as individuals, and our environment, whether material or spiritual. . . .[88]

Our goal, as a unionist in one of my classes said, must be to learn "what new technology can do for you, and what it can do to you." And armed with that knowledge, our responsibility must be to insure that technology is employed to serve humankind, and to improve the quality of life.

The "new social contract" is not working. Until organized labor — and the public at large — are brought into reindustrialization and high technology planning as full and equal partners, America may well find itself out of the running in the "fast lane" race.

END NOTES

1. *Business Week*, June 30, 1980, pp. 96-101.
2. *The Lansing State Journal*, March 4, 1982.
3. Governor William G. Milliken, *A Plan to Increase the High Technology Component of Michigan's Economy* (Lansing, Michigan: September, 1981).
4. *The Detroit Free Press*, May 22, 1983.
5. Henry J. Levin and Russell W. Rumberger, *The Educational Implications of High Technology*. Institute for Research on Educational Finance Governance, Project Report No. 83-A4 Stanford: (Stanford University, 1983).
6. Ibid., p. 4.
7. Levin and Rumberger, *High Technology*, pp. 4, 17 citing Max L. Carey, "Occupational Employment Growth Through 1990," *Monthly Labor Review* (August, 1981), pp. 42-55.
8. Levin and Rumberger, *High Technology*, p. 5.
9. Ibid., pp. 4, 5, 17.
10. Ibid.
11. Jack Russell, "Michigan's Ailing Economy: Is Robotics The Cure?" speech delivered at the Conference on Robots and High Technology, University of Michigan, Ann Arbor, March 20, 1982.
12. Ibid.
13. H. Allen Hunt and Timothy L. Hunt, *Robotics: Human Resource Implications for Michigan* (Kalamazoo: W.E. Upjohn Institute for Employment Research, 1983), p. 8.
14. Ibid., p. 9.
15. *Business Week*, March 28, 1983, p. 85.
16. Ibid.
17. *Business Week*, March 14, 1983; *Solidarity*, March, 1983, p. 2.
18. Robot Institute of America, Supplement No. 5, February 7, 1981.
19. Robert Ayers and Steve Miller, *The Impact of Industrial Robots*, The Robotics Institute, Department of Engineering and Public Policy (Pittsburgh: Carnegie-Mellon University, 1981), p. 28.
20. *The Detroit Free Press*, July 22, 1982.
21. Harley Shaiken, "Detroit Downsizes U.S. Jobs," *The Nation*, October 11, 1980, p. 346.
22. *Iron Age*, December 15, 1982, p. 20.
23. *Business Week*, May 23, 1983, p. 168.
24. David Cockroft "New Office Technology and Employment," *International Labour Review* (November-December 1980), p. 690.
25. J. Rada, *The Impact of Micro-electronics* (Geneva, Switzerland: International Labour Organization, 1980), p. 3.
26. Diane Werneke, *Microelectronics and Office Jobs: The Impact Of the Chip On Women's Employment* (Geneva, Switzerland: I.L.O., 1983).
27. Rada, *Micro-electronics*, p. 32.
28. *Employment In Perspective: Working Women*, U.S. Department of Labor, Bureau of Labor Statistics, Report 674, Third Quarter, 1982, p. 1.
29. *Statistical Abstract of the U.S., 1982-83* (Washington, D.C.: U.D. Department of Commerce, Bureau of the Census), pp. 388-90.
30. This phenomenon is described in some detail in: *Race Against Time: Automation Of The Office* (Cleveland: Working Women, National Association of Office Workers, 1980), pp. 15-16.
31. Rada, *Micro-electronics*, pp. 75-76.
32. William J. Abernathy and Robert H. Hayes, "Managing Our Way To Economic Decline," *Harvard Business Review* (July-August 1980).
33. *Working Papers*, November-December, 1980, p. 51.
34. *Viewpoint*, Industrial Union Department, AFL-CIO, (Spring, 1981), p. 13.
35. These and subsequent oil price increases have had far more to do with the concentration and influence of American oil companies (and to some extent European)

and their control over oil drilling, refining, marketing and pricing than the actions of Arab countries and oil producers. See: John M. Blair, *The Control of Oil* (New York: Pantheon Books, 1976); also Joe Stork, *Middle East Oil and the Energy Crisis* (New York: Monthly Review Press, 1975).

36. "International Comparisons of Manufacturing Productivity and Labor Cost Trends Preliminary Measures for 1982," *News*, U.S.D.O.L., B.L.S., May 26, 1983, p. 1.

37. *Viewpoint*, I.U.D., AFL-CIO, Spring 1980, p. 4.

38. Ken Susnjara, *A Manager's Guide to Industrial Robots* (Shaker Heights, Ohio: Corinthian Press, 1982), pp. 125-140.

39. Ayers and Miller, *Robots*, p. 25.

40. Norman L. Naidish, Director, Applications Industrial Engineering, Revlon, Inc., quoted in *Iron Age*, March 19, 1982, p. 76.

41. *Race Against Time*, pp. 12-13.

42. *The Evening Press*, Bay City, Michigan, July 21, 1885.

43. Walter P. Reuther, *The Impact of Automation*, Statement before the Subcommittee on Economic Stabilization of the Joint Committee on the Economic Report of the U.S. Congress, October 17, 1955, pp.12-13.

44. James B. Carey, *The Challenge of Automation — Labor's Stake*, Papers delivered at the National Conference on Automation (Washington, D.C.: Public Affairs Press, 1955), p. 65.

45. Charles C. Killingsworth, "Automation, Jobs and Manpower," Statement before the Sub-Committee on Employment and Manpower, Senate Committee on Labor and Public Welfare, 88th Congress, 1st session, 1963 (Washington, D.C.: U.S. Gov't Printing Office, 1963), p. 1468.

46. *Business Week*, June 31, 1980, p. 96.

47. Thomas R. Donahue, "Labor Looks At Quality of Worklife Programs," Speech delivered at the Labor Relations and Research Center, University of Massachusetts at Amherst, January 7, 1982.

48. Ken Coates and Tony Topham, *The New Unionism: The Case For Workers' Control* (Middlesex, England: Penguin Books, Ltd., 1974), pp. 106-107.

49. For more details on the historical aspects of this struggle, see; David Montgomery, *Workers' Control In America*, (Cambridge: Cambridge University Press, 1979).

50. Coates and Topham, *New Unionism*, p. 59.

51. Robert Howard, "Second Class In Silicon Valley," *Working Papers*, September/October, 1979.

52. The Universal Product Code is a system of pricing items by printing black-and-white bars on the label of the item, rather than using Arabic numerals. This code can be read only by electronic scanners. This phenomenon is explained more fully in William Burns, "Changing Corporate Structure and Technology in the Retail Food Industry," Donald Kennedy, Charles Craypo and Mary Lehman, eds., *Labor and Technology: Union Response to Changing Environments* (Penn State University: Department of Labor Studies, 1982), pp. 38-40.

53. *I.M.F. News*, International Metalworkers' Federatrion, 14/28, p. 3.

54. Doris B. McLaughlin, *The Impact of Labor Unions On The Rate and Direction of Technological Innovation*, Institute of Labor and Industrial Relations-University of Michigan-Wayne State University, Report to the National Science Foundation (Springfield, VA: National Technical Information Service, 1979), pp. 28-36.

55. Ibid.

56. Kevin Murphy, *Technological Change Clauses in Collective Bargaining Agreements* (Washington, D.C.: AFL-CIO Department for Professional Employees, 1981).

57. Ibid.

58. Ibid.

59. Leslie Nulty, "Case Studies of IAM Local Experiences With The Introduction of New Technologies," Kennedy, et al., *Labor and Technology*, p. 132.

60. "New Technology Agreements," Post Office Engineering Union, London.

61. Ibid.

62. "General Agreement On Technological Development and Computer Based Systems," Norweigan Federation of Trade Unions, March 15, 1982.

63. Ibid.

64. Ibid.

65. Inge Grangvist, "The Swedish Labor Perspective," *Technological Change and Unions*, Dennis Chamot, ed. (Washington, D.C.: AFL-CIO Dept. for Professional Employees, August, 1982), pp. 20-21.

66. Dennis Chamot and Michael Dymmel, *Cooperation or Conflict: European Experiences With Technological Change at the Workplace* (Washington, D.C.: AFL-CIO, Dept. for Professional Employees, 1981), p. 12.

67. Susan Attenborough, *Microtechnology* (Ottawa: National Union of Provincial Government Employees, 1982), p. 24. The Canada Labour Code covers only federal sector employees in Canada.

68. Social and Labour Bulletin (Geneva: International Labour Office, June, 1981), pp. 262-63.

69. Steve Early and Matt Witt, "How European Unions Cope With New Technology," *Monthly Labor Review* (September 1982), pp. 37-38.

70. *Social and Labour Bulletin*, 2/82, p. 156.

71. Chamot, *Cooperation or Conflict*, p. 9.

72. Ibid.., p. 10.

73. Harley Shaiken, "A Technology Bill of Rights" (Washington, D.C.: International Association of Machinists and Aerospace Workers, 1981).

74. Susan Attenborough, *Mircotechnology*, pp. 29-32.

75. Killingsworth, *Automation*, pp. 1479-80.

76. Ayres and Miller, *Robots*, pp. 39-41.

77. Dan Pilcher, "Job Training In The States," *State Legislatures* (June 1981), p. 10.

78. Job Partnership Training Act of 1982, Public Law 97-300, Section 302 (a).

79. Pilcher, *Job Training*, p.11.

80. Ibid.

81. Ibid.

82. Ayres and Miller, p. 43.

83. Jill Casner-Lotto, "Retraining Displaced Workers Is Seen As Urgent," *World of Work Report*, Vol. 8, No. 1, January 1983; *Ford Facts* (Dearborn: UAW Local 600), January 17, 1983, p. 1.

84. Ibid.

85. Ibid.

86. "Technology-Its Impact on CWA Today And Tommorrow," *The 1979 Conference: A Final Report* (Washington, D.C.: Communications Workers of America).

87. Three such universities whose labor education programs have recently sponsored major conferences on unions and technological changes are: The Pennsylvania State University, Michigan State University and The University of Michigan.

88. Melvin Kranzberg and Carroll W. Pursell, Jr., "The Importance of Technology in Human Affairs," *Technology in Western Civilization*, Vol. 1, Kranzberg and Pursell, eds. (New York: Oxford University Press, 1967), p. 10.

Some Principles Concerning Union Involvement in Quality Circles and Other Employee Involvement Programs

Robert Cole

There are no panaceas in the field of worker-manager relationships. Neither quality circles nor any other participative management approach holds the answers to our work-related problems. Such programs and practices are not intrinsically good or bad. It is how the various parties respond to them that determines whether these ideas make a useful contribution to improving working conditions or not.

Quality Control Circles

Although the observations presented here will be about my experiences with quality control circles (QCCs), I believe they apply more generally to employee involvement programs of various sorts. QCCs are a national movement in Japanese industry involving about one out of every eight Japanese employees. They are the norm in large scale manufacturing firms. In the United States as of early 1983, there were an estimated 5,000 work sites that had some version of QCCs. According to a 1983 study carried out by the New York Stock Exchange, quality circles as such were the most rapidly growing "human resource activity" over the past two years in firms with over 500 employees.

What is a QCC? A QCC is a relatively autonomous problem-solving group of workers at a given workshop. It is usually led by a foreman or senior worker and meets once a week or every two weeks for about an hour. Participants are taught elementary methods of problem-solving, including some statistical methods, and are then turned loose to select and solve work problems. Job-related quality problems are broadly conceived as improving methods of production as part of company-wide efforts. Some typical efforts include reducing defects, reducing

Robert Cole is a Professor of Sociology at the University of Michigan. This article originally appeared in the Labor Studies Journal, *Winter, 1984.*

scrap, reducing rework, and reducing machine down time. Broader problems such as safety and absenteeism may also be chosen.

Twin Sources and Goals of Employee Involvement Programs

Broadly speaking, employee participation programs have two sources; personnel management philosophies that stress increased productivity and quality, with some modest emphasis on improving employee welfare; and the tradition of industrial democracy, with the focus on giving people more control over their work environment. The initial measurement of the cost effectiveness of QCCs by such companies as Honeywell, Northrup, Lockheed, and Delco suggests that they are quite effective in improving quality, bringing about cost reduction, and even reducing absenteeism. Nonetheless, such evaluations must not obscure the other focus of QCCs, that is, the self-development of workers. This includes development of the leadership abilities of foremen and workers, skill development among workers, increased intrinsic work satisfaction among workers, improvement of worker morale and motivation, and stimulation of teamwork within work groups. So in principle there are these two sides to QCCs, which have twin goals; one contributing to organizational goals such as improved quality and cost reduction, and the other contributing to human development, or quality of work life. Note that I said *in principle*, because in practice one side may be more emphasized than the other. Given management's tendency to concentrate on the bottom line, you can pretty much predict which side they are likely to emphasize if there is not a countervailing force such as the union involved.

Management Initiatives

The central point here is that however unionists feel about these kinds of employee involvement activities, there is no doubt that they are going to confront such programs with increasing frequency. Attendance at management seminars and a careful reading of the management literature in recent years has made it clear to me that influential management people believe that their hourly employees represent an unmobilized resource, and that American firms are suffering in competition, especially vis-à-vis the Japanese, because of their failure to mobilize this resource.

There is some basis for this belief. In a recent two-year period, for example, the Ford Motor Company averaged 85,000 suggestions from its employees. For the same two-year period, Toyota — with a smaller number of employees — averaged 385,000. American management is increasingly aware of these discrepancies. They are coming to believe that you can make great improvements in quality if you start allowing the hourly people to participate in more shop floor decision-making and problem-solving. They may be right or wrong, and I think much depends on how they go about it. The important point here is that increasingly, management believes that employee involvement activities are the wave of the future.

That is not to say that QCCs are the answer or that some other particular approach is. We all know that there is a faddish quality to all this; one program succeeds another without leaving a trace. But even after taking this into account, the fact is that unionists are going to be faced with proposals for this kind of participative activity with increasing frequency. It is not just the organizational development people who are pushing it — we all know that they are not very powerful. But when individuals such as Philip Caldwell, the chairman of the Ford Motor Company, get excited about this kind of activity, you know that the company is going to generate serious initiatives and that unions had better be prepared to deal with them.

Union Responses — Three General Options

What then are the alternatives open to the unions in responding to management initiatives in the area of participatory practices? It seems to me that unions have three options:

1. They can ignore it.
2. They can fight it.
3. They can get involved and try to shape it to serve union and worker interests.

To just ignore it strikes me as dangerous. An ostrich strategy means that if the program succeeds, then management gets the gravy and the union gets nothing. Not only that, it means that management can potentially use these employee involvement practices to undermine union support among the membership. To be sure, there are times when for internal political reasons, the local union people will want to stand off to the side in the beginning; but over the long haul that will be a self-defeating strategy.

The second strategy is to fight employee participation programs. If the union is in a plant where everything about the past history of union-management relations there tells them that management is going to use it as a speedup, then it seems to me it's not unreasonable to fight it. But the union should avoid a knee-jerk negative reaction, for two reasons. First, American management is running scared today and nowhere more so than in the auto industry. They are faced with an unprecedented set of problems and pressures, including Japanese competition, the energy problem, pressure from the government, and resistance from the consumer. Under these conditions, many managers are starting to question whether the old methods of dealing with problems will work. Some of them are thinking that maybe they have to find a better way to work with the unions and to draw upon the talents of their work force. This creates situations in which the union may be able to work constructively with management.

The second reason why unions should avoid a knee-jerk negative reaction is that these participative programs sound awfully good to a lot of hourly people, especially some of the younger workers who haven't been burnt badly in the past by experiences in this or that management program. Participative management has a nice demo-cratic ring to it. It's packaged in an attractive fashion. Unions have to be careful that by rejecting such activities outright they don't leave an opening for management to drive a wedge between the so-called "obstructionist" union leaders and the "needs" of the rank and file.

This brings me to the third option. It is the route that opens up in those situations in which the union senses management is sincerely trying to find a new way of doing things. Although it often takes a crisis to bring management to the point of looking for a better way of working with employees, once they get there, then the union has an opportunity to work with them and to shape new practices so that they can serve union and worker interests. In the right circumstances and over the long haul, this alternative will yield the most benefits. As discussed above, participative programs serve two sets of goals; those of management and those of the workers. While the two interests are not necessarily incompatible, they do often come into conflict. Only by active union involvement can the workers be assured that they will not be manipulated simply to meet the narrow objectives of personnel management policies.

Union Responses — Specifics

Let me turn now to the question of how unions can deal specifically with management initiatives in this area. These observations are based on conversations with local union people who have to deal with QCCs, including members of the UAW, Teamsters, and Machinists. First, if membership support is weak — perhaps the union official has an election coming up and he or she is worried about charges by oppo-nents of being in bed with management — and if union relations with management are poor, they may want to keep their distance or actively oppose. If the union decides to keep its distance but not oppose, they can ask that management keep them informed on all developments, keeping the door open for participation at a later date. Basically, the union adopts a "low posture," as the Japanese call it. If QCCs start to catch on with the membership and the union believes that a strong base of support is beginning to develop, then they can consider a more active response.

Let me outline the nature of such a response starting from a different premise. Suppose the union is a local union with pretty good mem-bership support and reasonable relations with management. And the union decides to test management's commitment to all those pretty words. The first thing they may want to say to management is that they want to participate in all discussions right from the beginning so that they are not presented with any decisions in which they have had no input. So any policy decisions relating to QCC activity must have a union input. In the case of QCCs, companies often want to set up steering committees. If that's the case, then the union needs to be represented on it.

Six Issues

But before the union buys in, there is a whole set of issues that they need to resolve to their satisfaction. If they can't get satisfaction, then they may decide to withdraw support. What are those issues? I have identified six.

First, the union will want to be sure that the management initiators of the new program can deliver top management support, and that means demanding a meeting with top management to be sure. In some cases, these employee involvement activities are the brainstorm of a particular management official and when he or she goes, so does the program. The point is that the union official doesn't want to go out on a limb with the membership and endorse something that is later suddenly discontinued. He or she will want to be sure there is strong support for these activities from top management right from the start. Nothing can kill a program like this more quickly than the lack of full top management support. That's what happened to the supposedly successful program at Lockheed Air Missiles.

Second, there is the impact of QCCs on job security. To protect membership, the union will want some guarantee that the implementation of suggestions by the QCCs doesn't lead to layoffs. To be sure, it may be difficult to separate the causes of layoffs from QCC activity. But to the extent possible, the union obviously wants to protect its membership from this outcome. They may want something in writing from management on this.

Third, the union will want to be sure that the QCCs do not take up matters that fall under collective bargaining agreements. You can tell this to the circle members and management and even get it in writing; but in some companies local unions have found that in the first several months until the ground rules are clear, they have to insist on a union committeeman being present at every meeting to be sure that this principle is maintained. There are those unionists who would argue that the circles should be involved in collective bargaining, but I suggest that the outcome is likely to be chaotic, with circles coming into conflict with union leadership positions and with one another.

Fourth, a point already touched on above, is union concern that the adoption of QCCs not turn into a speedup. Here unions have got to make it clear to management, first, that they won't tolerate this, and second, that they will withdraw their participation and actively oppose the program if that is what seems to be happening. I do want to emphasize in this connection that the well-known premise of QCCs is not that people work harder or faster, but that they work smarter. Moreover, the union should not underestimate its members. The hourly people are not going to select those problems and come up with those solutions that result in their having to work harder and faster.

Rather, they are going to select those problems and come up with those solutions that make their work easier — ones that get rid of obstacles and nuisances. So I think the union needs to have confidence in the hourly people at the same time as they carefully monitor management's behavior.

Fifth, the union will want to make sure that management maintains a balance between the two aims of the program. While QCCs can support management goals like improved quality and cost reduction, it had better contribute to the quality of employee work life in terms of such things as skill development and giving workers more control over their everyday work environment. It has got to be made clear to management that they will not be allowed to tilt these programs to one aim at the sacrifice of the other aim. The twin goals have to be emphasized and here I think you can be up front with the membership. They know management is not in this because of their essential goodness. But the union can say to the membership that there is another set of goals that directly serve worker interests, and that they will cooperate with the program only as long as the membership feels that the twin goals are being realized.

Sixth and last, there is the question of what happens to the productivity increases resulting from the reduced scrap, reduced rework, reduced costs, and so on. Does the company get it all or are these benefits shared with the employees? There are a wide range of company practices in this regard. Some companies give what I call jellybean rewards — that is, nominal payments. I was at one company whose incentive program for suggestions involved all sorts of gimmicks like dinner certificates, nail clippers, and other such trivial gifts. It showed that despite having adopted QCCs, which assumes that the company treats workers as adults fully capable of making a contribution to the firm, they were still treating the workers as children. Elsewhere, a more serious commitment to sharing the productivity increase is being made. At one company, 10 to 15 percent of the productivity increases generated by the circles is being paid back to the workers making the suggestions. Most companies fall between the two extremes. In a number of companies, the QCC members have the option of plugging their solutions into the suggestion system.

A different way to put the matter is that participatory practices require individual employees to take greater responsibility for work operations. Traditionally, management is expected to reward individuals for the amount of responsibility they bear. Thus, with greater responsibility resulting from participatory activities, it is only natural that workers should receive commensurate rewards.

Financial Incentives

My own judgment is that the only way employee involvement practices are going to survive in the long run is if some strong financial incentives are built into them. It is easy enough to run a program of this kind without financial incentive for six months or a year. But in the long run you increase the probability of holding worker interest if you build strong financial incentives into their operation. But most management people, being shortsighted, don't recognize that this would serve their own long-term interests. Thus, I think the union has an important role to play here. They can keep management honest and help insure that these participative approaches have a real impact by pushing for a significant sharing of any productivity increases generated.

Summary and Conclusion

Let me close with the following observation. As already stated, there is nothing intrinsically good or bad about employee involvement practices. It is a matter of how it gets carried out. All the evidence suggests that workers do want to have greater control over their everyday work environment. This can be achieved both by developing representative forms like collective bargaining and direct forms such as employee involvement in decision-making. While there can be some problems in operating on both these tracks simultaneously, there is no inherent conflict. What is important is that unions develop a sense of ownership of these participatory practices so that they can shape them to meet union and employee interests. Otherwise management will focus exclusively on their own interests.

It is important that union involvement in employee involvement practices be as depoliticized as possible so that it does not become a basis for campaigning by pro and con leadership groups within the union. This requires a broad consultation and consensus-building within the union prior to making a commitment. Also, it requires that the union educate management so that they do not inadvertently create dissension within the union.

In helping shape participative practices to meet worker interests, unions will further strengthen member recognition that the union is doing something for them. This will give members a greater sense that the union is necessary. When I talked with a Teamster plant steward at Honeywell a few years ago, he said that before the union got involved with the QCC program, he always had trouble getting people to run for committeemen. But now, three years later, he doesn't have that problem. People are concerned about what is going on. There is a sense of involvement and he is pleased with that. At this particular plant, the union became a part of that involvement.

On the whole I see QCC and other employee involvement practices as an opportunity for union leaders. If unions do not respond positively, they risk setting up a self-fulfilling prophecy. That is, if they start with the assumption that management can't be trusted and will exploit the employees, by their own inaction they may help bring about the very thing they feared.

Participative Decision-Making at Work: A Guide to Bibliographic and Program Resources

William Parsons

A significant trend toward new forms of participative and cooperative labor-management relations is occurring in many American workplaces. This new trend has gained importance during the past decade. The growth and implementation of these new forms is matched by the myriad of labels used to describe them. In the early and mid-1960s the terms *job enlargement* and *job enrichment* were used to describe changes in the scope of the tasks performed by workers. However, beginning in the 1970s a new level of development occurred, in which management often approached union organizations with opportunities for expanded roles in the workplace. (In the past when union organizations sought greater participation in workplace decisions, they had found management very protective of its prerogatives.) This new approach of joint labor-management consultation has resulted in the formation of labor-management committees at industry and plant levels where parties have agreed.[1] Pioneered by the auto industry and the United Auto Workers, this program has been labeled "Quality of Work Life" or "QWL." Similar approaches have arisen in other settings, labeled as employee involvement (EI), worker participation, or participative management.

Typically, management expresses an interest in opening greater communication with union organizations and the work force and including them in limited decision-making processes at the workplace. Management's interests arise from a growing recognition and acceptance of the need (whether for rational economic reasons or to adjust to social values) to involve employees in some sharing of information and decisions that are directly related to their work tasks. This managerial

William Parsons is Labor Studies Coordinator at Lansing (Mich.) Community College and Research Director of the Lansing Area Joint Labor-Management Committee. This article originally appeared in the Labor Studies Journal *(Winter, 1984).*

acceptance of the principle of employee participation, probably based on a mix of the rational economic and social value motivations, is a realization that the traditional approach of scientific management has become increasingly counterproductive to effective control and direction of the new, more educated work force of the 1970s and 1980s.

Whatever the rationale, management in major American corporations is increasingly pursuing policies using the participative management approach. The expanding application of participative management and QWL is also occurring in small firms, some service industries, and many public sector workplaces. The extent of this spread has led some observers to herald an era of "new industrial relations." QWL/EI has become a rallying cry for involving employees in solving workplace problems, shoring up productivity, guarding against quality defects, and courting higher employee loyalty. For unions, QWL/EI appears either as a road to greater legitimacy, acceptance, and influence within the workplace, or as a wedge driven into the workplace to sever workers from unions.

The fact that this policy is becoming so widespread requires union leadership and labor educators to seek a clear understanding of the implications of this new approach to labor-management relations. Collective bargaining agreements, the role of union leadership, relations between supervisors and workers, and even the attitudes of workers toward union organizations may be influenced by the introduction of these new participative programs. It is imperative that the leadership and membership of the labor movement assess the implications of this trend and evaluate their own interest and alternatives.

This article will introduce readers to the diverse literature and resources available. The first section provides a summary of the major dimensions of labor-management cooperation and QWL, the historical development of various forms of managerial control, the ideas of participation and industrial democracy, international experiences in participative approaches, American experiences with participation, and practical concerns regarding the process and politics of participation.

The second section outlines the sources for further information and networking support. There is a considerable range of interests covered among these sources, and each offers assistance to interested parties. The key resource centers and materials in the labor-management cooperation approach will be identified.

Historical Development of Various Forms of Managerial Control

Extensive readings are available on the historical development of labor-management relations in the United States. The principal issue is the struggle between owner/managers and workers over control of the labor process. Power in the workplace has rested upon the rights of property ownership and the control of the technical knowledge of the production process itself. The development of managerial policy, through scientific management and hierarchical authority structures, functioned to dispossess the workers of their skills, knowledge, and ultimately control over the actual process of production.[2] This analysis has been extended to examine the role of technology and bureaucracy as further elements in the process of increasing managerial control over the workplace.[3]

These efforts to extend managerial control were frequently resisted and countered by workers in their daily performance of tasks. Conflict in industrial societies was a constant tension between the management and labor elements of the industrial setting.[4] Industrial conflict may be viewed as ongoing cycles of control and resistance.[5] A major concern is the recognition of how worker participation fits into the social and historical perspective of these cycles of control.[6]

Edwards' acclaimed work, *Contested Terrain*,[7] contains one of the most effective discussions on the development of workplace control mechanisms, the resulting conflict, and worker resistance. Edwards identifies three predominant forms of control used to direct workers toward management's design of the production process. These three — simple control, technical control, and bureaucratic control — were historically evolved patterns for maintaining hegemony over the work force and control over the work process. Dickson raises the concern that participation, rather than an escape from scientific management and hierarchical control, is itself a new form of organizational control.[8] If these writers are correct, then worker participation on its face would be a wolf in sheep's clothing to unions and workers' control advocates. This is the question raised by many unionists who remain skeptical of QWL after encountering years of hostility and deception in the labor-management relation, while others feel unions can avoid this problem.

This cycle of control structures and worker response is an ongoing feature of the struggle in the workplace between management and labor. The evolving character of control mechanisms highlights two important aspects in this historical dynamic; first, struggle over control in the workplace is a persistent and deeply rooted aspect of industrial settings; second, the forms of control are increasingly embedded in the technical and social division of labor in the workplace. Thus, the very structure of the labor process, with all its rules and specialists, becomes a central element of control processes. Consequently the issue is, as Dickson outlines,[9] whether the present approaches are participation in control, or participation *as* control.

Participation and Industrial Democracy

Participation has long been an important concern in our democratic society. The right to have a voice in political decision-making, and providing guaranteed opportunities to exercise those rights, is a cornerstone of American political democracy. Yet the rights of political participation do not spill over to the workplace. The worker's right to a voice in decision-making and the legitimate opportunity for involvement in various levels of decision-making in the workplace have not been a hallmark of American industry. The opportunity for participation, and the effectiveness of that participation, varies greatly. The scope of participation and the extent of involvement in the workplace decision process also seem to vary, but generally remain limited in nature. This does not mean that democracy in the workplace has not been a goal.

Industrial democracy is a concept that extends the rights of participation into the economic as well as the political activities of society. Industrial democracy means that the rights of involvement in decision-making should be extended to all the citizens in the workplace, just as they are politically in society at large. The concept of industrial democracy as an ideal has long played an important role in the American labor movement.[10] Collective bargaining itself is a manifestation of the efforts of workers to push for greater participation and democracy in the workplace. Douglas Fraser, past President of the United Auto Workers, has declared that industrial democracy has always been and still remains an important goal of the labor movement.[11] Fraser emphasizes participation as a necessary step toward the goal of greater involvement and democracy for citizens at the workplace. Yet the step of participation does not necessarily mean that either democracy or increased real control will result.

Blumberg[12] and Pateman[13] provide an effective introduction to the scope of participation in political theory and in practice. Participation is strongly rooted in our political theory, yet the application of this right has often been limited, resulting in a case of less than full democracy in society. Ideally all may have the right to participate, but some may have greater opportunities than others. This inequality of participation has plagued the political process, and certainly is the practice in economic decision-making. Greenberg, in a clarification of the theoretical literature on participation, discusses the diverse schools of thought on worker participation.[14] These perspectives vary from management and humanistic psychology to democratic theory and participatory left interpretations of the concept and applications of participation in work. A central argument is that confusion arises in both the precise meanings and the inconsistent practices of participation. Loveridge reinforces this concern that participation has been ambiguously and inconsistently practiced.[15] In an attempt to specify the boundaries of the terminology, Dachler and Wilpert, for example, have examined the conceptual dimensions of participation in organization.[16] The conclusions from these readings are that participation, like QWL, is a term which has been inconsistently and ambiguously applied, leading to more confusion than clarity.

One need only review the *management literature* to recognize the divergence of interpretations used in defining and designating participative activities. Management discussions of participation focus on patterns of low intensity and narrow applications of involvement.

Participative management has been described as a method to achieve the goals of managers through greater attention to the human resources of the organization.[17] A style of management that encourages selective participation in work-related problem solving is the major aspect of this approach. *Humanistic psychology* reinforces this approach by identifying important human social needs of workers for recognition and a voice in work activity.[18] The role of humanistic psychology and the human relations school in management theory is very important. Yet one must not forget the overarching constraints that influence management behavior. Berg and his colleagues examine the work reform movement and managers' responses.[19] Berg recognizes skeptical concerns among managers as strong deterrents to experimentation in work design, but suggests that the organizational and economic environmental constraints are possibly the most influential in limiting the extent of work reform that managers will undertake in the workplace.

The interpretations of participation are widely divergent when contrasting the management/humanistic psychology approaches with the democratic theory and participatory left views of some in the labor movement. The concept of industrial democracy, while not a consensus interest of all workers or unions, nevertheless is an important goal to many in the labor movement. The right to participate, and the goal of participation in the workplace, are concerns for many in the left and labor movement. Workers' control as a means for advancing these industrial democracy interests is a theme explored by Hunnius, Garson, and Case.[20] The importance of labor's stake in a democratic workplace is emphasized by Olson.[21] Carnoy and Shearer argue that economic democracy is a participative pattern that exceeds the confines of the work site and ultimately incorporates the entire economic realm of society.[22] Their book is an excellent discussion of the important linkages between workplace democracy, political democracy, and extending economic democracy.

When democracy and participation are pushed to their full potential, the result might be worker ownership of the enterprise. Zwerdling surveys the range of participative approaches from advisory opportunities to worker ownership.[23] In a seminal study, Bernstein identified several basic elements necessary for effective worker participation in decision-making, and set up a useful framework for viewing the interrelationship of different levels of enterprise decision-making and democratic participation.[24] Bellas examines worker ownership in the plywood industry as an example of the extension of industrial democracy.[25] Many issues central to this worker ownership direction are discussed in a collection of essays that identifies the critical problems involved in workers' attempting to participate at the highest levels of control in the workplace.[26]

Theoretically, participation can extend to full control for workers in both the enterprise and in the total economy. Obviously there are pressures from management and property owners against such an evolution, however. Walker provides a valuable discussion and taxonomy of the problems and practices within the range of workers' participation in management.[27] He examines the tension of these diverse interests and suggests that the practice of participation will continue to unfold in conflict and contradiction as organizations attempt to evolve from traditional authoritarian structures toward more participatory forms.

International Experiences With Participation

An examination of the actual experiences of workers and unions with participative approaches indicates that quite distinctive patterns arise in different countries, with the most extensive experiences occurring in Europe. While there have been many initial American experiments in introducing forms of worker participation into the workplace, none has developed as far as the formalized or legislated practices found in many European settings.

The major European countries have developed approaches which vary considerably in their forms and extent of participation. Northern European nations are examples of the most advanced forms of industrial democracy. Thorsrud and Emery provide a seminal work with an empirically based rationale for democratic participation at work.[28] Qvale[29] and Gustaven and Hunnius[30] present the Norwegian strategies for creating new work reforms and democratization of industries, while Gardell decribes the process of work reorganization in a Swedish setting.[31] The Swedish model features both co-determination and autonomous work group elements for extending industrial democracy. The Swedish Institute and the Ministry of Labor have published numerous articles describing the political and economic participation that workers have developed to gain control of their working lives and of national economic planning.

The experiences in Western Europe vary across the continent, with co-determination forms in West Germany and shop steward participation in Great Britain as distinctive examples of alternatives that trade unions may pursue under the industrial capitalist system. The importance of comparative developments in Europe must be emphasized because European economic structures are similar to the American economic system, and these models represent potential adaptable approaches for American industries. Garson, for example, presents an effective introduction to the Western European experiments in worker self-management in industry.[32] Cooper and Mumford also survey experiences in both Western and Eastern Europe.[33] For an American perspective on various European plans, see Bernstein and Bernstein on the comparisons of industrial democracy patterns across 12 nations.[34]

Eastern Europe is characterized by a planned economy rather than a market economy and by the elimination of private ownership of the means of production. Yugoslavia is the most documented case in the area, and Adizes provides a basic overview of how industrial democracy operates in that country.[35] Wachtel describes the methods of workers' management in theory and practice in Yugoslavia.[36]

Japan has been the focal point of much interest regarding labor-management cooperation. Cole provides a comparative examination, with a valuable discussion of the historical background of industrialization in the Japanese economy.[37] He contrasts American and Japanese auto industry patterns of work organization and participation. One of the most noted features of this Japanese management style is the "Theory Z" organization system.[38] Some analysts attempt to explain the success of Japanese management styles as a product of cultural and social factors as well as basic economic cooperation,[39] while others seek to debunk the impression that Japanese management has some unique or magical solution to labor-management conflict.[40] This second view stresses the links of American ideas to Japanese methods and underscores the fact that Japanese labor and cultural conditions are significantly different from the American experience. There is a considerable (some would say excessive) attention to Japanese management methods in the literature.

American Experiences With Participation
The bulk of American experiences with participative approaches and employee involvement has been principally within the past decade. Davis[41] and Walton[42] both survey the major developments in the past few years. Weinberg[43] and Batt and Weinberg[44] complement this with a viewpoint from officials from the U.S. Department of Labor. The predominant forms of worker participation are the QWL/EI activities found most notably in the auto industry.

There are several readings that set a context for understanding the overall growth of these QWL/EI activities. Major works in this regard are that of Davis and Cherns[45] and the more recent documentation by Siegel and Weinberg[46] of various applications. A May 1981 *Business Week* article is another must item for reviewing the growing American management experimentation with worker participation.[47] Finally, Simmons and Mares offer the most recent book in this field, which examines the scope of participative levels and effectively discusses the problems that arise on the road to developing significant worker participation in the workplace.[48]

The actual description and evaluation of QWL/EI activities currently being experienced in many workplaces is an important check on the practices of this approach. Most of the citations center on joint approaches by labor unions and management to improving the workplace and work process through increased employee involvement in decision-making. Some examples include the General Motors-UAW experiences;[49] the Bolivar, Tenn., project, also a UAW effort;[50] a hospital setting experience;[51] the six years of experimentation at General

Foods Topeka;[52] and an elaborate analysis of workplace democratization in an insurance company.[53] Two valuable articles which briefly outline the QWL process and implications for work site applications are those by Drexler and Lawler[54] and Driscoll.[55] Witte's study of participation in a nonunion workplace represents one of the most documented efforts at understanding the dynamics of employee involvement in an organizational setting.[56] Finally, for lessons of critical value on the QWL process and prospects, Goodman presents 10 issues that are vital to the ongoing effectiveness of any participation effort.[57]

The Process and Politics of Participative Approaches
There is a need for labor educators and union leaders to become familiar with the details of implementing workplace participation processes. There are a number of guidelines available from resource centers such as the U.S. Department of Labor, various QWL centers, and some local area labor-management committees. The Lansing Area Joint Labor-Management Committee, for example, has recently published an orientation pamphlet on the QWL/EI process.[58]

The design of participation requires careful attention to several aspects of the existing organizational relationships, and several articles describe the introduction and structuring of the process. Bohlander,[59] Bourdan,[60] and Stymme[61] examine these design questions and provide some model suggestions. Guest[62] and Westley[63] also point out several elements of design that should be incorporated in developing an effective QWL/EI process. For those examining the quality circles approach, Gregerman[64] and Klien[65] are helpful in alerting participants to the issues involved. The process of participation poses a potential risk of disrupting the politics within both the union organization and formal management structures if done improperly, and attention to these interests is necessary. Nadler and Lawler overview many of these perspectives and directions within the QWL/EI efforts.[66]

The literature indicates that most participatory approaches are initiated, designed, and controlled by management. Even when the union is a joint partner, management frequently seems to be the more active partner. The concerns of union leaders regarding these approaches usually center on whether management appears intent on sharing control over the process and what goals management holds respecting the scope and direction of QWL/EI policy. Many unionists support participatory efforts as advancing the interests of the union when the design and control is a joint labor-management effort. Bluestone,[67] Horner,[68] and Watts[69] are union leaders who argue the supportive side of the issue.

Cohen-Rosenthal, however, questions whether unions should become involved, and examines the appropriate conditions under which they should.[70] Understanding what is in QWL/EI for the unions and workers is an important concern as unions seek to match their own interests with the prospects within participation.[71] Two other impor tant resources in this area are Greenberg and Glaser on the viewpoint and interests of union leaders,[72] and *Extending Workplace Democracy*, an extensive discussion of the pros and cons of QWL activities directed to union leaders.[73]

There are many who have reservations about, or are against, union involvement in workplace participation programs. While there are many joint labor-management ventures, there is also extensive use of the participative approach in nonunion work sites. Employee participation efforts are an important tool used by union-free management consultants to address employee concerns and to keep unions out of the workplace. This double-edged application of participative programs has led some unionists to condemn the cooperative effort as really a co-optive strategy. The periodical *American Labor*[74] and Lagerfeld[75] have directly raised this issue and expressed their concerns regarding such activities as union-busting. Barbash[76] and Winpisinger[77] also express skeptical viewpoints on the sincerity and appropriateness of this approach. There are problems for the role of the stewards in the workplace which is introducing participative efforts.[78] The caution that participation might in practice become a tool for deception and greater managerial control over the work force is proposed by Ramsey[79] and Dickson[80] to alert unionists to the need to examine very closely the employee involvement activities. All these authors question the basic premise and sincerity of management-designed participation and express doubt that any significant changes in decision-making or control in the workplace could develop from such programs. Donahue[81] and the *IUD Viewpoint*[82] provide further arguments regarding the cautions necessary when engaging in participative approaches. Finally, Parker and Hansen term this approach the "circle game," disdainfully evaluating the consequences resulting from such participative circle activities.[83]

One final area for attention is the impact of participation programs on collective bargaining. Rosow identifies this area as one of the key issues to watch carefully in future participative activities.[84] Concerns have been expressed that QWL/EI should not interfere with the normal collective bargaining relationship or with the day-to-day administration of the contract.[85] Crowley and his colleagues explore union members' preferences for how their representatives should behave in this activity, especially regarding the ongoing protection of traditional issues.[86] St. Antoine suggests that the legal scope of collective bargaining might be expanded as a response to this shift in labor-management relations.[87] In a related note on the legal framework, Schneider examines the National Labor Relations Act, section 8(a)2, to determine whether certain conditions of participatory cooperation might in fact be violations of the law. He contends that nonunion settings might risk violation if management is dominating or interfering with the labor organization, creating a kind of company union.[88]

There are several topics of further interest available for review. The primary concerns include information on the viewpoints of management toward participative approaches, the exploration of participation impacts upon the roles of supervisors and stewards in the workplace, specific participation and problem-solving styles and their consequences, basic definitions, and examples of alternative participation approaches.

Additional Sources of Information

Besides the articles and books mentioned above, there are many other sources of information on the topic of worker participation in decision-making about which labor educators should be aware. Not limited to print materials, these sources include organizations that work within the subject area, periodicals that regularly focus on these topics, and films which may be useful to labor education programs about QWL issues.

Organizations

There are a number of organizations working within the general area of expanded decision-making in the workplace. Some of these are dedicated to a specific form or mechanism for employee involvement, for example quality circles, or are tied to a very specific geographical area. The list below involves some of these specific organizations as illustrations of their type, and is not meant to slight other such organizations by exclusion.

Association for Workplace Democracy, formerly the Association for Self-Management, is a nationwide network of activists, academics, and practitioners interested in the larger topic of participation in the workplace. The network involves everyone from QWL advocates to worker-owned business members. AWD sponsors both nationwide and regional conferences. *Workplace Democracy,* the quarterly journal of the organization, is a good source of information on the wide range of topics that can be related to the concept of workplace democracy. AWD is a membership organization. Association for Workplace Democracy, 1747 Connecticut Ave., N.W., Washington, D.C. 20009. Phone 202/265-7727.

Industrial Cooperative Association is an organization that has worked in a variety of settings assisting workers who have converted their workplaces to cooperative ownership. ICA has also changed its focus to include advising labor unions in relation to corporate research areas. ICA is one of the groups working in this very specific form of expanded worker control — worker ownership — and have approached it in a way to ensure the greatest amount of employee involvement in decision-making within worker-owned enterprises. Industrial Cooperative Association, 249 Elm St., Somerville, Mass. 02144. Phone 617/628-7330.

National Center for Employee Ownership has been a major clearinghouse for information on employee ownership issues and also has offered services of consultation and technical assistance. Their publications include bibliographies, case studies, and handbooks on the subject. National Center for Employee Ownership, 1611 S. Walter Reed Drive #109, Arlington, Va. 22204. Phone 703/979-2375.

Ontario Quality of Worklife Centre is a division of the Ontario Ministry of Labor and is dedicated to education, consultation, and research on issues in the broadly defined QWL area. *QWL Focus* is the quarterly journal of the Centre and is a well-written, high quality journal. The journal's bibliographic references, along with its announcements and reports from national and international conferences, are well worth the trouble of writing for this free publication. The Centre also disseminates periodic working papers and reports which equal the journal in quality. Ontario Quality of Worklife Centre, Ontario Ministry of Labor, 15th Floor, 400 University Ave., Toronto, Ontario, Canada M7A 1T7. Phone 416/965-5958.

Michigan Quality of Worklife Council is an example of the type of state and regional QWL centers that are developing. The Council does technical assistance, promotion, education, and publishing in the area of quality of work life. The Council's *Quality of Worklife Review* is a quarterly that should interest those outside the state of Michigan as well as those within it. Michigan Quality of Worklife Council, 755 W. Big Beaver Rd., Suite 508, Troy, Mich. 48084.

Lansing Area Joint Labor-Management Committee is an example of what can be done on a city or areawide basis. It promotes QWL through its newsletter, other publications, conferences, and other activities. Lansing Area Joint Labor-Management Committee, 1801 West Main St., Lansing, Mich. 48915. Phone 517/482-1654.

U.S. Department of Labor's Division of Cooperative Labor-Management Program was established in 1982 to provide publications and information network assistance to all interested in participation programs in the workplace. The agency has issued a number of very useful publications on forming a joint labor-management committee and on plant closings, and has compiled the *Resource Guide to Labor-Management Cooperation* (see note 1), which lists 181 in-plant, industry, and areawide committees (of which the Michigan QWL Council and the Lansing Area Joint Labor-Management Committee are examples). Division of Cooperative Labor-Management Programs, Labor-Management Services Administration, U.S. Department of Labor, Washington, D.C. 20216.

Periodicals

Workplace Democracy, QWL Focus and *Quality of Worklife Review* are described immediately above. Another important periodical that covers the issues of worker participation on a regular basis is *Economic and Industrial Democracy*. Started in 1979, this publication is a source of well-written, more academic explorations into the diverse topics within its area of concern. Past issues have focused on Eastern Europe and workers' self-management and the political economy of education. It is a definite must for anyone who wants to know the area in both a theoretical and practical way from an international perspective. *Economic and Industrial Democracy*, c/o Sage Publications, 275 S. Beverly Drive, Beverly Hills, Calif. 90212. Please especially note Donald Van Houten's "Bibliography: Industrial and Economic Democracy," *Economic and Industrial Democracy* 3 (August 1982): pp. 366-79.

Films

There are a number of films that discuss aspects of worker participation and the QWL process. Some are brief, but convey their point clearly.

The Detroit Model (produced by WNET, 1980, distributed by California Newsreel) depicts the stark crisis of the auto industry, responses of rationalization, and possibilities for democratization of production decision-making. [For a review, see *LSJ* 7, no. 1 (1982): pp. 61-63. — Ed.]

We've always Done It This Way (produced by ATV Television, 1978, distributed by California Newsreel) depicts how Lucas Aerospace workers in Britain worked to save their jobs by joining together to intervene in production decision-making.

Temiscaming (produced by National Film Board of Canada, 1975, distributed by California Newsreel) describes how workers, government, and businessmen in Canada worked to reopen a shut-down U.S.-owned paper company, Temiscaming Mill, and how this effort impacted labor-management relations.

Why Work? Part I (produced by WNET, 1976, distributed by California Newsreel) explores the "work crisis" of alienating and unsatisfying production jobs. The film illustrates alternative approaches to workplace democracy in several diverse work sites.

Blue Collar Capitalism (produced by JBS Films, 1978, distributed by Michigan Media) describes the worker-community buyout of an asbestos mine in Vermont, and explores the complex problems involved in worker ownership.

I Told Them Exactly How to Do It (produced by Video Aides, Tuxedo, N.Y. 10987) is a short (12-minute) film on the problems in the workplace when supervisors tell employees exactly how to do the job, but fail to listen to the employees. Consequences are poor communication, incomplete instructions, frustration, and production flow breakdowns.

Joshua in the Box (produced by Steven Basustow Productions, California, 1970) is a 5-minute animated illustration of the process of change; opportunities, desire for change, fear of change, and the circular results of change within uncertainty. It is useful for activating discussion on the meanings of and resistance to change, and the contradictory needs and emotions of all of us in a change situation.

End Notes

1. For a listing of those labor-management committees, see *Resource Guide to Labor-Management Cooperation*, U.S. Department of Labor, Labor-Management Services Administration (Washington, D.C.: U.S. Government Printing Office, 1982).

2. S. Braverman, *Labor and Monopoly Capital* (New York: Monthly Review Press, 1974); K. Stone, "The Origin of Job Structures in the Steel Industry," in *Labor Market Segmentation*, Edwards, Reich, and Gordon, eds. (Lexington, Mass: D.C. Heath, 1975); S. Marglin, "What Do Bosses Do? The Origins and Functions of Capitalist Hierarchy in Production," in *The Division of Labor*, A. Gorz, ed. (Sussex, England: Harvester Press, 1976).

3. David Noble, *America by Design: Science, Technology and the Rise of Corporate Capitalism* (New York: Oxford University Press, 1977); D. Montgomery, *Workers' Control in America* (Cambridge: Cambridge University Press, 1980); Dan Clawson, *Bureaucracy and the Labor Process* (New York: Monthly Review Press, 1980).

4. Douglas Hibbs, "Industrial Conflict in Advanced Industrial Societies," *American Political Science Review* 70 (1976), pp. 1033-58.

5. H. Ramsay, "Cycles of Control: Workers' Participation in Sociological and Historical Perspective," *Sociology* 11 (1977), pp. 481-506.

6. Michael Burawoy, *Manufacturing Consent: Changes in the Labor Process Under Monopoly Capitalism* (Chicago: University of Chicago Press, 1979).

7. Richard Edwards, *Contested Terrain: The Transformation of the Workplace in the Twentieth Century* (New York: Basic Books, 1979).

8. John W. Dickson, "Participation as a Means of Organizational Control," *Journal of Management Studies* 18, no. 2 (1982), pp. 159-176.

9. Ibid.

10. Milton Derber, "Collective Bargaining: The American Approach to Industrial Democracy," *Annals of the American Academy of Political and Social Science* 431 (May 1977), pp. 83-94.

11. Douglas Fraser, speech delivered at the conference of the Lansing Area Joint Labor-Management Committee, Michigan, Nov. 9, 1982. A collection of remarks by labor and management leaders is contained in *The Cutting Edge: Seven Voices for Workplace Democracy* (Lansing, Mich.: Lansing Area Joint Labor-Management Committee, Inc., 1983).

12. Paul B. Blumberg, *Industrial Democracy: The Sociology of Participation* (New York: Schocken, 1969).

13. Carole Pateman, *Participation and Democratic Theory* (Cambridge: Cambridge University Press, 1970).

14. Edward S. Greenberg, "Participation: A Clarification of the Theoretical Literature," *Social Science Quarterly*, (September 1975).

15. R. Loveridge, "What Is Participation: A Review of the Literature and Some Methodological Problems," *British Journal of Industrial Relations* 18, no. 3 (1980), pp. 279-319.

16. H.P. Dachler and B. Wilpert, "Conceptual Dimensions and Boundaries of Participation in Organizations," *Administrative Science Quarterly* 23 (March 1978), pp. 1-39.

17. W.P. Anthony, *Participative Management* (Reading, Mass.: Addison-Wesley, 1978).

18. The principle sources in this area are Frederick Herzberg, *Work and the Nature of Man* (Cleveland: World Publishing Press, 1966); and Douglas McGregor, *The Human Side of Enterprise* (New York: McGraw-Hill, 1960).

19. Ivan Berg, Marcia Freedman, *Managers and Work Reform: A Limited Engagement* (New York: Free Press, 1978).

20. Gerry Hunnius, G. David Garson, and John Case, *Workers' Control* (New York, Vintage Books, 1973).

21. David Olsen, "Labor's Stake in a Democratic Workplace," *Working Papers* (March-April 1981), pp. 12-17.

22. Martin Carnoy and Derek Shearer, *Economic Democracy* (White Plains, N.Y.: M.E. Sharpe, 1980).

23. Daniel Zwerdling, *Workplace Democracy* (New York: Harper & Row, 1980).

24. Paul Bernstein, "Necessary Elements for Effective Worker Participation in Decision Making," *Journal of Economic Issues* 10, no. 2 (1976), pp. 490-522.

25. Carl Bellas, *Industrial Democracy and the Worker Owned Firm* (New York: Praeger, 1972).

26. Frank Lindenfeld and Joyce Rothschild-Whitt, eds., *Workplace Democracy and Social Change* (Boston: Porter Sargent, 1982).

27. Kenneth F. Walker, *Workers' Participation in Management — Problems, Practice, and Prospects*, IILS Bulletin no. 12 (Geneva: International Institute for Labor Studies, 1975).

28. Einar Thorsrud and Fred Emery, *Democracy at Work: The Report of the Norwegian Industrial Democracy Program* (Canberra: Australian National University, 1974).

29. Thoralf Ulrik Qvale, "A Norwegian Strategy for Democratization of Industry," *Human Relations* 29, no. 5 (1976), pp. 45-70.

30. Bjorn Gustaven and Gerry Hunnius, *New Patterns of Work Reform: The Case of Norway* (Oslo: Oslo University Press, 1981).

31. Bertil Gardell, "Worker Participation and Autonomy: A Multilevel Approach to Democracy at the Workplace," *International Journal of Health Services* 12, no. 4 (1982), pp. 527-528.

32. G. David Garson, ed., *Worker Self-Management in Industry: The Western European Experiment* (New York: Praeger, 1974).

33. Cary Cooper and Enid Mumford, eds., *The Quality of Working Life in Western and Eastern Europe* (Westport, Conn.: Greenwood, 1979).

34. Harry Bernstein and Joanne Bernstein, *Industrial Democracy in Twelve Nations*, U.S. Department of Labor, Bureau of International Labor Affairs Monograph no. 2 (Washington, D.C.: U.S. Government Printing Office, 1979).

35. Icheck Adizes, *Industrial Democracy Yugoslav Style: The Effect of Decentralization on Organizational Behavior* (New York: Free Press, 1971).

36. Howard Wachtel, *Workers' Management and Workers' Wages in Yugoslavia: The Theory and Practice of Participatory Socialism* (Ithaca, N.Y.: Cornell University Press, 1973).

37. Robert Cole, *Work, Mobility and Participation: A Comparative Study of American and Japanese Industry* (Berkeley: University of California Press, 1979).

38. William Ouchi, "Theory Z. Corporations: Straddling U.S.-Japan Molds," *Industry Week*, May 4, 1981.

39. Peter F. Drucker, "Behind Japan's Success," *Harvard Business Review* 59 (January-February 1981), pp. 83-90; Robert Hayes, "Why Japanese Factories Work," *Harvard Business Review* 59 (January-February 1981), pp. 56-66.

40. James L. Hall and Joel K. Leidecker, "Is Japanese-Style Management Anything New? A Comparison with U.S. Participative Models," *Human Resource Management* 20, no. 4 (1981), pp. 14-21; James N. Ellenberger, "Japanese Management: Myth or Magic?" *American Federationist* 89 (April-June 1982), pp. 3-12.

41. Louis E. Davis, "Enhancing the Quality of Working Life: Developments in the U.S.," *International Labour Review* 116 (1977).

42. Richard Walton, "Work Innovations in the United States," *Harvard Business Review* 57, no. 4 (1979), pp. 88-98.

43. Edgar Weinberg, "Labor-Management Cooperation: A Report on Recent Initiatives," *Monthly Labor Review* (April 1976).

44. William L. Batt, Jr., and Edgar Weinberg, "Labor-Management Cooperation Today," *Harvard Business Review* 56 (January-February 1978), pp. 96-104.

45. Louis E. Davis, and A.B. Cherns, eds., *Quality of Working Life*, 2 vols. (New York: Free Press, 1975).

46. Irving H. Siegel and Edgar Weinberg, *Labor-Management Cooperation: The American Experience* (Kalamazoo, Mich.: Upjohn Institute for Employment Research, 1982).

47. "The New Industrial Relations," *Business Week*, May 11, 1981.

48. John Simmons and William Mares, *Working Together* (New York: Knopf, 1983).

49. Irving Bluestone, "Implementing Quality of Worklife Programs," *Management Review*, (July 1977), pp. 43-46; Stephen H. Fuller, "How Quality of Worklife Projects Work for General Motors," *Monthly Labor Review* 103 (July 1980), pp. 37-39.

50. Michael Maccoby, "Changing Work: The Bolivar Project," *Working Papers*, (Summer 1975), pp. 43-55; Barry Macy, "A Progress Report on the Bolivar Quality of Work Life Project," *Personnel Journal* 58 (August 1979), pp. 527-30.

51. David A. Nadler, "Hospitals, Organized Labor and Quality of Work: An Intervention Case Study," *Journal of Applied Behavioral Science* 14, no. 3 (1978), pp. 366-81.

52. Richard Walton, "Work Innovations at Topeka: After Six Years," *Journal of Applied Behavioral Science* 13, no. 3 (1977), pp. 422-33.

53. Daniel Hoeschen, "Workplace Democratization: A Case Study of the Implementation of Worker Participation in Decision-Making" (Ph.D. diss., American University, 1980), *Dissertation Abstracts International 41*, no. 8 (1980), p. 3745A.

54. John Drexler and Edward Lawler III, "A Union-Management Cooperative Project to Improve the Quality of Worklife," *Journal of Applied Behavioral Science* 13, no. 3 (1977), pp. 373-86.

55. J.W. Driscoll, "Labor-Management Panels: Three Case Studies," *Monthly Labor Review* 103 (June 1980), pp. 41-44.

56. John Witte, *Democracy, Authority, and Alienation in Work: Participation in an American Corporation* (Chicago: University of Chicago Press, 1980).

57. Paul S. Goodman, "Realities in Improving the Quality of Work Life: Quality of Work Life Projects in the 1980's," *Labor Law Journal* (August 1980), pp. 487-94.

58. Martin Bakken, William Parsons, Marvin Finke, *QWL/EI Orientation Pamphlet* (Lansing, Mich.: Lansing Area Joint Labor-Management Committee, Inc., 1983).

59. George W. Bohlander, "Implementing Quality of Work Programs: Recognizing the Barriers," *MSU Business Topics* 27 (Spring 1979), pp. 33-40.

60. R.D. Bourdan, "A Basic Model for Employee Participation," *Training and Development Journal* 34, no. 5 (1980), pp. 24-29.

61. Bengt Stymne, "Design Principles for a Participative Organization of Work," *Economic and Industrial Democracy* 1 (1980), pp. 263-88.

62. Robert H. Guest, "Quality of Work Life — Learning From Tarrytown," *Harvard Business Review* 57, no. 4 (1979), pp. 76-87.

63. William Westley, "Problems and Solutions in the Quality of Work Life," *Human Relations* 32, no. 2 (1979), pp. 113-24.

64. I.B. Gregerman, "Introduction to Quality Circles: An Approach to Participative Problem-Solving," *Industrial Management* 21, no. 5 (1979), pp. 21-26.

65. Gerald D. Klien, "Implementing Quality Circles: A Hard Look at Some of the Realities," *Personnel* 58 (November-December 1980), pp. 11-20.

66. David A. Nadler and Edward E. Lawler III, "Quality of Worklife: Perspectives and Directions," *Organizational Dynamics* (Winter 1983), pp. 20-30.

67. Irving Bluestone, "A Changing View of the Union-Management Relationship," in *Breakthroughs in Union-Management Cooperation*, J. Loftus and B. Walfish, eds., (Scarsdale, N.Y.: Work in America Institute, 1977); Bluestone, "Human Dignity Is What It's All About," *Viewpoint* 8, no. 3 (1978), pp. 21-24; Bluestone, "Quality of Worklife Goals Fulfill Union Objectives," *World of Work Report* 6, no. 12 (1981), pp. 89-92.

68. William T. Horner, "Tarrytown: A Union Perspective," *National Productivity Review* (Winter 1982), pp. 37-41.

69. Glenn Watts, "Quality of Work Life," presented at the National Labor-Management Conference, September 1982 (reprinted in *Labor Arbitration Information System*, Washington, D.C., Labor Relations Press, 1982); Watts, "New Direction in QWL" in *The Cutting Edge: Seven Voices for Workplace Democracy* (Lansing, Mich.: Lansing Area Joint Labor-Management Committee, Inc. 1983).

70. Edward Cohen-Rosenthal, "Should Unions Participate in Quality of Work Life," *QWL: The Canadian Scene* 4, no. 1 (1981).

71. Charles D. Burck, "What's In It for the Unions," *Fortune* 104 (August 24, 1981), pp. 88-94.

190   *William Parsons*

72. Paul D. Greenberg and Edward Glaser, "Viewpoints of Labor Leaders Regarding Quality of Worklife Improvement Programs," *International Review of Applied Psychology* 30 (April 1981), pp. 157-75.

73. Andrew Nickelhoff, ed., *Extending Workplace Democracy: An Overview of Participatory Decisionmaking Plans for Unionists* (Ann Arbor: University of Michigan Labor Studies Center, 1981).

74. "Worker Involvement: What Other Unions Have Learned," *American Labor* 14 (1981), p. 5; "Quality of Work Experiments: Progress or Union Busting?" *American Labor* 14 (1981), pp. 1-4.

75. Steve Lagerfeld, "The Pop Psychologist as Union Buster," *American Federationist* 88 (November 1981), pp. 6-12.

76. Jack Barbash, "Humanizing Work — A New Ideology," *American Federationist* 84, no. 7 (1977), pp. 8-15.

77. William Winpisinger, "In the Real World, We Have to Eat," *Viewpoint* 8, no. 3 (1978), pp. 2-7.

78. M. Marchington and R. Armstrong, "Employee Participation: Problems for the Shop Steward," *Industrial Relations Journal* 12, no. 1 (1981), pp. 46-61.

79. J. Ramsey, "Phantom Participation: Patterns of Power and Conflict," *Industrial Relations Journal* 11, no. 2 (1980), pp. 46-59.

80. Dickson, "Participation as a Means of Organizational Control." See footnote 8.

81. Thomas R. Donahue, "Labor Looks at Quality of Worklife Programs," speech delivered at the University of Massachusetts, Amherst, Jan. 7, 1982. Available from the AFL-CIO Public Relations Department, Washington, D.C.

82. "The Quality of Working Life," Special Issue, *Viewpoint* 8, no. 3 (1978).

83. Michael Parker and Dwight Hansen, "The Circle Game," *The Progressive* 47, no. 1 (1983), pp. 32-35.

84. Jerome Rosow, "Quality of Work Life Issues for the 1980's," in *Work in America: The Decade Ahead*, Kerr, Clark, and Rosow, eds. (New York: Van Nostrand Reinhold, 1979).

85. David Lewin, "Collective Bargaining and the Quality of Work Life," *Organizational Dynamics* 10, no. 2 (1981), pp. 37-53; Louis Davis and C.S. Sullivan, "A Labor-Management Contract and Quality of Working Life," *Journal of Occupational Behavior* 1, no. 1 (1980), pp. 29-41.

86. James C. Crowley, Hubert Feild, and William Holley, "Negotiating Quality of Work Life, Productivity, and Traditional Issues: Union Members' Preferred Roles of Their Union," *Personnel Psychology* 34, no. 2 (1981), pp. 309-28.

87. Theodore J. St. Antoine, "Collective Bargaining, Individual Voice, and Inadequate Law," typescript, Interdisciplinary Program on Working Life Working Paper no. 1 (Ann Arbor: University of Michigan Labor Studies Center, 1982).

88. Thomas J. Schneider, "Quality of Working Life and the Law," speech delivered at Harvard University, Kennedy School of Government and Public Policy, Nov. 19, 1981.

Publications Available from The Department of Labor Studies
The Pennsylvania State University

Monograph Series
Labor and Technology: Union Response to Changing Environments
Labor and Reindustrialization: Workers and Corporate Change

Pamphlet Series
A Union Member's Guide to the New Right
Hazardous Chemicals: A Guide to Reducing Exposure

Quarterly Newsletter
Pennsylvania Labor

Copies of the above should be ordered from:

The Department of Labor Studies
The Pennsylvania State University
901 Liberal Arts Tower
University Park, PA. 16802